Age of Fear

D1542946

AGE OF FEAR

Othering and American Identity during World War I

ZACHARY SMITH

JOHNS HOPKINS UNIVERSITY PRESS, BALTIMORE

© 2019 Johns Hopkins University Press
All rights reserved. Published 2019
Printed in the United States of America on acid-free paper
9 8 7 6 5 4 3 2 1

Johns Hopkins University Press
2715 North Charles Street
Baltimore, Maryland 21218-4363
www.press.jhu.edu

Library of Congress Cataloging-in-Publication Data

Names: Smith, Zachary, 1980– author.
Title: Age of fear : othering and American identity during World War I / Zachary Smith.
Description: Baltimore : Johns Hopkins University Press, [2019] | Includes bibliographical references and index.
Identifiers: LCCN 2018020735 | ISBN 9781421427270 (hardcover ; alk. paper) | ISBN 1421427273 (hardcover ; alk. paper) | ISBN 9781421427287 (electronic) | ISBN 1421427281 (electronic)
Subjects: LCSH: Germans—United States—Public opinion—History—20th century. | Germany—Foreign public opinion, American—History—20th century. | Propaganda, Anti-German—United States—History—20th century. | World War, 1914–1918—Social aspects—United States. | Moral panics—United States. | United States—Ethnic relations.
Classification: LCC E183.8.G3 S56 2019 | DDC 305.800973—dc23
LC record available at https://lccn.loc.gov/2018020735

A catalog record for this book is available from the British Library.

Special discounts are available for bulk purchases of this book. For more information, please contact Special Sales at 410-516-6936 or specialsales@press.jhu.edu.

Johns Hopkins University Press uses environmentally friendly book materials, including recycled text paper that is composed of at least 30 percent post-consumer waste, whenever possible.

To Curt and Deb

CONTENTS

ACKNOWLEDGMENTS

My initial interest in the Great War grew out of a video game. As a preteen, I spent countless hours on my parents' Texas Instrument desktop, joystick in hand, dogfighting Spads, Albatrosses, and Fokkers over the Western Front. *Red Baron*, a flight simulator game based in World War I, was not only addictive—it could be downright irritating to anyone within earshot. Of course, whenever the opportunity arose the speakers had to be cranked to or near full blast. To me, the rat-a-tat-tat of the machine guns and the growl of the plane's engine were symphonic, if not hypnotic, allowing me to lose myself completely in the life-or-death struggle in which I was engaged. To everyone else, the game sounded as if someone was mowing our living room carpet, with every landed round on my adversary's fuselage mimicking the clink of the mower's blade on an unseen rock. Looking back, it's a little surprising that my parents showed remarkable restraint under these circumstances, permitting me to complete my mission before dishing out a much-warranted rebuke. That they allowed scenes such as this to be repeated was one of their many contributions to this book.

Curt and Debbie Smith's primary contribution to the book, however, has been their example. My parents worked themselves to exhaustion for their kids—my brothers, Jeremy and Casey; my sister, Chelsea; and me. Yet I learned from them the resolve one must have in order to keep battling when times are tough. My parents taught me how to grin and bear it during life's difficult stretches, a necessary skill if one is to make it in academia these days. They showed me that if I can push through the difficulties, all will work out in the end. At the same time, my parents' healthy skepticism, especially of people in positions of power and authority, has shaped my worldview and understanding of history. This did not instill a deep cynicism or lack of trust in some vague notion of "the system" or "the man"; rather, it inspired a desire to understand those who wield or have wielded formal and informal power as well as the societies and cultures that have conferred that power upon them. Without intending to, my parents raised a historian. I dedicate this book to them.

The process of researching and writing this book would not have been possible without the advice, assistance, support, and encouragement of a large number of people to whom I owe a tremendous amount of debt. I will forever be grateful to John Morrow, my doctoral advisor at the University of Georgia (UGA), where this project first took flight. He was generous and encouraging, provided invaluable counsel, and allowed me to make my own way intellectually. I could not have asked for a better mentor. I also owe much to Jim Cobb, Steve Berry, Kathleen Clark, Ben Ehlers, Laura Mason, and Michael Kwass, all of whom were generous with their time and provided essential feedback in the project's early stages, helping propel it toward its present form.

Much of the research and writing of this book would not have been possible without the financial assistance of the Department of History at UGA and the UGA Graduate School, the latter having awarded me a generous research travel grant and a yearlong writing fellowship. A significant portion of the time I devoted to this project was spent driving to or sitting in an archive in Washington, DC. The archivists at the National Archives in College Park, Maryland, and the Library of Congress's Manuscript Division went above and beyond in answering my questions and helping me tap into the deep recesses of their collections. The librarians at UGA were a tremendous help in navigating the university's extensive microform collections. The Samford University interlibrary loan office made the final rounds of research as painless as possible. I would be remiss if I did not acknowledge Gretchen Sexton, who conjured her technical wizardry to help turn my rough poster and cartoon files into the captivating images found in these pages.

The staff at Johns Hopkins University Press have been a pleasure to work with. I am grateful to Elizabeth Demers for taking an interest in an unsolicited book proposal and then taking a chance on the manuscript. Lauren Straley guided me through much of the publication process with both patience and professionalism. Thanks to Laura Davulis and Juliana McCarthy for guiding the project through to the end. Lisa Bintrim's copyediting improved the prose and saved me from several cringe-worthy mistakes.

The personal debts I accumulated while taking on this project were just as significant as the professional ones. My years in Athens, Georgia, were among the most enjoyable and rewarding of my life. Along with the Pebble Creek crew of Jennifer Wunn, Steve Nash, and Jim Gigantino (as well as Dori, who was gracious enough to not eat me), I also must thank LaShonda Mims, Tammie Rosser, Kathi Nehls, Bea Burton, Kathryn Tucker, Jenny Schwartzberg Wilson, Jason Manthorne, Kurt Windisch, Ashton Ellett (thanks for running down Kaiser

Wilhelm's noggin), Jessica Fowler, J. D. Jordan, Aaron Safane, and Charles Carter. I am grateful that I was able to share that bizarre yet infinitely gratifying liminal space known as graduate school with each of you. Michael Kazin, Sally Shaul Kazin, and Avery regularly welcomed me to their home for good burgers and good brews while pretending to be interested in my Purdue Boilermakers and teaching me that there is no amount of writer's fatigue that a marathon of *Mystery Science Theater* can't cure. Athens is a wonderful, magical place, and all of you made it feel like home.

I am eternally grateful to Tina, Doug, Alli, and Alex Anderson for being my Georgia parents and siblings. Thank you for providing me with a refuge, a home for the holidays, and the very memorable lesson that a Thanksgiving turkey cooks better when it actually fits in the roaster. My in-laws, Lois and Arlin Reynolds, have been a constant and essential source of support and encouragement throughout much of the life of the project.

The loves of my life—my wife, LeeAnn Reynolds, also a historian, and our daughter, Lila—sustain me and motivate me each day to be a better husband, father, and human being. The fortitude and grace with which LeeAnn faces the challenges that her work and her dependents (that would be Lila and me) place in front of her every day is nothing short of inspiring. She has brought out of me a strength I was not aware I possessed. As we awaited Lila's entry into the world four years ago, my primary hope for our daughter was that she would grow into a sweet, empathetic, and kind soul. The fact that she is also hilarious and beautiful—and already has a higher IQ than her dad—is simply icing on the cake. Watching her grow has been the delight of my life. The next book, God willing, is for you girls.

Age of Fear

Introduction

Generally, however, we create the bogey by pulling the bed-clothes over our heads. . . . For in the seclusion and half-light of class tradition and private superstition, in a whispered and hesitant atmosphere, phantoms thrive.

WALTER LIPPMANN, 1914

"The United States must be neutral in fact as well as in name during these days that are to try men's souls," President Woodrow Wilson declared on August 19, 1914, just three weeks after the opening shots of the First World War in Europe. Neutrality might be difficult for the American people, the vast majority of whom could trace their ancestry to one of the European belligerents. Wilson pleaded with his fellow citizens to remain "impartial in thought as well as in action" and to "put a curb on our sentiments as well as upon every transaction that might be construed as a preference of one party to the struggle before another." Maintaining an objective position was of paramount importance because the country had a "duty as the one great nation at peace" to rescue the Old World from self-destruction by convincing its leaders and people to choose a path toward peace instead of war.[1]

Wilson's privately shared concerns, however, leave some doubt as to whether he was capable of the impartiality he demanded from his fellow citizens. Even while publicly reiterating the justice of American neutrality, the president worried about the potential danger a victorious and assertive Germany could pose to the United States, its institutions, and its democratic identity. As early as September 3, 1914, a mere two weeks after issuing his call for calm and evenhandedness, he confided to the British ambassador to the United States that his nation's democratic heritage was at stake in the war. "If they [Germany] succeed," he claimed, "we shall be forced to take such measures of defense here as would be fatal to our form of Government and American ideals."[2] Days earlier, Wilson's friend and advisor Colonel Edward House recorded in his diary that the president broached with him a similar anxiety, "that if Germany won it would change the course of our civilization and make the United States a military nation." Wilson's concern over Germany, House wrote, was not limited to its autocratic and militaristic regime. The president came close to blaming "the German people as a whole rather than the leaders alone" for Germany's alleged penchant for aggression, adding that Wilson believed "German philosophy was essentially selfish and lacking in spirituality."[3] To the president, the United States could end up being just as much in need of rescuing as Europe was.

Though expressed in confidence, Wilson's apprehension regarding German motives and the consequences of a German triumph for the United States foreshadowed the fear and anxiety that would grip a large segment of the American population during World War I. This book examines how white Anglo-Saxon Americans defined their country's role in the conflict, their German enemy, and their identity as "Americans" during their time as a neutral party and, after April 1917, as an active belligerent in the Great War. Over the past century, scholars have written volumes on the various aspects of the United States' experience during the First World War, but few have explored why so many Americans acted so fearfully and, in some cases, violently in support of the war effort. The best studies have avoided reducing Americans' nervousness and assent to the wartime state to "hysteria" or the result of manipulative propaganda. They have instead emphasized the importance of civic duty, local politics, and the pressures of conformity.[4]

I argue that the support for American belligerency and the fear of all things German that Wilson and countless other white Americans displayed during the First World War reflected their long-standing apprehension over the security and stability of their national and ethnic identity. Over the several decades preceding the war's outbreak, white Americans had become increasingly worried that the comforts of modern life and the influx of massive numbers of allegedly inferior (although white-skinned) immigrants from southern and eastern Europe were threatening to slow or reverse the country's national and cultural advancement, thus potentially compromising Anglo-Saxons' position as a dominant and civilized race. As the presumed German threat loomed over the United States during the war, many white Anglo-Saxon Americans became increasingly preoccupied with their own perceived vulnerability while redirecting their anxiety regarding ethnic pluralism onto their German enemy. Consequently, Germans in Europe and those of Teutonic ancestry in the United States took the form of the proverbial Other, a dangerous and uncivilized people who directly threatened the nation and all that

Anglo-Saxons believed themselves to be. To many white Americans, urgent calls for sacrifice, civic engagement, and conformity were necessary because the conflict was a war of self-defense that required Anglo-Saxons to reassert their power and identity.

I base this argument on the premise that most white Anglo-Saxons in this period understood their world and defined themselves primarily through racial and religious conceptions of progress. To explain perceived cultural, cognitive, and physical differences among the world's ethnicities, racial scientists at this time applied Charles Darwin's theory of "natural selection" and the "survival of the fittest" to human relations and development. In *On the Origin of Species*, published in 1859, Darwin maintained that biologically superior species flourished over time by effectively adapting to their environment, an evolutionary process that crossed generations. Many Americans and western Europeans believed that some races, like the animal and plant species Darwin studied, had evolved more than others. Accordingly, the less advanced peoples were stuck in a more primitive stage of technological, political, and cultural development, one that more sophisticated races had long since surpassed. The rise of nationalism in the United States and Europe acted as a catalyst to such hierarchical racism as anthropologists, biologists, and sociologists affirmed their nations' superiority and justified imperial exploitation by ranking the world's races on a biologically determined scale. The lower down the scale a race was thought to have landed, the more boorish and volatile they were believed to be. This hierarchical assessment of race also became part of the western vernacular, as whites in imperialist nations employed such terms as *savage, primitive, brutish,* and *uncivilized* to describe dark-skinned colonial subjects, aboriginal peoples, and those white ethnicities believed to be lagging behind in their development.[5]

The most civilized race on the world stage, at least according to American and British scientists, were the Anglo-Saxons. Throughout the century preceding the Great War, English and American racial theorists had determined that Anglo-Saxons (as well as their German cousins) had descended from the Teutonic Goths who conquered autocratic Rome in the fifth century. After populating the British Isles, the Anglo-Saxons were believed to have developed into the greatest of the Germanic races due to their enlightened, freedom-granting political institutions.[6] This most advanced and democratic branch of the Teutonic family eventually found its way to the New World, where it soon began fulfilling its racial destiny by eliminating and replacing the inferior non-whites who already inhabited the continent.

It is no coincidence that such a racial-historical philosophy came to promi-nence in the United States during the so-called age of imperialism, when questions of power and progress could not have been more intertwined. Ameri-can expansion across North America in the early and mid-nineteenth century, the drive for an overseas empire in the 1890s, and the progressive crusade to uplift the lesser white immigrants at the turn of the century were regarded as central to the Anglo-Saxon race's mission to spread its democratic institutions and Protestant faith (i.e., "civilization") to inferior peoples at home and abroad. Social gospel minister Josiah Strong put it best in 1893 when he rhetorically asked whether "there [was] any room for doubt that this race . . . is destined to dispossess many weaker races, assimilate others, and mold the remainder, until, in a very true and important sense, it has Anglo-Saxonized mankind?"[7] Although perhaps not sharing Strong's degree of confidence, by 1914 most white Americans—particularly those who could trace their ancestry to Great Britain—would continue to share his views on their race's calling.

Missionary Anglo-Saxonism remained prominent in the early twentieth-century United States in large part because of a popular belief that a race's traits and place in the hierarchy of peoples were not necessarily set in stone. Perhaps the most prevalent racial theory in the country was Lamarckism, or "use-inheritance," the hypothesis that the behaviors that members of a race employed to adapt to an environment could become biologically encoded and passed on to future generations. Theoretically, use-inheritance suggested that some non-Anglo white immigrants could become part of the Anglo-Saxon race by altering their behavior, homes, and communities to imitate those es-poused by the dominant culture. Over time, the theory went, the Lamarckian impact of environmental circumstances could bind various peoples together into a distinct, homogenous race and nation under a common language and culture. Interestingly, Darwin himself rejected Lamarckian use-inheritance, which predated his own evolutionary theory, because he believed evolution happened largely by chance instead of by the species' choice. Yet future pro-ponents of Darwinism comfortably embraced Lamarckism because the con-cept of acquired traits was central to both theories.[8]

To progressive reformers, willful assimilation was the key to Anglo-Saxonizing mankind in the nation's overcrowded urban centers. Their attraction to Lamarckism was clear in their targeting of immigrant communities, which were objects of anxiety and curiosity for Anglo-Saxons because of the aliens' dress, language, traditions, and alleged depravity. Through campaigns to "Americanize" alien newcomers from southern and eastern Europe by altering their environment and behavior to mimic that of middle-class Protestant Anglo-Saxons, progressive-minded Americans assumed that the instincts and even brain size of some foreigners and their children would self-modify. Such a transformation would reshape them into something more advanced, familiar, and similar to Anglo-Saxons.[9]

Although some white-skinned ethnicities were thought to be less capable than others of such an elevation, this popular understanding of the link between race and culture opened the synonymous "white," "Anglo-Saxon," and "American" identities to non-Anglo European immigrants and their children. Dressing, acting, and thinking like an Anglo-Saxon, then, were necessary prerequisites to being "white" or "American" in the Progressive Era. Consequently, white Americans could describe the Anglo-Saxon American race as simultaneously a conglomerate of various white peoples as well as a singular, separate, and unique ethnicity. For the sake of clarity and as an acknowledgement of the fluid nature of racial identification in this period, throughout the book I refer to Americans of British descent as well as assimilated non-Anglo whites as both *white* and *Anglo-Saxon* Americans.

Conceptions of religious progress were no less tied to white Anglo-Saxons' identity and their desire to assert their cultural dominance. The belief that Anglo-Saxons bore a divinely ordained responsibility to spread the Christian faith across the North American continent and ultimately the world, through passively modeling godly behavior or actively pursuing war or reform, has been among the most critical and enduring aspects of white American identity formation. Yet, most American Christians understood that the world's progress toward the millennium was not guaranteed. Just as sin and possibly the Devil himself were believed to stand in the way of the world's advancement toward God's kingdom, regressive or evil forces in the physical world stood as obstacles to the realization of a sophisticated, just, free, and secure society.

This popular apocalyptic understanding of peoples and events had its origins in the revivalism of the second Great Awakening of the early 1800s (the first occurred in the eighteenth century). Seeking an emotional response to warnings that an individual's or the world's final judgment could be imminent, evangelical ministers emphasized the importance of making oneself and one's world right with God. At the same time, evangelicalism's emphasis on spiritual equality was easily wed to secular notions of white egalitarianism codified in the Declaration of Independence and Constitution. This, along with ministers' insistent calls to battle sin, facilitated the dramatic spread of revivalist denominations throughout the less affluent classes in American society and into popular American culture. By the final quarter of the nineteenth century, this urgent brand of religion had spread well beyond the bottom rungs, as second-generation and upwardly mobile Protestants, many of whom would become secular-minded reformers or imperialists hoping to spread Anglo-Saxon democracy to the backward and downtrodden, embraced the message while toning down the outward display of emotion.[10]

To many Christians in the early twentieth century, the immoral and wicked impediments to the Anglo-Saxon United States' redemption were most often foreign in nature. Whites frequently viewed potential and real conflicts with immigrants—over language, patriotism, alcohol, workers' strikes, or radical ideologies—in dire and absolute terms, as matters of black versus white or good versus evil. The supposedly unstable and therefore more primitive races were believed to be a powder keg that, if set off, would pose an existential danger to the United States by threatening to overturn not only capitalism but also middle-class Protestant Anglo-Saxon society and culture, thus reversing or impeding the nation's spiritual progress and the world's march toward the Second Advent. While interpretations of the German enemy as an existential threat during the war were not always explicitly religious, many Americans spoke of the conflict and the enemy in such absolute language. Accordingly, I use the terms *millennial* and *apocalyptic* in reference to both secular and religious explanations of the threat the Teutonic Other was believed to pose.

It was through these interconnected understandings of racial and millennial progress and conflict that many white Americans forged their identity as Anglo-Saxon Americans and their view of the wartime German enemy as a racial and spiritual Other. Scholars commonly have defined Othering as the practice of labeling a people or culture as different or separate from one's own group. Much of the scholarship on this phenomenon centers on the theme of Orientalism, or western views of colonial subjects and non-western cultures. Generally, these studies agree on several interconnected aspects of the Othering process. First and foremost, they maintain that Othering is a function of self-identity in that conceiving of another group as one's binary opposite allows the in-group to more easily define itself. Second, a group's Otherness often is identified through their observable features, be it skin color or some aspect of the out-group's culture. Third, it is not easy for the out-group to shed the Other label that the in-group places on them. This definitely has been the case with westerners' views of Middle Easterners as well as historic attitudes toward African Americans in the United States. Finally, to Other an entire people or culture is to create, at least in the mind of the in-group, a hierarchical relationship that justifies the domination and subordination of the out-group.[11]

White Americans' Othering of Germans during the First World War, however, did not directly follow this paradigm. For one, the Germans' rapid transition into full-blown Otherness and then the comparatively rapid dissipation of this perception after the war were unique. Once the apparent German military threat to the United States had passed and many Teutonic immigrants had assimilated into Anglo-Saxon culture during and shortly after the war, their demonization largely ended. At the same time, the typical themes of domination and subjugation also developed in unique ways. By and large, white Americans were more concerned about the enemy Other dominating *them* through military or clandestine means than they were about keeping Germans perpetually subordinate. In part, the Othering of the German people grew out of Anglo-Saxons' fears of their own inadequacy, not out of a sense of their own power.[12]

Four primary factors contributed to the unique wartime Othering of the German enemy. First, rationalizations of German Otherness were often grounded in interpretations of real wartime events. Germany's invasion of neutral Belgium, its cruelties against civilians in Europe and on the Atlantic, and its secret agents' and diplomats' intrigues within and against the United States confirmed to many Americans that something may very well be wrong with the German people. Second, contemporary thoughts about racial progress and the elasticity of white identity opened the possibility that an advanced white race like the Germans could devolve into a lesser or regressed state. Use-inheritance worked both ways. Just as many believed a democratic and fair society could elevate semi-civilized races, the oppressiveness of militarism and autocracy could have a barbarizing effect on a civilized and cultured race such as the Germans. German whiteness, therefore, was in dispute during the war. Third, the apocalyptic worldview, in both its secular and explicitly religious incarnations, provided a cultural framework within which white Americans could articulate German Otherness, their anxiety over the consequences of losing the war to such an enemy, and their perception of their own racial and spiritual standing. Propagandists of all types defined the Great War in apocalyptic terms, or even as Armageddon itself, warning that through infiltration, invasion, subjugation, and threats, the pagan or satanic German Other would ensure the annihilation of white Anglo-Saxon American identity and interrupt the world's march toward the millennium. Finally, Anglo-Saxon Americans had at their disposal familiar Othering templates they could apply to their Teutonic foe, most notably the common view that African Americans and immigrants from the less developed parts of Europe were inherently volatile and untrustworthy. Although the German Other did not perfectly match either of these specific models, the accessibility of the templates helped white Americans make sense of German behaviors that did not fit prewar stereotypes of the Teutonic race.

Propaganda—from government agencies, politicians, news media, or private citizens' groups—was the primary medium through which white Anglo-Saxons negotiated and conveyed German Otherness and their sense of their own identity and vulnerability during the First World War. Although the word *propaganda* today carries a very negative connotation, prior to the war it was not regularly considered harmful or a cynical ploy for economic profit or political gain, although at times these elements undoubtedly were present. Instead, most wartime propagandists believed that what they said, wrote, or drew was based in fact.[13] In reality, the "truth" the propagandists espoused often was based in half-truths and rumors that through stereotypes, prejudices, and fear were perceived as genuine facts. Yet the insistence of most propagandists that their claims were accurate demonstrates that their propaganda was not merely manipulative. It also reflected the racial and millennial anxieties of its creators. In fact, propagandists were equally likely as, or perhaps more prone than, the average citizen to believe that something was genuinely dangerous and different about the Germans. The propagandists' task required that they immerse themselves in these thoughts and constantly search for supporting evidence, thus reinforcing the ostensibly truthful nature of their messages. Most American propaganda during World War I was meant as a public service above all else, as a means of convincing Americans to act for the preservation of their nation and their Protestant Anglo-Saxon values in the face of the foreign danger they purportedly encountered.[14]

Evidence that Americans' fear was genuine can be found not just in the rhetoric and art of propagandists but also in the words and actions of those their propaganda targeted.[15] Civilians' regurgitation of the messages of wartime propaganda in thousands of letters to government officials and the reports of federal investigators speaks to the degree to which the propagandists' version of the truth was accepted as such. Fearful white Americans from across the country wrote to the federal government about Teutonic agents in their neighborhood, rumored German plans to invade the country, and some of their fellow citizens' alarming lack of awareness of the German peril. At times, they also violently lashed out at German Americans and the allegedly disloyal by damaging their property, beating them, or even lynching them. To further protect themselves from the Teutonic Other, they acquiesced to an unprecedented expansion of federal power and contraction of civil liberties during the war. To a significant number of white Anglo-Saxon Americans, Germany had to be defeated at all costs.

By all outward appearances, Germany was an easy nation to fear. In fact, Germany was a country born of aggression and intrigue. In 1870, Otto von Bismarck, the chancellor of Prussia, orchestrated a diplomatic crisis that led to a victorious war against France and the unification of twenty-six separate states into a single German Empire, with the Prussian king as its kaiser (or emperor) in 1871. With the accession of Kaiser Wilhelm II in June 1888, Germany turned its attention to *weltpolitik*, a policy of acquiring an overseas empire that corresponded to the country's growing industrial and military might. Yet despite Germany being no more aggressive than its imperial competitors, this shift from a continental to a global focus inevitably created new tensions with the other great European colonial powers and the United States, itself a burgeoning world empire.[16]

Germany's image problem was invariably caused by insistent government officials, some German intellectuals, and the emotionally erratic, bombastic, and ultimately timid kaiser who often couched their nation's imperial aims in overtly antagonistic and assertive language. Thus, when tensions arose between the United States and Germany over Samoa (1889 and 1899), the Philippines (1898), and Venezuela (1903), American military and political leaders interpreted German actions as excessively hostile.[17] Yet the German government's policies and actions rarely corresponded to their rhetoric, as its aggressive bluster and bluff implied belligerent designs where they did not exist. Still, Americans' often understandable misunderstanding of German intentions aroused much anxiety in the press at various points in the 1890s and into the 1910s, ultimately establishing Germany's standing in the United States and much of Europe as an international bully.[18]

The circumstances surrounding the eruption of the First World War damaged Germany's reputation in the United States even further. After the assassination of the heir to the throne of Austria-Hungary in June 1914 by a Serbian nationalist, the kaiser's government offered its unconditional support in its ally's quest to enact revenge on Serbia. Although each member of Europe's competing alliance systems—the Entente, or Allied Powers (France, Russia, and Great Britain, who formally joined in August), and the Central Powers

(Germany and Austria-Hungary)—were also willing to risk a world war to further their individual national interests, much of the blame for the global conflict at the time stuck to Germany thanks to its "blank check" to Austria-Hungary, its invasion of its neutral neighbor Belgium, and its overenthusiastic prewar saber rattling during Wilhelm II's reign.[19]

The conflict that ensued quickly took the name the "Great War" because of the massive destruction and loss of life it would bring. Germany's opening offensive through France and Belgium nearly reached Paris, only to be turned back at the Battle of the Marne in September 1914. A four-year stalemate ensued as both sides dug the trenches that would define the Western Front. The trenches, though, were in part meant to protect soldiers from the massive quantities of the most destructive and deadly weapons yet created. Generals were not shy about using the machine guns, heavy artillery, poison gas, tanks, airplanes, and other modern arms that Europe's factories churned out by the millions. Casualty figures were astonishingly high—over one million during the five months of the Battle of the Somme in 1916, for example—when soldiers were ordered to leave the relative safety of the trenches.[20]

Brutality also reigned behind the German army's lines in Belgium and northern France. Nervous German soldiers, tormented by stories of armed civilian resistance during the Franco-Prussian War, executed thousands of Belgian and French civilians, many of whom were female, young, or elderly, suspected of spying or taking pot shots at the occupiers. The accused who did not fall victim to German firing squads had their homes destroyed and much of their property confiscated. Tens of thousands of Belgians also were placed on trains and driven east to Germany where they would be forced to work in factories that supplied the kaiser's army. Allied propagandists did not have to exaggerate the truth of German outrages much in order to raise the ire of their own citizens as well as those in neutral countries.[21]

With industrial warfare exhausting the warring nations' raw material bases, strong relations with neutral countries were of paramount importance if one was to keep up in the wartime arms race. From July 1914 to April 1917, the United States was far and away the wealthiest and most industrially developed neutral. By all accounts, the American people were happy to follow their president's advice and stay impartial toward a war that most believed had little to do with them. But American capitalism, like the president himself, had little interest in true neutrality. With the British Royal Navy enforcing a tight blockade on the Central Powers, the Allies were in a far better position to fully exploit American industrialists' and bankers' willingness to sell munitions and provide loans to belligerents. American lenders had become so accommodating to the Allies that in late 1916 the Federal Reserve feared the United States would endanger "this position of strength and independence" by betting too much on an Allied victory.[22]

The United States' less-than-neutral relationship with the Allies meant problems with Germany were certain to arise. Being at an overwhelming material disadvantage, Germany felt it had little choice but to find ways to cut off the flow of American goods, arms, and money to the Allies. The means by which it chose to do this, however, were not conducive to rehabilitating its image internationally or within the United States. The German Embassy in Washington orchestrated small-scale espionage, sabotage, and propaganda campaigns to disrupt American arms production and shipments while attempting to turn public opinion toward a more balanced neutrality. German agents' few successes, though, did practically nothing to slow the movement of war materials to the Allies nor alter the United States' partisan neutrality.[23] Germany was more successful on the high seas. With its capital ships bottled up by the Royal Navy's blockade, the German navy deployed submarines, or U-boats, in the Atlantic to sink Allied merchant vessels carrying war supplies. On several occasions, U-boat captains mistook American vessels and civilian ships for British merchantmen. The sinking of the *Lusitania*, a large British passenger ship, by a U-boat off the coast of Ireland on May 7, 1915, was a public relations nightmare for Germany despite the fact the *Lusitania*'s hull held munitions meant for the Western Front. Of the two thousand civilians onboard, 1,198 were killed; 128 of those killed were American. Germany, hoping to keep the United States from officially joining the Allies, responded to the ensuing diplomatic crisis by significantly restricting its U-boats' rules of engagement.[24]

Meanwhile, the Wilson administration was struggling to manage a volatile situation south of the American border. Mexico had been gripped by revolution since 1910, and the United States had intervened diplomatically and militarily on several occasions. After Wilson chose to recognize Venustiano Carranza as the head of a new Mexican government, Carranza's rival, Pancho Villa, sought revenge by striking at Americans in Mexico and, occasionally, across the border in the United States. Wilson responded in March 1916 by ordering the Punitive Expedition into the deserts of northern Mexico in pursuit of Villa. After eleven months with 110,000 troops engaged, the force failed to catch Villa and his men. The American army's debacle in Mexico and the increasingly realistic prospects of a war with Germany spurred a movement for improved military preparedness, a cause that Wilson himself would eventually support.[25]

As the calendar turned to 1917 and the American army continued to flail in Mexico, circumstances led Germany to grow less concerned about risking war with the United States. Knowing its army and citizens could not hold out much longer under the strains of a multifront conflict, German leaders reasoned that they could win the war before the home front collapsed if their U-boats could effectively blockade Great Britain into starvation and force it to exit the war. To accomplish this, on February 1, the German General Staff lifted all restrictions on the U-boats' terms of engagement, which it knew would likely lead to the loss of more American lives and, consequently, war with the United States. Germany was gambling that it could defeat the remaining Allies before a significant number of American soldiers could reach France. Just in case, Germany devised a scheme in January 1917 meant to keep the American army in North America. In the notorious Zimmermann Telegram, the kaiser's government proposed to Mexico that it invade the United States in the event of an American war declaration on Germany. In exchange, Germany promised to return several southwestern states that Mexico had lost in the Mexican–American War in 1848. Germany also suggested Mexico contact Japan about joining the conspiracy. The British intercepted the message in February and passed it on to Wilson, who shared it with the press in early March. While the announcement of unrestricted U-boat warfare led Wilson to break off diplomatic relations with Germany, the Zimmermann Telegram further limited his peaceful options and shattered much of the remaining good will the American people had for the German nation.[26]

On April 2, 1917, a month after going public with the Zimmermann Telegram, Wilson addressed Congress to ask for a declaration of war on Germany, which he was granted four days later. Claiming the United States had no quarrel with the German people, only its government, the president laid out his case for war and his view of his nation's role in the conflict. The United States would fight to make the world "safe for democracy," by which he meant the spreading of national self-determination to peoples living under despotic regimes. Yet despite the drive for improved military preparedness, the country was nowhere near ready to fulfill this mission. Ironically, the president and Congress would have to make the United States more like Germany—a massive, bureaucratic, military state—in order to accomplish Wilson's millennial aims of world peace and global democracy. American methods, though, were less coercive. The federal government's power expanded far and wide during the war, but most of the growth came through encouraging voluntarism. Spurred on by government propaganda, many Americans rationed food and coal, grew their own vegetables, bought "Liberty Loans" to help pay for the war, and informed on disloyal or suspicious persons. Farmers, bankers, and industrialists were also asked, not forced, to provide for the war effort, though often with very healthy financial incentives. Not every federal measure, however, was voluntary. The federal government ordered twenty-four-million men to register for a military draft, took complete control of the nation's railroads, confiscated the property of thousands of "enemy aliens," and squelched dissent, much of it from pacifists and socialists, with severe sedition laws. Patriotic vigilantes also punished alleged "pro-German" elements, often under the pretext that the federal government was not taking a strong enough stand against internal enemies.[27]

In the end, Germany's exhaustion was more critical to the war's outcome than the expanding American state or the arrival in France of America's inexperienced army. Facing an overwhelming Allied offensive and revolution at home, Wilhelm II abdicated on November 9, 1918. Two days later the warring powers signed an armistice that ended the Great War. The final peace settlement, the Treaty of Versailles, provided no comfort to the hated Germans. Instead of fair peace terms based on Wilson's so-called Fourteen Points, which he hoped would fulfill his larger mission of spreading democratic principles and eliminating armed conflict, Wilson and the Allied leaders offered the new republican German government a humiliating and vengeful treaty that placed full blame for the war on Germany, stripped it of large sections of its territory, greatly limited the strength of its military, and exacted stiff monetary reparations. Wilson acquiesced on these issues in order to ensure the formation of a League of Nations, an international body that promised collective security to its members and would act as an independent arbiter in disputes between nations. With no binding mechanisms to enforce its resolutions, though, Wilson's League was powerless to prevent future wars both small and large. The United States' failure to join, because the Senate followed popular American opinion by refusing to ratify the treaty, undermined much of the League's credibility and effectiveness from the outset.[28] Eternal peace would have to wait.

This book deviates from this traditional narrative by showing that during the First World War most white Anglo-Saxon Americans were less interested in universal peace than in saving themselves from subjugation and preserving their identity. I have divided the book into five thematic chapters and an epilogue. The chapters are organized as chronologically as possible in order to emphasize the steady growth of Anglo-Saxons' fear over the course of the war while also highlighting the ways in which concurrent and overlapping events intensified their racial and millennial anxieties. Chapters 1 and 2 focus on the neutrality period. In chapter 1, I argue that concerns about the decline of the Anglo-Saxon race's masculine identity contributed to an increasing fear that the relatively weak state of the US military left the country open to foreign conquest. Modern comforts and the timidity they engendered, some argued, had stripped Anglo-Saxon men of their vitality. Military preparedness advocates claimed that these men must arm and reengage with their race's primitive virtues or else a tougher and more vigorous foreign enemy, most likely Germany, would complete the Anglo-Saxons' degeneration through an apocalyptic invasion.

In chapter 2, I explore how Anglo-Saxons' perception of vulnerability also led them to look inside their own country for possible threats to their nation and identity. More specifically, I examine how white Americans transformed their impression of the German American community from one of trust and kinship to one of treachery and racial Otherness. The conversion was not easy. Anglo-Saxon Americans tried, ultimately unsuccessfully, to reconcile their positive prewar views of their Teutonic neighbors with episodes of German sabotage and intrigue. These acts reminded many Americans of the dangerous foreign Others of the past and present and helped reshape their own understanding of Germans' racially determined capabilities.

Chapters 3 and 4 cover the nineteen months during which the United States was officially at war with Germany. Chapter 3 continues where chapter 2 leaves off. Many white Americans came out of the trauma of neutrality and into the even greater intensity of wartime believing that German Americans were a scheming and volatile force that aimed to strip the nation of its Anglo-Saxon identity through cultural conquest, or "Germanization." Despite the fact that there was no tangible evidence of German intrigue in the United States after 1915, the federal government and a significant number of Americans acted as if the country was under siege by enacting stiff sedition laws, calling on the federal government for help, or, in the most extreme cases, resorting to vigilante violence.

In chapter 4, I examine racialized conceptions of the German enemy in Europe and a common apocalyptic understanding of the American stake in the war. Propagandists, politicians, and some racial theorists claimed that decades of Prussian militarism and autocracy had created an environment in

Germany that had caused the once great Teutonic race to regress to a dangerously violent and primitive state. To many Americans, the people of Bach's and Wagner's Germany had become a wild, bestial, and evil race that sought nothing short of world domination and the destruction of civilization. Propagandists and nervous citizens cried that the consequence of isolationism and apathy was defeat in Europe, which would mean either an apocalyptic invasion of the United States or the indefinite militarization of the entire nation, both of which promised to undermine Anglo-Saxon identity.

In chapter 5, which encompasses both neutrality and wartime, I address explicitly religious and millennial interpretations of the European German's apparent degeneration, Anglo-Saxon identity, and the United States' spiritual mission in the war. White Americans' racialized conceptions of themselves and their German enemy cannot be divorced from their religious understanding of the war's meaning. The supposedly inherent link between democracy and the teachings of Christ were believed to be clear indicators of Anglo-Saxons' spiritual superiority in comparison to the innately autocratic Teutons, who revealed through their alleged worshipping of themselves, pagan war gods, or even Satan that they had lost the ability (if they ever had it) to comprehend the compassion and benevolence underpinning democracy and Christianity. In the minds of many Americans, the Great War between democracy and autocracy also was a battle, perhaps the final one, between the forces of good and evil, progress and regression.

Finally, in the epilogue, I briefly sketch the ways in which concerns about American identity and potentially dangerous foreign Others have shaped how Americans have constructed their impressions of their nation's enemies since World War I. In many ways, our conception of foreign villains since 1918 has not changed much from the racially and millennially charged images of the wartime German Other. Americans have feared their overseas adversaries— be they Germans, Japanese, Russians, or Islamic radicals—not only because these enemies could do bodily harm to Americans or their family but also because Americans have interpreted the Other's practices and beliefs as aggressive and uncivilized threats to everything they have identified as "American."

My hope is that readers can see a bit of their own time in the pages that follow. Even though a century has passed since the United States and the Allies proved victorious over Imperial Germany, too often we Americans still envision and portray our enemies, both real and imagined, as monolithic, savage, conniving, evil, and existential threats to our country and way of life. As with the German enemy in the First World War, such sentiments have grown out of actual events. For instance, Al Qaeda terrorists really did fly planes into the World Trade Center and the Pentagon on September 11, 2001, and ISIS (Islamic State in Syria) fighters really have beheaded scores of hostages and attacked civilians in the West.

Yet, at the same time, we have consistently based our interpretations of such events on exaggerated fears and heated rhetoric that overstates the scale of the threat before us, thus reducing our ability to accurately calculate the genuine risks of living in the modern world. With all the attention politicians and the news media have paid to terrorism, most Americans likely would be shocked to hear that that they are one hundred times more likely to be killed by an asteroid than by a terrorist attack.[29] No reasonable person would assume that the asteroid also has designs on their culture and institutions. It is this assumption that has fueled American hatred, fear, and disgust toward the country's enemies and has led us to surrender some of our most sacred and cherished civil liberties for the sake of security. If the experience of Americans in the Great War era can teach us anything, it is that giving in to fear can be more dangerous to us, democracy, and our identity than the threats we assume loom over us.

CHAPTER ONE

Identity, Decline, and Preparedness, 1914–1917

> The men who are the torch carriers of world civilization are those, and only those, who acknowledge the supreme duty of protecting sacred spiritual things when attacked.
>
> THEODORE ROOSEVELT, Memorial Day, 1916

Funerals typically are not joyous occasions. Yet according to Lieutenant-Governor W. L. Harding of Iowa, the Mid-West Conference on Preparedness at which he was speaking in 1915 was just that, a cheerful memorial service celebrating the passing of a depraved individual. The meeting was "the funeral of the mollycoddle," by which he meant an effeminate and overindulged man or boy, "one funeral which I will enjoy." The specific question at hand in the conference was the degree to which the United States was militarily prepared to defend itself against foreign invasion, an issue that Americans began debating in earnest after the May 1915 sinking of the *Lusitania*. Yet as many other advocates for increased preparedness would do during the period of American neutrality, Harding conflated the United States' relative lack of military strength with a perceived crisis in white American masculinity. "I want to assure you I am not in favor of war," Harding professed. "I am in favor of men, great, big, red-blooded men, who will fight for the right and their country, if necessary. . . . I like to be a citizen of a country where we have manhood that is willing and able to take care of itself." With the world such a dangerous place, the country could ill afford the continued enabling of mollycoddles. An invading enemy (Harding specifically cites Japan) "may come over here and . . . think she is dealing with chambermaids and not men."[1] Harding's concerns reflected common assertions that Anglo-Saxon men were failing to maintain both their patriarchal authority and the vitality of their race. During American neutrality, many of the most well-known and boisterous supporters of increased military preparedness loudly proclaimed that these failures had resulted in a weakened Anglo-Saxon disposition and, consequently, a lack of interest in strengthening the nation's military.

To many white contemporaries, the perceived decline in Anglo-Saxon male strength and mental fortitude was due to an overabundance of civilization, which they insisted had feminized American society and its politics. Scientific, technological, and civic advances, which many Anglo-Saxon Americans claimed as evidence of their superiority among the world's peoples, were making white men too comfortable. Modern luxuries and desk jobs were softening Anglo-Saxon men's bodies, hands, and demeanors, thus diminishing their elemental and warrior-like ancestral qualities. This concern grew from the mainstream Lamarckian understanding of how environment can shape a race's development. A popular myth was that Anglo-Saxon American racial superiority had grown from generations of white settlers who had violently spread democracy and Christian civilization across the American frontier. While taming such a wild, primitive environment, Anglo-Saxon trailblazers had to rely on, and in the process enhance, their own primal characteristics. Yet with no more frontier to subdue (it was famously deemed "closed" in the early 1890s), some feared that sedentary workplaces and female-dominated homes and schools had become the predominant environments in which men and boys came of age. To many racially minded Americans, this feminization and overcivilization of American society and culture could have tragic consequences. As their frontier-taming Anglo-Saxon ancestors had shown, great races maintained some semblance of primitivism, without which they would never have become great. How could the "fittest" races have survived and thrived without being strong, virile, and willing to kill (brutally if necessary) potential threats and obstacles to their progress?

The softening of the Anglo-Saxon race appeared even more alarming in the late nineteenth and early twentieth centuries as groups that had been deemed economically and politically dependent on white men began to openly challenge this patriarchal relationship. Industrial laborers frequently and often violently confronted their white male employers in attempts to more equally redistribute wealth (and thus power) across classes. Immigrant races from backward areas of Europe with unfamiliar cultures often took part in these altercations as they flooded American metropolises, supplanting native-born whites as the majority in many cities. Meanwhile, the increasingly successful drive for women's suffrage had allowed women to violate the male space of politics while an increasing number of female industrial workers directly undermined the patriarchal tradition of the primary male breadwinner.[2]

These two perceived crises—the decline of Anglo-Saxon male vigor and masculine authority—intersected during the nationwide debate over the necessity of improving the nation's defenses in case the United States became embroiled in the Great War. Much propaganda espousing military prepared-ness depicted the Anglo-Saxon race and nation as slowly but surely degenerat-ing into a weak, apathetic, flabby, and materialistic version of its former self—in a sense, an Other—that had withdrawn from the "masculine" world of struggle and competition and into a more "feminine" life of comfort and ease. If the race and nation were to be secure and maintain their place among the strongest and most enduring races, advocates claimed, Anglo-Saxon men must maintain a vigorous lifestyle and, consequently, an appropriate degree of primitiveness. A small but loud number of preparedness supporters claimed that racial-masculine decline due to an increasingly feminine and pacifistic environment left the United States open to conquest by a more brutish people. In short, men needed to be men again, and the Anglo-Saxon race needed to rediscover its primal instincts or else the nation would face apocalyptic consequences. Concerns about the nation's lack of military preparedness, then, masked a deeper and long-held anxiety about the vulnerability of Anglo-Saxon racial and masculine identity.

White Anglo-Saxons' decline was particularly evident to preparedness advocates when they compared their countrymen to the seemingly more martial and, presumably, masculine races of the world. Fictional invasion scenarios were central to much preparedness propaganda. The attackers often stood as models of civilized brutishness as they maintained at least a modicum of savagery, which made them superior soldiers to their Anglo-Saxon oppo-nents. Such representations were very similar to depictions of Native American warriors on the late nineteenth-century frontier, who white officers respected for the doggedness with which they defended their land. The primitive and martial characteristics of the "noble savages" allowed the military to identify them as simultaneously a racial Other worth destroying and an object of envy.[3] Similarly, some Anglo-Saxons believed that the nation's prospective enemies in 1915 and 1916 had not lost the primal instincts that an overexposure to civi-lization was expunging from the white American makeup. In short, zealous preparedness supporters did not seek to identify themselves and their nation as the binary opposite of possible battlefield foes. Instead, during neutrality they wished that the Anglo-Saxon race was *more like* those tougher, more masculine Others.

Racial–masculine concerns also contained an apocalyptic component that was more secular and Darwinian than it was religious. Many preparedness proponents argued that an attack by one of these more militant and thus primitive nations likely would result in the absolute destruction of the Anglo-Saxon United States and everything their ancestors had built. Maintaining an appropriate balance between the race's civilized traits and primal characteristics would keep the nation both physically sturdy and militarily capable of staving off the imminent apocalypse that an impotent race would otherwise have deserved. Preparedness proponents' repeated allusions to the dire and unforgiving consequences of unpreparedness and overcivilization suggest that the millennial component of popular American culture had some influence on their rationale for a more well-armed and well-toned United States. Although this connection between race, masculinity, and preparedness was primarily the concern of the Anglo-Saxon patrician class during neutrality, apocalyptic prophecies of war and regression became commonplace in 1917 and 1918, when white Americans had a clear enemy Other on which to focus their trepidation.

Native-born Americans' concerns about overcivilization leading to Anglo-Saxon skittishness and decline, however, predated the war by several decades. In 1881, physician George M. Beard created what would become the common diagnosis of "neurasthenia." "The chief and primary cause" of "the very rapid increase of nervousness" that characterized the ailment, Beard affirmed, "is modern civilization." Modern society was "the one constant factor without which there can be little or no nervousness, and under which . . . nervousness in its many varieties must arise inevitably." Beard concluded that "savages or barbarians, or semi-barbarians or partially civilized people" rarely contracted the disorder; the same was true of those "in the lower orders in our great cities," farmers, and manual laborers ("those who represent the habits and modes of life and diseases of our ancestors of the last century"). In short, neurasthenia was the curse of the world's most advanced, cultivated, and potentially overcivilized peoples. By the end of the century, as excitement over the nation's overwhelming victory in the Spanish-American War helped bond ideas about military force and masculine strength in the popular American mind, overcivilized male neurasthenics came to be thought of as physical and emotional weaklings, their symptoms a retreat from manliness and a decline into femininity.[4]

To avoid a neurasthenia epidemic and buttress Anglo-Saxon masculinity, the cultivation of the inherent savagery of Anglo-Saxon male youth became the model of male socialization. Educational psychologist G. Stanley Hall warned in 1899 that male overcivilization had to be nipped in the bud early or else white American boys' inborn primitive instincts would dissolve away before being adequately honed. "The child repeats the history of the race. The child is in the primitive age," Hall maintained. "The instinct of the savage survives in him." Degeneration could be avoided and masculine strength fostered if boys were encouraged to cultivate their primal instincts through physical and aggressive activity along with temporary yet repeated exposure to outdoor life, as opposed to indulging the predominantly indoor comforts of modernity. "I think we are in danger of becoming over-sentimental rather than over-brutal," Hall surmised. "Physical courage is the foundation for moral courage later in life." A boy who is coddled, however, "will become a degenerate, selfish man. Luxury brings decay."[5] To avoid regression through overcivilization, Anglo-Saxon boys and men needed to reconnect with their inner brute. Naturally, primitive peoples, and presumably those races that preserved some semblance of savagery, would be more physically and psychologically hardy and capable on a battlefield.

While most white Americans agreed that Anglo-Saxon identity could not be maintained without adopting habits from the race's more primitive past, there was much disagreement on how to put this theory into practice. Most hoped to accomplish the task through peaceful pursuits. While memories of Civil War heroism continued to pique some Americans' interest in the military academy as the proper arena for masculine development, by the end of the nineteenth century most Americans preferred their sons pursue this goal through team sports. The benefits of sports were similar to those of military drill—physical assertiveness, self-restraint, and complete subservience to group objectives—but without the explicitly martial character.[6] In 1910, psychologist William James likewise sought a "moral equivalent of war" that could foster "the martial type of character . . . without war" by conscripting boys in the "immemorial human warfare against nature." Whether it be working in mines, constructing skyscrapers, building roads, or even washing dishes, "the military ideals of hardihood and discipline would be wrought into the growing fiber" of America's youth. "Such a conscription . . . and the many moral fruits it would bear," James concluded, "would preserve in the midst of a pacific civilization the manly virtues which the military party is so afraid of seeing disappear in peace."[7] The same could be said for outdoor clubs such as the Boy Scouts of America (BSA), which maintained young boys' primitive qualities without the violence of contact sports or danger of militarism. Most of the BSA's national administrators, including pacifists like Stanford University president David Starr Jordan and steel magnate Andrew Carnegie, implored Scout leaders to build physical strength, character, and virtue—believed to be defining traits of white Anglo-Saxon Americans—without instilling military discipline.[8]

Popular literature at the turn of the century also offered non-military lessons in developing and maintaining the primitive aspects of Anglo-Saxon identity while avoiding the pitfalls of overcivilization. Aside from the famous westerns by Owen Wister and Zane Grey, the most explicit of the era's best-sellers on the benefits of sharpening young men's primal instincts were Jack London's *The Call of the Wild* (1903) and Edgar Rice Burroughs's *Tarzan of the Apes* (1914). London, an outspoken Anglo-Saxon supremacist, chose a dog named Buck as his protagonist. Buck is stolen from his home in California and sold to a man in the extreme northwest who forces him to work as a sled dog. The extremely harsh experience, however, turns out to be a godsend. By the end of London's novel, Buck's prolonged primitive existence and distance from the trappings of civilized society has stripped him of any semblance of domestication. Running away into the wilderness, Buck becomes "the dominant primordial beast," physically and emotionally stronger than ever. Similarly, Burroughs's Tarzan is not born in the wilderness. Instead, he is the orphaned son of British aristocrats who, after their deaths, is found and raised by apes in the African jungle. Yet along with his immersion in the primeval world of "our fierce, hairy forebears," as Burroughs Darwinistically calls the apes, Tarzan also has access to his deceased parents' remaining possessions. The combination of these civilizing influences, along with his gender, racial pedigree, and primitive upbringing, mold Tarzan into a superhuman figure and king of the apes.[9]

Although influential writers like James, London, and Burroughs reflected popular concerns about the softening influence of overcivilization on the nation's male youth, most white Americans did not view the problem as immediately dire when the First World War began. Even those who argued for modest improvements in the nation's defenses between 1914 and 1917 did not feel a great urgency.[10] Ironically, race-conscious preparedness supporters were quite nervous, in part because they faced an uphill climb in convincing the public that the nation's racial-masculine decline left the door wide open for a foreign military invasion. Popular anxieties about overcivilization, however, provided fertile soil from which apocalyptic preparedness arguments could grow, especially with the addition of the fertilizing influence of the Great War. The global conflict had raised the stakes of the great Darwinian competition between nations and races, a contest that some believed could sweep up the

United States and, if it was caught unprepared, mark its subjugation by a foreign power.

For many preparedness advocates in late 1914, the reactions of most Americans, their leaders included, to the war's outbreak was a disappointing example of the nation's overcivilized, effeminate, and degenerated condition. Inspired by the opening of hostilities, the editors of the *Forum* revealed their aversion to physical confrontation with gory descriptions of the horrors of Great War battlefields, followed by a pronouncement: "This is the glory of war. God damn all war."[11] In his annual address to Congress on December 8, 1914, Woodrow Wilson warned that American hawkishness would suggest to the world "that we had been thrown off our balance by a war with which we have nothing to do, whose causes can not touch us, whose very existence affords us opportunities of friendship and disinterested service which should make us ashamed of any thought of hostility or fearful preparation for trouble." Democratic Congressman Martin Dies of Texas concurred. "Separated from all the warring nations of the earth by broad oceans," he maintained, "it would seem that God had planted this great people here to work out a shining example of liberty."[12]

According to advocates for a reinvigorating preparedness, the vast majority of whom opposed American intervention in 1914, such idealistic talk was naïve, pacifistic, and indicative of a nation, culture, and race in decline. The pacifism of their political opponents, anti-war activists (most of whom were women), and the American people at large was tantamount to a national outbreak of neurasthenia, evidenced by the country's rejection of the hardy primitive virtues that were necessary if a potentially more masculine foe attacked the United States. Apathy and an aversion to physical confrontation, preparedness propagandists asserted, had come to define an overcivilized nation that remained devoid of honor while continuing to be drunk on luxury and ease. Such a mindset not only left the feminized nation physically, psychologically, and morally prostrate but also left it susceptible to foreign aggression.

Most preparedness advocates deemed militaristic Germany as the nation most likely to exploit the country's overcivilized condition. This was in part due to British propaganda in the United States that deemed German aggression the primary cause of the war and, through the famous Bryce Report published in 1915, highlighted and at times exaggerated the brutality of Germany's invasion and occupation of Belgium. Equally important to the decision to focus on Germany in preparedness propaganda, however, were the sporadic episodes of German intrigue—espionage and sabotage in particular—within the United States throughout 1915 and 1916 (discussed in detail in chapter 2). As the incidents continued, in 1915 especially, an increasing number of Americans began to feel as if Germany was already bringing the war to American shores. German atrocities in Europe, Germany's plotting in the United States, and its bellicose prewar reputation made the kaiser's forces an obvious antagonist for preparedness propaganda.

Yet early in the war, more racially focused Americans viewed Teutons' close racial kinship to the Anglo-Saxon and their policy of universal conscription as evidence of the German's hardiness, a trait sorely lacking in many American men. Theodore Roosevelt, for instance, said in September 1914 that he had "nothing but . . . praise and admiration" for the Germans, who were "a stern, virile and masterful people, a people entitled to hearty respect for their patriotism and far-seeing self-devotion." Although news of German crimes in Belgium and northern France would cause Roosevelt to change his tune, his early assessment of German strength and dedication would contrast sharply with his evaluation of alleged American apathy in the coming months.[13]

With Germany seemingly the most likely adversary in a future conflict, its aggression and atrocities against civilians in the early months of the Great War exacerbated concerns among preparedness advocates about the softness of Anglo-Saxon men. No specific event did more to popularize the preparedness campaign, spread its warning against national apathy and emasculation, and damage Germany's reputation in the United States than the sinking of the *Lusitania* in May 1915. The attack, combined with occasional headlines regarding German intrigue, suddenly made Europe's war seem far less distant. Woodrow Wilson's immediate response was to declare, "There is such a thing as a man being too proud to fight. There is such a thing as a nation being so right that it does not need to convince others by force that it is right." Although he retracted the statement the next day, May 10, and sent several stiff notes to Germany warning of the consequences of future attacks on the high seas, Wilson's initial response and Americans' generally favorable reaction to it drew the ire of the most ardent preparedness advocates, many of whom also happened to be the president's Republican political opponents.[14]

Some of the most ardent preparedness enthusiasts were frustrated with the president's and American people's response to the sinking, not because they actively sought war with Germany but because it signified that the crisis of white masculinity was worsening. Although Roosevelt publicly heaped praise on the toughness and character of American men, in private he had no problem implicating the American people in Wilson's faintheartedness. In June, he confided to a British friend that "Wilson's delightful statement . . . seemed to me to reach the nadir of cowardly infamy."[15] Two days earlier he wrote to a confidant, Massachusetts Senator Henry Cabot Lodge, "They [Americans] are cold; they have been educated by this infernal peace propaganda of the last ten years into an attitude of sluggishness and timidity."[16] On May 11, four days after the *Lusitania* went down, General Leonard Wood, another close friend of Roosevelt, wrote in his diary of a similar concern with the American people's "rotten spirit in the Lusitania [*sic*] matter" and bemoaned the fact that a "yellow spirit [was] everywhere in spots."[17] According to Wood, Henry Stimson, the former and future secretary of war, was "also deeply disgusted with our prevailing yellow streak" in the face of German bullying and considered, likely with his tongue firmly implanted in his cheek, "giving up his citizenship, if no change comes."[18] To these very prominent men, the Anglo-Saxon United States had lost its edge.

To those in the press who were equally flabbergasted with the nation's apparent timidity, the *Lusitania* disaster called up long-standing popular suspicions of Anglo-Saxon and national decline. The American victims on the *Lusitania* and other subsequently sunken ships died, claimed the editors of the *New York Tribune*, because Germany knew the president and his cabinet would not follow his tough talk with manly deeds, and neither would the American people demand he do so. "Here in America, under the inspiration of Mr. Wilson's Administration, the American people are day by day absorbing more and more of the cult of cowardice and the gospel of selfishness" instead of the dogma of physical courage and manly sacrifice. The president and the overcivilized American people, the editors suggested, had forsaken the primal and ancestral traits that had formed the core of their Anglo-Saxon identity. "It is better that American honor, all that America has meant in the years of our national existence, should be discarded than that this country should put to touch its comfort, its prosperity, its glorious peace, which is the peace of cowardice."[19] Along with exposing that Anglo-Saxon Americans were not as hardy as their ancestors, the sinking also was surefire proof that the United States was not as safe as its apathetic people liked to believe. "If anything more were needed than the last year of European history to demonstrate the necessity of a proper preparedness," the *World's Work* argued, "the rapidity with which the storm cloud gathered out of the wreck of the *Lusitania* should convince us." It "showed plainly again that such dangers rise suddenly and that we alone cannot decide whether there shall be peace or not."[20] With the president and the general public seeming to be willfully ignorant of the danger that a militarized Germany and Anglo-Saxon timidity now posed, something needed to be done to cure them of their naïveté.

Many prominent citizens, politicians, and patriotic organizations offered universal military training (UMT) for all young men and boys as an antidote to the United States' precarious defenses as well as to the overcivilization and cowardice they felt had been weakening the nation since long before the *Lusitania* affair. UMT often was described as a cure-all: it would impart discipline, physical strength, and camaraderie while Americanizing non-Anglo white immigrants. But lying underneath much of the UMT propaganda was a desire to enact G. Stanley Hall's educational philosophy of cultivating the savage instincts of Anglo-Saxon boys before an increasingly overcivilized culture reduced them to sissified Others. Military training and camping in the outdoors, UMT advocates maintained, would allow American youth to sharpen the hardy virtues their ancestors had displayed on the frontier and better equip the nation militarily and emotionally for an enemy attack.

The National Security League (NSL) was the most persistent and perhaps most effective organization at selling UMT as a means of both reconnecting Anglo-Saxons with their primitive, masculine past and strengthening the nation's military defenses. Founded on December 1, 1914, in New York City with the support of many wealthy and "public spirited" northeasterners, such as Henry Stimson, Massachusetts congressman Augustus P. Gardner, publisher George Putnam, former head of both the State and War Departments Elihu Root, and Congregationalist minister and editor of the *Outlook* Lyman Abbott, the NSL printed over one million copies of dozens of pamphlets and organized over one hundred pro-preparedness rallies and meetings in just its first year of existence. The NSL and its politically partisan spinoff, the American Defense Society (ADS), primarily argued for UMT by couching it in the apocalyptic context of what could happen if the United States and its men remained apathetic and weak.[21] The president of the NSL, S. Stanwood Menken, a corporate lawyer from New York, argued that universal military training would "increase the vigor of our race," which he claimed was necessary because a foreign invasion could be imminent. Menken also hoped to awaken Americans to the possibility that "the danger of our natural isolation" (by which he meant the Atlantic and Pacific oceans) had made the nation weak and complacent, the consequences of which could be devastating to the United States and, consequently, American identity. In Pittsburgh in 1916, he begged his audience to read up on "the history of good and industrious nations who have ceased to exist, who have committed national suicide thro' lack of preparedness and power."[22]

Few were more obsessed with the concepts of decline and power than Theodore Roosevelt, who often spoke on behalf of the NSL and ADS. In an April 1916 speech, Roosevelt did not mince any words in explaining what avarice, faint-heartedness, and apathy could cost the United States: "Love of ease, shirking of effort and duty, unwillingness to face facts, the desire to comfort ourselves by words that mean nothing—all these spell worthlessness while our civilization lasts, and spell also a speedy and an ignoble end of that civilization." If his audience was unmoved by his apocalyptic prophecy for the overcivilized nation, the former president also cited feminized Belgium, the nation that militarized Germany had been dominating and defiling since the Great War began, as an example of the national humiliation and effemination that unpreparedness could wreak. Preparing American arms and, more importantly, toughening American mettle were the only means of ensuring "that there might not befall us on an even greater scale such a disaster as befell Belgium." The American people must heed Roosevelt's warning against physical weakness, emotional frailty, and un-Americanism "or else they will when it is too late learn the lesson from some terrible gospel in which it is written by an alien conqueror in letters of steel and flame."[23]

Major H. S. Howland's nervous call to reconnect the Anglo-Saxon nation to its hardy and martial identity lacked Roosevelt's flair but not his urgency. In a speech published by the American Defense Society, the retired army officer promoted UMT as the solution to Anglo-Saxon impotence and the nation's unpreparedness. While acknowledging the crisis of masculinity, Howland believed that white American men possessed the inherent valor necessary to eventually overcome the nation's pacifism and negligence of the military. In the event of an invasion, he claimed, a long line of heroic yet untrained Anglo-Saxon volunteers would sacrifice for their nation's defense, but they would be no match for the proficient army of a militarized foe. To avoid such disgrace, Howland proposed UMT, which "is most important and essential to the health, strength and defense of the nation." By "nation," Howland meant the Anglo-Saxon race, within which he appears to include all American whites. "It is estimated that one million young men become of age in the United States every year," he explained, "and they constitute a physical and mental asset which should be conserved, in order that we may endure as a nation; but this asset can only be conserved by subjecting our young men to training, military and athletic, that will render them physically fit, not only to be defenders of the Nation in time of need, but to be the fathers of the Nation as your ancestors were before you, as you are today, and as they must be in the future." The nation's youth would not let their country down, Howland concluded, because "bravery is the common heritage of the Anglo Saxon."[24] Through UMT, white Americans could rediscover the innate and masculine qualities that were central to white Anglo-Saxon identity.

Henry Stimson also believed that overcivilization had left the country open to invasion. The reason for the race's racial–masculine degeneration and the deterioration of the nation's defenses was the "preponderance of modern city life" on the race. "From a nation of vigorous and hardy frontiersmen," the former cabinet secretary argued, "we have become rapidly transformed into a nation of city-dwellers. The majority of our people now live the sedentary indoor life of the city. The effect of such a transformation cannot but have an insidious effect upon the fibre of body and resolution alike." The urban environment, which was responsible for the weakened state of white manhood, "is enormously against those hardy outdoor virtues of mind and body under which the traditions of the Anglo-Saxon race were crystallized." Unfortunately, Stimson bemoaned, only "a pitiful minority . . . of the great mass of young men shut up in brick and mortar" have had the "opportunity to develop those outdoor hardy virtues which are the secret ideal of every right-thinking boy!" Universal military training, however, would leave no flabby, weak-kneed boy untouched. Describing popular concerns about the militarizing effects of UMT as "wholly imaginary," Stimson explained that the camp at Plattsburg—the UMT experiment in upstate New York populated by the privileged Anglo-Saxon sons of the Northeast—was a prime example of democratic militarism and the benefits of reintroducing males to their primal roots in the outdoors. If one witnessed the campers' "duties and vicissitudes" as well as "the steady ranks standing at attention while the call of the colors sounds," Stimson argued, they would not "wish to have any element of our manhood escape its influence."[25]

Yet if the point of UMT was to maintain schoolboys' primitive instincts while instilling the discipline, strong work ethic, and physical strength that were believed to be hallmarks of Anglo-Saxonism, the Plattsburg camps Stimson referenced did not advance the cause directly. Although the majority of the attendees were approaching or beyond middle age, by most accounts, their drill sergeants did not spare them the strenuous experience they desired. Some likely attended in hopes of proving their manhood or overcoming a midlife crisis. But as William Menkel of *Review of Reviews* wrote, the attendees forfeited their time and money out of a genuine anxiety over the prospect of a foreign attack and the weak state of the army. "So grimly did these men go at their tasks," Menkel commented, "one would easily obtain the impression that the enemy had fixed a time for landing on our shores, and that the day was not far off." If or when the invasion occurred, the nation would need a reserve of officers from the better classes to help train and lead the makeshift army of citizen-soldiers that would have to be organized. Plattsburg campers sacrificed, Menkel wrote, "to fit themselves for service to their country in time of need. To make of themselves efficient units in a system of national defense."[26] For them, military training was more than just a means of forging national unity and reaffirming Anglo-Saxon manhood. It also was a necessary measure to protect the nation from imminent foreign dangers while maintaining their class authority and identity.

Preparedness advocates, though, made serious attempts to remedy the faintheartedness and undisciplined state of the nation's male youth. With Plattsburg as the archetype, state governments in Massachusetts and New Jersey studied the establishment of UMT in public schools in 1916. That same year, the New York legislature passed one law mandating three hours of military training a week for boys between the ages of sixteen and nineteen and another that required physical education classes, taught by members of the state's Military Training Commission, for both girls and boys ages eight to sixteen. Some in Congress also attempted to make military training central to public education. Senator George Chamberlin of Oregon introduced a bill that would oblige young men and boys between twelve and twenty-three years old to begin military training, with the older trainees being prepared for war by the Boy Scouts, an organization that had shown itself to be averse to any degree of militarism. Perhaps reflecting national sentiment at the time, the bill did not pass.[27] Similarly, New Jersey Representative Richard Wayne Parker encouraged Congress to raise armies through the obligatory training of hundreds of thousands of young men in colleges, universities, and public high schools. Exploiting boys' inherent competitiveness by arranging contests in shooting and such exciting enterprises as drill and inspection, Parker asserted, would instill "a spirit of self-defense" without requiring stern military discipline, a sentiment similar to that of Boy Scout leaders and proponents of team sports.[28] Despite slight differences in means, the aim of each proposal for UMT was the same: to defend the nation against external enemies and the Anglo-Saxon identity from decline through overcivilization.

Ultimately, however, arguments for UMT largely fell on deaf ears because a large number of Americans, perhaps most, did not view the state of the nation's defenses in the same racial, masculine, and Darwinian terms as many of the leading preparedness proponents. Moreover, because of the United States' distance from Europe and Americans' traditional distaste for militarism and military adventure, rarely had the military been anything but small throughout the country's history. To make matters more difficult for UMT supporters, the United States was only a decade removed from a very unpleasant imperial undertaking in the Philippines that was characterized as much by American brutality as by military strength, an experience that revealed that war could unleash the inner savage to a far greater degree than psychologists at the time thought healthy.[29]

Yet some preparedness supporters in 1915–1916 believed they could persuade Americans to move beyond the uncomfortable realities of the Philippine episode and forsake their age-old distrust of standing armies by establishing the dangers that military impotence directly posed to the nation. They hoped to accomplish this through wild stories of foreign invasion by a manlier race that was more in touch, but not overly so, with its primitive side. The employment of apocalyptic invasion scenarios was not a new tactic for preparedness advocates. Looking back to the War of 1812, most leading military intellectuals during the nineteenth century had viewed a seaborne invasion as the greatest military threat to the United States. In the latter decades of the nineteenth century, despite much objective evidence that a massive invasion of the country was both militarily and financially impossible, military officers regularly painted vivid pictures of a mighty European power invading American shores, sacking and holding for ransom the country's most important commercial cities.[30]

The invasion scenarios concocted in 1915 and 1916 differed from those of previous decades in that they had clear racial and gender undertones, took place during a world war, and were more widely circulated through popular media. Throughout the neutrality period, advocates produced apocalyptic and, at times, racially tinged magazine articles, editorials, cartoons, novels, and films claiming that at some point a foreign power, most often depicted as or implied to be Germany, would descend upon the United States, forcing the unwarrior-like Anglo-Saxon nation into the role of a submissive weakling, thus completing the deterioration of Anglo-Saxon identity that the race itself had set in motion. At the same time, the aggressors in such stories provided clear examples of how maintaining contact with a race's inherent primitiveness could result in national (or racial) strength and unity of purpose. Yet due to the melodramatic nature of most of these narratives, their effectiveness in converting an audience more interested in neutrality than military intervention seems to have been minimal, at least in the short term.

One of the most sensational tales appeared as a serial in *McClure's Magazine* from May to August 1915 and was published as a full-length novel in 1916. In "Conquest of America, 1921," Cleveland Moffett, a member of the American Defense Society's Board of Trustees, claims to have randomly chosen Germany as the antagonist, the color of the enemy's flag being superfluous to the reality of the United States' vulnerability to attack. "Conquest of America" previewed the nation's submission to a more virile and, as evidenced by its brutal actions, primitive power if Anglo-Saxon Americans continued down their degenerative path. The story begins with Germany's destruction of the Panama Canal in late April 1921 and its official declaration of war the following week. Thousands of German troops, hardened by their victory in Europe in 1917, then land in New York's harbor, meeting very little resistance due to the lack of coastal defenses and a small, poorly deployed navy.[31] The Germans quickly consolidate their beachhead and take control of Manhattan, their prize being the J. P. Morgan & Co. Banking House on Wall Street. They conquer their next target, Boston, with equal ease and burn it to the ground.[32] In the final installment, Paul von Hindenburg, the real-life commander of German forces on the Eastern Front in Europe in 1915, splits his armies to the west and south, successfully sacking both Philadelphia and Washington, forcing the federal government to flee to Chicago.[33]

More dramatic than the story and more revealing of Moffett's feelings about German destructiveness are the corresponding sketches, which suggest that Anglo-Saxon timidity could result in a real-life Armageddon reaching American shores. In the May edition, covering the initial invasion and fall of New York City, *McClure's* printed a sketch of a wrecked skyscraper with the top quarter of the building falling toward the street. In the following installments, images of a burning Richmond, Virginia, and German howitzers leveling Philadelphia accompanied Moffett's story. The apocalyptic consequences of the nation's overcivilization and unpreparedness, if confronting Germany or any other well-armed aggressor, were unmistakable. Moffett's prophetic tale was meant to strike at Americans' sense of decline and powerlessness against unpredictable dangers and more virile enemies. "It is America that is attacked; it is America that is unprepared; and we are Americans. What would happen to us?" Moffett asked rhetorically.[34]

Thomas Dixon, a former college classmate of Woodrow Wilson, also hoped to stimulate the American people to support preparedness with a tale warning about the pitfalls of overcivilization. Dixon's 1916 novel *The Fall of a Nation* was released as a feature motion picture in June of that year. In the film, which more directly alluded to masculine decline than the book, the real enemies are women's suffrage and female anti-war activists, who, after gaining the right to vote, elect equally pacifistic men to Congress; these men, in turn, largely disarm the nation's military. The "Imperial Confederation of Europe," whose army looks suspiciously like Germany's, capitalizes on the United States' vulnerability by invading the East Coast with the help of Old World immigrants. The assistance the Confederation received from foreigners was a clear allusion to the growing distrust of German Americans due to Germany's campaign of intrigue within the United States. At the same time, anti-war male characters based on caricatures of prominent pacifists William Jennings Bryan and Henry Ford are portrayed in a manner similar to how preparedness advocates frequently described female pacifists—as naïve, unthinking, and unsuspecting dupes of Germany. The parodied characters also are explicitly feminized, the enemy forcing them to cook for the invading army after the men had welcomed their presumed friends with flowers. The story, however, ends on a hopeful note as the feminists who got the United States into this mess help to organize an army of citizen-soldiers who drive out the invaders. The women also play an active role in the nation's defense, not by fighting but by seducing all 200,000 Confederation soldiers into leaving their posts, allowing the men, who under dire circumstances had rediscovered their manhood, to do the real fighting and defeat the unsuspecting foe.[35]

Dixon's ending, while somewhat confusing, appears to have been a plea for white men to reestablish their patriarchal control over an increasingly softening society. He implies that such circumstances (which were often portrayed through veiled allusions to rape in the film) leave everyone, including women, vulnerable to the designs of a more virile Other who has sustained some of its primitive virtues. Perhaps it should come as no surprise that the nation's strength is regenerated and its people saved from subjugation once white men reclaim their masculine power and women subordinate themselves to it. Dixon, though, may have overstated his case. While the *New York Times* claimed that *The Fall of a Nation* was "full of thrills," it also determined that "as propaganda, it is a pity it is so reckless." Audiences apparently did not think very highly of *The Fall of a Nation* either. Chicago theaters screened the film for only two weeks.[36]

That the movie fell flat is somewhat of a surprise considering that Dixon's approach to national weakness followed a template that he had used to great effect in his 1905 best-selling novel *The Clansman* and in the adapted screenplay for D. W. Griffith's now infamous 1915 film *The Birth of a Nation*. In both the written and film versions of the story, Anglo-Saxon northerners prioritize political gain over racial solidarity during Reconstruction by bestowing social and political equality on African Americans in the South, which results in widespread black crime, violence, and rapaciousness. Like the embrace of unmanly pacifism in *The Fall of a Nation*, the consequences of Anglo-Saxon moral decline are devastating. African Americans essentially conquer the South and its female population in a manner similar to how the Imperial Confederation and its immigrant collaborators conquered the nation. Only after the white knights of the Ku Klux Klan arise to rescue the country from northern whites' degeneracy and black depravity is the Anglo-Saxon United States redeemed.[37] The themes that Dixon had employed so effectively in *The Clansman* and *The Birth of a Nation*—the decline of Anglo-Saxon male power, subjugation by a more aggressive and primitive race, and national liberation through virtuous white citizens—were at the heart of many calls for increased preparedness. That this message in his 1916 film did not resonate with many Americans, however, likely had as much to do with citizens' relative disinterest in the Great War as with the tale's sensational nature.[38]

Other writers took what they believed to be a more systematic and less hyperbolic approach in their description of the doomsday scenario that would likely descend upon the overcivilized nation. According to Hudson Maxim, brother of the machine gun mogul Hiram, in his 1915 book *Defenseless America*, "War is inevitable" and would likely take place in Americans' own backyards. As the title suggests, the United States was not ready. Maxim described the supposedly unavoidable war in very specific detail, including but not limiting himself to maps of likely enemy advances, the number of foreign troops that could land on American shores, and the paltry defenses that the United States could bring to bear. His warning about the inevitable perils of the country's military impotence, he hoped, may at the very least "save the lives of a few of our people—may save a few homes from the torch—may lessen the area of devastation—may by adding a little power to our resistance, help to get slightly better terms from the conquerors for our liberation." His pessimism was grounded in an explicitly Darwinian and Lamarckian conception of the environment's elemental role in fostering a race's traits. Decades of anti-war sentiment and relative economic prosperity, Maxim declared, had weakened the hardy constitution of the nation's manhood. While Americans "generally recognized" that a man's "body and mind [are] the sum of his own ancestral experiences," they had "fail[ed] to recognize that he is also of necessity a war-ring animal." They also had forgotten that "the formative influences of the fierce struggle for existence have made him what he is." In short, "the absence of strife would be as fatal to him in the end as would be the absence of food, air, or water." Without conflict Anglo-Saxon identity was dying and would soon be gone for good. Yet white men could reclaim their masculinity and warrior identity and prevent atrocities similar to those German soldiers had committed in Belgium by supporting increases in the nation's military pre-paredness. "If it is wrong to insure with armaments against invasion of this country, which invasion would mean the violation of our homes, the rape of our wives and daughters and sisters and sweethearts," Maxim concluded, "then it is wrong to be a man, it is wrong to resent dishonor of the home, and all of us who have any manhood in us should be emasculated."[39]

In these well-known fictional accounts of foreign invasion, the authors plead with Anglo-Saxon American men to rediscover the old warrior identity that had served their ancestors so well or else the nation would fall victim to a more virile foreign enemy. Also in each case, timidity, pacifism, and apathy—all signs of effeminacy and overcivilization—plague white American men, leaving them physically and emotionally unprepared to combat aggression and defend the nation (and its women) from being violated. The overcivilized nation had rejected or lost the virtues of strength and resilience its forefathers had once embraced. Its Anglo-Saxon heritage and identity were fading fast, the authors and filmmakers suggested, and this degeneration could lead to potentially dire consequences unless the United States recaptured some of the primal virtues its men had lost.[40]

Fictional stories of burning cities, weak-kneed pacifists, and foreign con-querors marching down American streets were not the only exaggerated ex-amples that preparedness advocates employed to awaken overcivilized Anglo-Saxons. They also consistently cited examples of other unprepared nations that had found themselves reaping the consequences of unmanly pacifism, most notably China.[41] China's relevance laid in its relationship with the European Great Powers and Japan, which had divided Chinese territory into individual spheres of economic influence. Preparedness proponents portrayed China's predicament as a cautionary tale of a once great nation that had embraced paci-fism and forfeited its warrior traits. More specifically, advocates consistently looked to Japan's assertive wartime maneuvering in China to illustrate to

Americans the dangers of being unprepared or unwilling to defend oneself in the face of aggression.

Military and imperial concerns regarding Asia, however, were nothing new. Preparedness proponents' references to China's quandary spoke equally to both their growing apprehension about the rise of Japan as the chief enemy in the Pacific and their concerns over the United States' military unpreparedness. For one, Japan showed itself to be a worthy adversary with its overwhelming victory in the Russo-Japanese War in 1904–1905. At the same time, although they were able to make secret compromises on spheres of influence in Asia, the United States and Japan almost came to blows on two occasions in the decade prior to the First World War. The first major incident occurred in 1906 over the San Francisco school board's decision to place Japanese students in segregated schools, thus violating an 1894 non-discrimination treaty. Theodore Roosevelt's administration and Admiral Alfred Thayer Mahan overreacted to the Japanese objections to the law by speaking openly of war. Even though the informal Gentleman's Agreement in 1907 temporarily settled the issue of Japanese immigration, months later Roosevelt flexed the navy's muscles by sending the "Great White Fleet" on a public relations tour of the Pacific while Mahan warned against the "Japanizing" of the country west of the Rockies through immigration or invasion. A similar situation arose again in 1913, this time over a California law excluding Japanese immigrants from land ownership. Again, Mahan, the nation's leading voice in all matters naval, envisioned apocalyptic consequences if "free Asiatic immigration," which could lead to "Asiatic occupation—Asia colonized in America," were not brought to an end.[42] To some prominent Americans, Imperial Japan was a natural choice, along with Germany, as the virile power most likely to pose an existential threat to the overcivilized United States.

China's submission to Japan's economic and territorial demands in January 1915 was the more immediate source of preparedness supporters' concerns about Japan's military strength as well as China's and the United States' comparative impotence. Japan attempted to expand its economic sphere of influence in quasi-colonial China by issuing its Twenty-One Demands, meant to exploit Europe's preoccupation with the Great War. Despite its open support for the revolutionary Chinese government, the Wilson administration claimed to care little about Japan's demands unless it showed signs of using its newfound influence to choke off American exports to the China market.[43]

Preparedness supporters, although cognizant of the strategic significance of the situation in Asia, often portrayed Japan's dominance of China in gendered and racial contexts that hinted at Anglo-Saxon Americans' own timidity and unpreparedness. As in the fictional accounts of a European (or transparently German) enemy, propaganda regarding preparedness and Japan's dominance over China offered white Americans a choice between two extremes: regress to the state of the overcivilized and prostrate Chinese or reclaim the primitive aspects of their Anglo-Saxon ancestry by embracing the virtues of the physically dominant and masculine Japanese. Theodore Roosevelt was one of many who portrayed the Chinese and American preparedness situations as analogous, claiming that for several decades China had "been helpless to keep its own territory from spoliation and its own people from subjugation" by more militarily prepared empires. The Chinese found themselves in submission, Roosevelt claimed, because over the centuries they had withdrawn from masculine struggle while denying social prominence to their military caste in favor of pacifists. Suggesting that white Americans were degenerating into Chinese-like Others, he concluded that "The vagaries and dreams and blindness of [China's] pacifist leaders and statesmen have paralleled our own" as the United States "ha[d] been sinking into the position of the China of the Occident."[44]

Nowhere was the connection between China's and the Anglo-Saxon United States' decline, as well as martial Japan's ability to dominate both, more evident than in political cartoons. The prevailing theme in the editorial imagery was of a diminutive yet virile Japan who physically asserts itself over a despondent, submissive, physically flabby, and militarily weak China. Such representations of dominant Japan and unprepared China directly corresponded to most preparedness advocates' Darwinian view of international relations and concerns about Anglo-Saxon decline. While soft-bellied China was a thinly veiled allusion to the Anglo-Saxon race's own timidity and degeneration, domineering Japan was an implicit example of the power that maintaining a race's warrior-like traits could bring. The consistent placement of an observant Uncle Sam in the background of these cartoons was a clear attempt to emphasize the importance of the United States focusing its attention not just on the strategic situation in Asia but on the lessons the Anglo-Saxon nation could learn about preparedness from both China and Japan.

In spring 1915, the *Newark Evening Star* printed a cartoon that exemplified both the Chinese model of unmanly submission and Japan's response to the US government's criticism of its expanding influence in China. With Uncle Sam watching from a distant island labeled "U.S.," tiny yet domineering Japan stands relaxed atop oversized China's squishy stomach while holding a spear to the larger nation's nose. "Well, you see, it's this way," Japan, in a kimono,

Figure 1.1. "The Japanese Answer," cartoon, *Newark Evening Star.* Reprinted in *Current Opinion*, May 1915.

confidently proclaims in Sam's direction (fig. 1.1). In this instance, Japan is a powerful and capable military rival to the United States in the Pacific. At the same time, its boyish size, tribal outfit, and primitive weapon imply Japanese manhood had not become overcivilized nor lost touch with its primordial and, thus, martial instincts. Japan's cockiness, China's position as an out of shape and conquered behemoth, and Uncle Sam's presence implied a specific warning about American meddling in Asia as well as the perils of faint-heartedness and unpreparedness.

The following month, June 1915, *Current Opinion* ran an article reporting on a sampling of American newspaper opinion concerning the relationship between China and Japan that mirrored the lessons of fictional tales of an invasion of the United States. "Whether it be vassalage or merely advice which China must accept at the hands of militant Japan," the article claimed, "most of our papers see her pitiably helpless and suspect the aggressor of unscrupulous ambition." Along with the article, the editors also reprinted cartoons from various newspapers that made an explicit connection between the consequences of American unpreparedness and the nature of Japan's and China's relationship. A cartoon from the *Columbus (OH) Evening Dispatch*, for instance, depicted the relationship between Japan and China as one of domination and submission. A rotund "China" sits angrily on a porch with his hands cuffed. In the distance, a small Japanese soldier, with bayoneted rifle in hand, walks merrily toward a rowboat waiting by the ocean. The sun on the horizon acts as a double entendre, as symbolic of Japan ("Land of the Rising Sun") and, as the cartoon's title suggests ("The Disadvantage of Being Busy, Peaceful, and Unprepared"), as a hint as to the direction of the Japanese soldier's next unprepared target: the United States.[45]

The *New York Herald's* pictorial representation of Japan and China's relationship and its relation to the unprepared United States' potential fate lacks all subtlety. The cartoon also presents China as massive and Japan as childlike, but the control the Japanese character wields is unmistakable. As a disgusted Uncle Sam watches from a window, Japan, a pint-sized soldier in full uniform marching with a sword, parades China down the road by a leash attached to a nose ring. China, eyes closed with the white feather of cowardice in his cap, carries a sign around its neck bearing the words "Unpreparedness," "Pacifism," and "Nonresistance" (fig. 1.2). Again, the physical size of the characters denoted an unnatural relationship, with the unexpectedly strong leading the surprisingly weak. The cartoon's message was clear—if the United States did not reject the feminine principles across China's chest and embrace their hardy warrior instincts as Japan had done, it too could suffer a similar fate at the hands of a more virile race that had maintained the tenacity the Anglo-Saxon had apparently lost.

Another potential lesson in apathy and unpreparedness arose much closer to home. Beginning in January 1916, Mexican rebels, led by Francisco "Pancho" Villa, began attacking and murdering American civilians in northern Mexico and destroying their property, as well as the property of the Americans' employers. On the night of March 9, Villa's men fulfilled preparedness advocates' dark prophecy when they invaded New Mexico and ransacked the small town of Columbus, killing nearly twenty Americans. Soon afterward, President Wilson ordered 4,800 US regulars, called the Punitive Expedition under the command of General John J. Pershing, to cross the Rio Grande in search of the Villistas. The pursuit proved fruitless through March and April. By June, Wilson had mobilized 110,000 National Guardsmen to supplement the small and ineffective regular force. The results, however, were no better.[46]

The debacle in Mexico was exactly the kind of military embarrassment that preparedness advocates could exploit. The editors of the *New York World*, Charleston (SC) *News and Courier*, and *Chicago Tribune* directed their ire

Figure 1.2. "For Those That Like This Sort of Thing This Is the Sort of Thing They Like," cartoon, *New York Herald*. Reprinted in *Current Opinion*, July 1915.

toward a disinterested American public that was too enamored with luxury and comfort to face the reality of their martial deficits. According to the *World*, the American people encouraged "the attitude of sneering indifference to military preparedness" displayed in Congress because they "have been asleep, dreaming dreams of a happy-go-lucky world in which America was the petted Fortunatus to whom no danger would approach."[47] Likely with images of German atrocities in Belgium on his mind, Theodore Roosevelt grossly exaggerated the gravity of the situation on the border when he charged that the American people had "submitted tamely to the murder of our men and the rape of our women." The nation's "spiritless submission" had resulted in hundreds of American deaths in Mexico and the United States, he claimed inaccurately.[48] Roosevelt also argued, with an unveiled affront to the nation's manhood, that the army's inability to capture Villa and his comrades exposed an "impotence . . . for meeting any kind of serious assault made on our shores by any military power of the old world."[49] To the *Omaha World-Herald* of the generally pacific plains region, the nation had no excuse for its complacency and military feebleness. "Mexico is a third-rate nation on its last legs. As a military power it is a joke. As a power of any kind it is a joke," the editors proclaimed. "The United States, on the other hand, with a hundred million people, is the wealthiest country in the world. It is fat and wheezy with plenty.... And it is so poorly protected, so little prepared we are to defend our wealth, not to speak of our lives and our liberties, that a burlesque 'soldier' like Villa can cross the border on which the mobile portion of our army is massed, burn our towns, kill our people, and hurry back again to safety, while it takes us a week to make ready to go after him!"[50] The Anglo-Saxon United States had become so detached from its masculine responsibility and warrior identity that it was powerless to avenge the murdering of its countrymen on American soil at the hands of a less civilized, "third-rate" race.

Despite the *World-Herald*'s contention that the public had been ignoring the country's military needs, Germany's various transgressions and over a year of hyperbolic preparedness propaganda had caught the attention of many in Congress. Days before Villa's attack into New Mexico, the House Military Affairs Committee released for debate what would become the National Defense Act, which the Columbus raid and the army's failure to punish Villa would spur into law in July 1916. The legislation called for a small and gradual increase of the regular army and the expansion and federalization of the National Guard as a second line of defense. The increases, though, did not properly reflect the angry and anxious mood of many preparedness advocates. Instead of enacting universal military training to allow the army to meet the immediate problem in Mexico or the threat of an impending invasion from Europe or Asia, the new army was not set to reach its maximum size of 250,000 regulars and 450,000 guardsmen until 1921. The urgency of the moment, preparedness supporters feared, had been overlooked as Wilson and Congress punted any real talk of defense legislation until long after the 1916 election.[51]

Due to their disenchantment over the limited reforms, pro-preparedness publications fumed that Mexico had forced the United States into accepting a watered-down preparedness. A fitting example is a cartoon entitled "The Little Accelerator," published in the *Brooklyn Eagle* after the passage of the National Defense Act. The image depicts Mexico as a small, dark, boyish figure in a sombrero forcing a tall and stout Uncle Sam to march down a road marked "Preparedness" by poking Sam in the calf with the bayonet at the end of his rifle—Sam's calf being as high as little Mexico can reach. At the end of the road lies an active munitions factory (fig. 1.3). The image is the inverse of the paternalistic cartoons from the turn of the century that infantilized the United

Figure 1.3. "The Little Accelerator," cartoon, *Brooklyn Eagle*. Reprinted in *Literary Digest*, August 5, 1916.

States' supposedly uncivilized imperial subjects in the Pacific and Caribbean while placing Uncle Sam in the role of parent or teacher. It is also reminiscent of cartoons depicting China's and Japan's wartime relationship, in this case with Uncle Sam assuming a position similar to China's. The absurd difference in size and apparent age between Mexico and Sam, perhaps symbolic of each race's level of advancement, conveys the notion that a backward, non-white country like Mexico should not be capable of forcing the hand of the civilized Anglo-Saxon United States. The analogy appears to be that of a young, primitive child (undoubtedly the tougher of the two) wielding full control over a grown adult, perhaps a father figure. The message the cartoon offers also is consistent with several of the fictional invasion stories—again a tougher race is teaching the pacifistic United States a lesson on strength and preparedness. The fact that Wilson, Congress, and an indifferent populace allowed such an imbalance of toughness and martial character to develop between white Americans and a presumably inferior race, preparedness supporters believed, revealed a dangerous neglect of the military and an unnatural swing in the relationship of dependency the country held with its economically and supposedly racially weaker neighbor. Proving itself incapable of defending its borders and whipping a less civilized people into shape, the Anglo-Saxon United States appeared to be in a steady racial-masculine decline. The race was degenerating into a weak Other in relation to previous, hardier generations.

Germany's return to their policy of unrestricted U-boat attacks on January 31, 1917, and the public revelation of the Zimmermann Telegram on March 1, however, made the National Defense Act largely irrelevant. With Germany's attempt to court both Mexico and Japan to join their plot, it seemed that the United States could be in danger of being surrounded by enemies, all of whom had recently shown themselves to be of a more martial disposition than most Anglo-Saxon Americans. Germany, the most common selection of a European enemy in most fictional accounts of invasion, appeared to be genuinely bent on world domination or, at the very least, supremacy in the Western Hemisphere. The mention of Japan in the German note likely was no surprise to many Americans as a scant four years had passed since the last West Coast war scare. And Mexico (or, more specifically, Villa's bandits) had already, more or less, invaded the United States, providing an example of the perils of apathy and the decline of martial values. The *Omaha World-Herald* best expressed many preparedness advocates' Darwinian anxieties: "The German Government stands willing to turn loose upon the United States—our own country—the hordes of alien and inferior civilizations unless we accept and bow to its ukases upon the high seas."[52] Germany's actions in early 1917 effectively ended the prewar preparedness debate and awakened most of the country—pacifists, militant preparedness advocates, and everyone in between—to the likelihood that soon war would no longer be a fantasy played out in speeches, newspapers, novels, magazines, and movies.

In truth, none of the potential enemies mentioned in the Zimmermann Telegram were likely to harm the United States in the ways preparedness advocates had described. The European powers were bleeding each other white and exhausting their resources, tensions between Japan and the United States were at a low ebb by 1917, and Mexico continued to reel from revolution. Perhaps the reason the seeming inevitability of war in March was so jarring to the American people was that race, gender, and fear-based preparedness propaganda was effective in unintended ways. Contrary to propagandists' intentions, manufacturing and facilitating a concern about national effeminacy and a fear of foreign rivals, along with the trauma over German intrigue and German American loyalty, likely had reaffirmed many Americans' belief that the United States was best served by staying out of other nation's affairs.

That is not to say, however, that preparedness propaganda was ineffective. In fact, propaganda produced after April 1917 as well as many Americans' interpretations of the German threat to the country indicate that some general themes of the preparedness argument carried over into wartime and became more widely accepted. After entering the war, the possibility of an invasion of American soil by a race that embraced its primal instincts—militaristic Germany—became a more conceivable prospect in the event the United States and the Allies lost the war in Europe. Many Americans would buy wartime propagandists' line that apathy meant subjugation, which in turn meant the physical destruction of the country. The loss of Anglo-Saxon independence meant that their racial-national identity could not survive.

Inherent in those concerns, however, was a belief in the power of environment to not only advance but also reverse the wheels of racial progress. As many racial scientists of the period had done, proponents of military preparedness made a clear distinction between which environments and types of degeneration were particularly healthy or harmful. On one side of the spectrum was the theory that a unique American race was forged from a variety of white nationalities while taming nature and Native Americans. On the other side was the belief that urbanization and materialism were responsible for the decline of the Anglo-Saxon race. During wartime, this same theme of environment shaping racial character and development would color Americans' understanding of their German enemies, whose traditions and environment were said to have shaped them into a more aggressive and immoral race and nation despite their close kinship with the Anglo-Saxon.

Yet while preparedness advocates warned that an overcivilized and apathetic environment could degrade the Anglo-Saxon race into oblivion, during neutrality other commentators were becoming increasingly concerned about potential enemies within American borders. Why had some immigrants not assimilated into liberty-loving Americans within the United States' free and democratic atmosphere? The answer, an increasing number of "real" Americans feared, was a deep-seated campaign of German propaganda, espionage, and sabotage.

CHAPTER TWO

The Emergence of the Internal Enemy Other, 1914–1917

I would not be afraid, upon the test of "America first," to take a census of all foreign-born citizens of the United States, for I know that the vast majority of them came here because they believed in America; and their belief in America has made them better citizens than some people who were born in America. . . . But I am in a hurry for an opportunity to have a line-up and let the men who are thinking first of other countries stand on one side—biblically it should be on the left—and all those that are America first, last, and all the time on the other side.

WOODROW WILSON, October 11, 1915

Prussia's overwhelming victory in the Franco-Prussian War of 1870–1871 was no mere feat of arms, wrote journalist Melville Davisson Post in the April 10, 1915, edition of the *Saturday Evening Post*. Equally responsible for Prussia's triumph was that "France was already occupied under an elaborate system of secret colonization" by "at least thirty-five thousand secret agents of the German Government." The effectiveness of the German spy system could only have improved in the forty-three years between 1871 and the renewal of the Franco-German conflict on August 3, 1914. "When the German war machine began to move" through Belgium and northern France "everything before it . . . was known and planned to the minutest detail" by the secret agents already in country. "Every foot of ground from the Rhine to the Seine had been surveyed and plotted," Post explained. "Every tree and bush was known; every road and path; every village, and every street of every village; every bridge, all streams and hedges—in fact, the very contours of the earth." Teutonic preparatory intelligence-gathering also allegedly went beyond mere espionage and included unity-corrupting propaganda and the sabotaging of French industry and transportation. "The German mind does not stop short of a complete thoroughness," Post concluded, implying that all Germans were naturally meticulous. While other European nations conducted espionage, Germany excelled because of the inherent "patience of the Teuton" and a "talent for minute organization characteristic of the German mind."[1]

Post likely wrote this story as a cautionary tale. By spring 1915, American newspapers had been reporting that German espionage, sabotage, and propagandizing had been taking place in the United States for months. Yet unlike in France in the early 1870s, millions—not tens of thousands—of allegedly patient, coldly efficient, and thorough Germans called the United States home in 1915. As allegedly happened in France, some German sabotage, espionage, and propaganda activity, albeit a small amount, had taken place. These offenses within American borders and those by U-boats under the Atlantic inched the United States ever closer to the European war, and Anglo-Saxon anxiety over the loyalty of German immigrants and their American-born children intensified. For some white Americans, the prospect of widespread German American disloyalty bred as much, if not more, anxiety as submarines and the prospect of a foreign military invasion. As their behavior after April 1917 would show (see chapter 3), an increasing number of Anglo-Saxon Americans were convinced—by the real and imagined evidence of German intrigue that mounted over the course of American neutrality—that it was possible, if not probable, that a Teutonic invasion of sorts had been underway for decades. By the time the United States entered the war, the specter of Teutonic plots and German American disloyalty seemed to be urgent, alien threats to Anglo-Saxon American civilization.[2]

The demonization of German Americans, however, did not come automatically or easily during the neutrality period. In the press and among political leaders, a confused ambivalence defined the prevailing feeling toward Teutonic immigrants as editors and politicians tried to reconcile the generally positive prewar understanding of German Americans with the disturbing accounts of intrigue that they were reporting in newspapers, in speeches, and on the campaign trail. Although not direct reflections of public opinion, most indications suggest that editorial opinion and political rhetoric both mirrored and shaped popular concerns about German American loyalty. Spurred by the authority of these voices as well as by contemporary understandings of race and culture, German Americans' transformation into a full-fledged Other in the minds of many white Americans during neutrality was a relatively quick yet tortuous process that is indicative of the instability and fluidity of "whiteness" in the early twentieth century.

Several factors came into play to alter Anglo-Saxon Americans' perceptions of German Americans. The most obvious issue that soured white Americans' views of their Germanic neighbors was that actual agents of the German government were caught working behind the scenes and within American

borders, committing sabotage, engaging in propaganda, and initiating contingency plans in the event of war with the United States. Although German
spies and saboteurs had few successes, the repeated publication of their mostly
failed ventures naturally increased suspicions of the millions of similarly accented American residents. At the same time, German propaganda campaigns
raised concerns that the kaiser's agents were attempting to de-Americanize
assimilated German Americans.

Additionally, popular Teutonic racial stereotypes were well-established by
the start of the Great War and vague enough to fit either positive or fear-laden
opinions of German Americans. By the American war declaration in April
1917, the stereotypes that had seemed to have cemented their place within the
Anglo-Saxon in-group before 1914—that Germans were hard-working, ambitious, systematic, and self-sufficient—were unchanged.[3] Anglo-Saxons' perceptions of these characteristics, however, had shifted from 1914 to 1917. The same
traits that had made German Americans appear to be such faithful and valuable
Americans eventually became explanations for their disloyalty and Otherness.
By the time the United States was at war with Germany, for instance, many
Americans understood Teutonic thoroughness and diligence as evidence of
their innate talent for espionage, not only their industriousness. Furthermore,
Germans' inherent self-reliance was perceived as clannish or parochial, be-
havioral traits not conducive to assimilation into Anglo-Saxon American
society and evidence of their continued or renewed loyalty to Germany. In short,
by 1917 a critical mass of white Americans had concluded that German Americans had always been a racial Other, plotting on behalf of their Old World
masters to challenge Anglo-Saxon supremacy in the United States.

Finally, German intrigue and alleged German American duplicity aroused
many white Americans' preexisting nativist fears that immigrant deviousness
and degeneracy posed a racial and apocalyptic threat to Anglo-Saxon culture.
Throughout the nineteenth and early twentieth centuries, Anglo-Saxon Americans viewed most European immigrants, especially those of the working
class, with at least a modicum of suspicion, often questioning their capacity
for self-restraint and self-government. For many Anglo-Saxons, particularly
racial theorists and those of the well-to-do classes, strikes and radical political
ideologies had been the most alarming means by which the allegedly inferior
white races had threatened to overrun the republic since the 1870s and 1880s.
As scholar Matthew Frye Jacobson has noted, "by its violation of 'civilized'
standards of conduct . . . immigrant radicalism offered incontrovertible proof
of the immigrants' troubling racial pedigree."[4] By the dawn of the 1890s, the

stereotype of the volatile, savage, bomb-throwing, un-American immigrant had become part of the American cultural landscape. Consequently, as the number of immigrants from central, southern, and eastern Europe grew and labor disturbances appeared to occur more frequently, many in the press and within the respectable classes mistakenly identified most immigrants with radicalism and social revolution.[5] Although this alarmist anti-radical nativism only appeared episodically, the widespread sense that foreigners with undemocratic and anti-capitalist beliefs had the potential to literally destroy the United States from within was never far from many Americans' minds. With the beginning of the war, concerns about the potentially destructive impact of foreign peoples on American society became more intense and narrowly applied. Actual attempts by German agents to foment unrest and destroy vital pieces of economic infrastructure during World War I offered Anglo-Saxon Americans an opportunity to redirect their lingering paranoia over the influx of Europe's transient and allegedly radical laboring class onto a more specific target.

Before the start of the Great War, however, few would have pegged the German American population as a powder keg. Although many scientists and laypeople before the war claimed that Germans were overbearing, snobbish, and insular, their supposed racial kinship with Anglo-Saxons placed them high in the hierarchy of white races. The popular idea that a nationality's culture was an expression of inherent yet potentially malleable traits implied that the more similar two races' cultures appeared, the more similar their innate characteristics were likely to be. Under this assumption, white Americans considered their German cousins to be among the most assimilable of aliens largely because their presumed industriousness and ingenuity mirrored that of the Anglo-Saxon. Germans, as well as the Irish, largely cemented their "whiteness" in the two decades following the Civil War. Their sacrifices for the Union Army, their desirability over African Americans in state and federal bureaucracies during Reconstruction, and the beginning influx of southern and eastern Europeans illuminated their close racial and cultural connection to Anglo-Saxons.[6]

Not only were German Americans respected and trusted, but their language, culture, and people were seemingly everywhere in the United States in significant numbers in the 1910s. Despite the cataclysmic ravings of prominent nativists that waves of eastern and southern Europeans were poised to overwhelm and outbreed the Anglo-Saxon race, by 1910 the widely accepted Teutons constituted the largest non-Anglo white nationality in the United States by a wide margin. First-generation German immigrants and their children totaled over eight million, which accounted for slightly over a quarter of all white immigrants in the country. Although most (over 85 percent) lived in the mid-Atlantic and Midwestern states, only in New England and the mountain regions of the West were Germans not the largest immigrant group. Nor were they bound primarily to cities. While two-thirds lived in urban areas, Germans were the most likely among European immigrants to reside in rural settings. Yet in several major cities—such as St. Louis, Detroit, Los Angeles, Milwaukee, and Chicago—Germans were the largest non-Anglo ethnic group. Additionally, a study of German American settlement patterns in the 1880s showed that they were quite willing to integrate into preexisting Anglo-Saxon communities, indicating they were less clannish than other immigrant nationalities that segregated into the ethnic neighborhoods of the nation's industrial centers.[7]

In *The Old World in the New*, an influential book on the racial characteristics of European immigrants in the United States published mere months before the start of the First World War, leading sociologist Edward A. Ross declared that German immigration had an overall positive impact on American society. Physically, the racial mixing of the "strong, but often too stocky for grace" German with the "taller and thinner American" produced "good results in figure." Socially, the "heavy, slow-moving German blood benefits us [Anglo-Saxons] by counteracting" the characteristic impatience and "overlively ferment" of Anglo-Saxons. This "sluggish Teutonic temperament," though, was not a sign of low intelligence in the German but a desire "to be comprehensive and final." This proved, Ross argued, that the earlier charges that Germans had a penchant for political and social radicalism, an opinion emanating from concerns over mid-nineteenth-century political exiles (the so-called Forty-Eighters), were misplaced. The German's "respect for authority" along with "his love of order and system" signaled his conservatism. Consequently, it was "the apparent destiny" of German immigrants "to lose themselves in the American people, and to take the stamp of a culture which is, in origin at least, eighty per cent British."[8]

Ross's assessment of Teutonic capabilities and assimilability, however, was not entirely complimentary. While not doubting German Americans' ability to assimilate, Ross discussed several Teutonic traits that left some doubt as to whether they would be willing to conform to American culture. For instance, he contradicted his statement on the Teutons' easy assimilation by claiming that "the German is hard-headed, and is not easily borne off his feet by the contagion of example." At the same time, his "relish for details and this passion for thoroughness make him a born investigator" who "has most distinguished himself in work that calls for long and close observation."[9] When placed in the context of the ensuing war in Europe, these presumed characteristics would suggest an inborn attachment to German culture and a natural talent for espionage. Despite placing a positive spin on the German's perceived racial traits and kinship to the Anglo-Saxon, Ross emphasized the foreignness, or Otherness, of Teutonic Americans. Ross's book is indicative of the ambivalence that American politicians, editors, and propagandists would display in regard to German American fidelity during neutrality. Despite declarations of faith in Teutons' reliability, popular assumptions of their racial composition left the door open to suspicion.

And suspicious some were. Although very rare and not close to the level of intensity seen after 1914 (or after 1917 especially), prewar skepticism over German American intentions shared much in common with what would come during wartime. The source of mistrust was German-language newspapers and clubs, some of which touted German cultural superiority and occasionally portrayed autocratic Germany in a positive light. But although most of those who started pro-German publications and groups in the late nineteenth century were newer German immigrants, who were more likely to have close cultural ties to Imperial Germany than previous German immigrants, an emotional connection to one's ancestral homeland did not automatically imply an immigrant was not loyal to the United States. Still, these associations and newspapers alarmed a small number of Americans because they signified that the country's largest immigrant population may not be assimilating and because disagreements over imperial spheres of influence since the 1880s had caused relations with Germany to sour. Prior to 1914, several prominent Americans came to suspect that German American communities were sleeper cells, waiting on instructions from the kaiser or private German imperialist clubs on how they could help further Germany's aims in the Americas.[10] One notable example is the statesman John Hay, who, when secretary of state in 1903, warned then-President Theodore Roosevelt, who also was wary of German ambitions, of Teutonic disloyalty and clannishness. "It is a singular ethnological and political paradox," Hay claimed, that "the prime motive of every German American is hostility to every country in the world, including America, which is not friendly to Germany."[11]

The National German American Alliance (NGAA) was the entity around which most of the rare prewar distrust of the German American community was based. From the moment of its inception in 1901, a few American conspiracy theorists wrongly accused the NGAA of being a subsidiary of the Pan-German League, an organization founded in Germany in 1899 that was bent on expanding Germany's world empire into the Western Hemisphere. American misgivings grew along with the NGAA, which became the largest immigrant organization in the United States, peaking at three million members in 1916. Some Americans viewed the NGAA as additional evidence of Teutons' unwillingness to Americanize and an attempt to conscript German Americans in the kaiser's plot to undermine a chief imperial rival. A tightly unified immigrant association like the NGAA, some feared, could steer elections and, consequently, policies in a direction more suitable to German imperial interests than those of the United States.[12] The combination of pro-German publications and ethnic organizations would become a recipe for more widespread suspicion as the United States drew closer to entering the First World War.

Unlike some nativists' unnecessary fear of the NGAA prior to 1914, much of what Americans read in the newspapers between 1915 and 1917 about the German government's transgressions was very real, which undoubtedly tilted some Americans' attitudes about German Americans away from their general admiration for the Teuton. Not only were German submarines stalking the Atlantic for merchant shipping but a small band of secret agents, working mostly through the German Embassy in Washington, was active in the United States during American neutrality as well. Although mostly unsuccessful and far smaller in scope than the generally successful British campaign of intrigue, which consisted largely of propaganda, German agents at times achieved impressive results. Yet they were often caught, before or after carrying out their plans, making headlines across the country. German Americans took more than their fair share of the blame for Teutonic scheming within the United States, although very few actively assisted the kaiser's provocateurs.[13]

In 1915, German agents were particularly active. The first major incident occurred on February 2, 1915, on the US–Canadian border in Maine, where Werner Horn, a German national and captain in the German reserve forces, attempted to demolish a Canadian Pacific Railroad bridge. After his arrest, Horn admitted that unnamed German agents made "arrangements" with him and provided on-the-scene support. He was also quick to point out that the plot was not an act of war against the United States but Canada, its membership in the British Commonwealth making it Germany's legitimate enemy.[14] Perhaps sensing that the incident could change American attitudes toward German Americans for the worst, Bernhard Ridder, whose father was editor of the widely circulated German-language paper the *New Yorker Staats-Zeitung*, tried to defend the Americanness of Teutonic immigrants by pointing out that there was "a great difference between Germans here and the German-Americans." The latter had clearly chosen to side with their adopted country, while the former, like Werner Horn, "would undoubtedly" lash out violently if war came with their Fatherland.[15]

Horn's escapades did little to cause Anglo-Saxon Americans to begin perceiving American Teutons as outsiders. The sinking of the *Lusitania* in spring 1915, however, raised the stakes of German American loyalty, just as it did the issue of the nation's military preparedness. Not only was the incident a defining moment for US–German relations, but it also began the slow deterioration of Anglo-Saxon Americans' sense of security and distance from the war. With the attack on the *Lusitania*, Germany had solidified itself as the primary military threat to the republic, which made German American loyalty to the United States an issue of national security.

The number of stories and editorials concerning the "hyphen" (a pejorative term used to label immigrants of allegedly mixed or feigned loyalty) increased significantly after the *Lusitania* disaster. One example of this shift is the spin *Literary Digest* put on the German American press's reaction to the sinking. "'Entirely justified' is the verdict that is passed by German American papers upon the sinking of the *Lusitania*," it claimed, misleadingly implying that this was the most common sentiment among the German-language press. The editors then craftily employed the passive voice when describing their own views of German Americans' ultimate loyalty while at the same time perhaps betraying their racial-cultural stereotyping of the supposedly clannish Teuton. "It has been predicted" that if war with Germany became a reality, "American citizens of German blood would be false to their allegiance to the United States and that civil war would ensue." The editors cited only two editorial pledges of loyalty to the United States by German American papers, as compared to four celebrating or excusing the sinking.[16]

Condemnations of American Teutons, though, were far from universal and, if the next week's edition of *Literary Digest* is any indication, may have been voiced by the minority. The editors cited over a dozen mainstream metropolitan newspapers—such as the *Chicago Tribune*, *Baltimore American*, *St. Louis Globe-Democrat*, and nearly all of the major New York dailies—that expressed confidence in Teutonic American loyalty and empathy for the uncomfortable position in which the *Lusitania* sinking had placed them. The incident, *Literary Digest* reported, forced German immigrants to choose between Germany and their new home. Most editors affirmed that German Americans had passed the test with flying colors. The *Springfield (MA) Republican*, for instance, proclaimed that "there are no stancher [*sic*] or more thorough Americans than those who come to the New World from Germany . . . their case is tragic, but their loyalty is unswerving." The editors of the *New York Tribune* drew a similar conclusion. "Among German-Americans in general there can be no doubt of their" loyalty if German crimes on the high seas led to war and forced "them to choose between the land of their fathers and the land of their choice." The *Tribune* explained, "The call of the adopted country is the stronger, beyond a doubt." Yet despite printing such glowing praise for German American fidelity, *Literary Digest* could not allow its readers to forget Teutonic Americans' apparent excusing of the *Lusitania* sinking and overlook the obvious signs that they may be disloyal outsiders. "It must not be forgotten that they [German Americans] are almost unanimously convinced of the justice of Germany's cause as against the Allies, that many of them still disapprove of the Administration's neutrality program, that many find justification for the sinking of the *Lusitania*, and that not a few" condemned Wilson's harsh words toward Germany after the incident.[17] *Literary Digest*'s uncertainty over German Americans' actual allegiance is profound and representative of where both editorial and public opinion was headed.

The continued plotting of German agents on American soil from the late summer to winter 1915 directed the country's attention away from the *Lusitania* and back to the internal threat of German sabotage. After the Horn story lost momentum, concerns over actual German intrigue subsided until August, when the *New York World* released documents proving authentic German propaganda and sabotage plots in the United States had been conducted under the watchful eye of the kaiser's embassy in Washington. The documents, which the Secret Service recovered after the German Commercial Attaché Heinrich Albert accidentally left them behind on a train, contained astonishing details of German intrigue, including but not limited to the purchasing of an American munitions plant, the funding of pro-German newspapers, and the financing of several German and Irish immigrant associations.[18] In October, authorities nabbed a group of German saboteurs in the Northeast who named Franz von Papen and Karl Boy-Ed, the military and naval attachés in the German Embassy in Washington, as their primary contacts.

The most extensive case involving embassy personnel was probably that of Captain Franz Rintelen von Kleist, whom the *New York Times* speculated was "a warm personal friend of the Kaiser." In November, the *Times* reported that authorities in London had detained Rintelen, the ringleader of a massive German sabotage ring, with a forged American passport. The stack of evidence against Rintelen's "Teutonic conspiracy" was "mountain high," the editors concluded. In a nod to the stereotype of Teutonic efficiency, they maintained that the scheme "involv[ed] scores of persons, operating as parts of a single, splendidly organized, well-oiled machine."[19] Rintelen's plotting included practically every possible means of sabotage—setting fires and dynamite charges in munitions plants, encouraging strikes, planting bombs on Allied cargo ships leaving American ports, and attempting to reinstate the German-friendly dictator Victoriano Huerta in Mexico. Rintelen, whom the Secret Service had been tailing for months, also had frequent contact with von Papen and Boy-Ed, further implicating the German Embassy and contributing to the attachés' recall in December.[20]

The reaction in the press, especially in the Northeast, to the twists and turns of the various spy sagas of 1915 was indicative of Anglo-Saxon Americans' building anxiety over German intrigue, growing confusion about the allegiance of their Teutonic neighbors, and lingering fear of foreign insurgence. After the *New York Times* in early November compiled a list of thirteen steamships and nine munitions plants that had mysteriously exploded, *Literary Digest* reported that "some attribute [the blasts] to German agents or to German sympathizers." Such "disclosures thus far only scratch the surface" of the true magnitude of German intrigue, opined the *New York Herald*. If the plotters' incrimination of von Papen and Boy-Ed could be believed, then "Germany is now waging war within the United States."[21] Editors at the *New York Tribune* stood at the extreme end of public opinion, grossly overstating the spy threat while alleging that some German Americans took pride in their un-Americanness and the uncivilized destruction saboteurs had wrought. The "country is filled from one end to the other with disorder and with violence, which shows itself with fires, explosions, plotting. Ships that sail from American ports break into flame. . . . Alien fringes of our population are making alien interests the test of their votes cast in our elections and openly boasting of it."[22]

The conviction that German Americans reveled in the success of un-American and destructive plots against American capitalism was little different from the popular suspicions of widespread socialist or anarchist sympathies among the foreign-born population. Some newspapers, like the *Chicago Daily News*, explicitly equated German intrigue with violent labor radicalism. In a *Daily News* cartoon from October 1915, a "spy" of unspecified nationality surrounded by dynamite crawls out of an American flag–designed tent marked

Figure 2.1. "His Shelter," cartoon, *Chicago Daily News*. Reprinted in *Literary Digest*, October 30, 1915.

with the word "citizenship," his eyes and bad intentions set on several large factories (fig. 2.1). The "spy" label is a clear inference of the character's German ancestry while the tent implies that American Teutons, like the more familiar radical immigrant infiltrators, used the cloak of citizenship as a cover for their dastardly deeds. More importantly, the implied charge that sabotage was the work of German Americans, not trained German nationals, and the likening of the once-trusted Teutonic American with the radicalism of newer and supposedly more backward immigrants was a means of validating white Americans' growing distrust of the German American community.

While German sabotage and intrigue mostly came to an end upon von Papen and Boy-Ed's expulsion, a very small number of German agents remained active and undetected into 1917, their only apparent successes being the massive explosions at a munitions depot on Black Tom Island on July 30, 1916, and the Kingsland Assembly Plant on January 11, 1917, both in New Jersey. But despite assumptions of German guilt in the press, which over twenty years later investigators for the postwar Mixed Claims Commission would prove to have been correct, federal and local detectives at the time found no evidence that German agents were responsible for either blast.[23] With the two most dramatic incidents of German sabotage after 1915 being deemed accidental explosions at the time, the United States did not experience any verified attacks by Teutonic saboteurs throughout the remainder of the war. Yet despite the fact that operatives sent from Germany, not German Americans, carried out the vast majority of the conspiratorial plans, the alarming incidents in 1915 were as damaging to Anglo-Saxons' trust of German Americans as they were to US–German relations. With a pattern established, perceptions of the Teutonic population within the United States shifted toward the more familiar paradigm of immigrant radicals whose inborn traits and devotion to anti-democratic ideologies made them a direct threat to the country and individual communities.

Of greater concern during neutrality and wartime than sabotage or espionage was the possibility of anti-American propaganda spreading within German American communities. Faith in American Teutons' "Americanness" likely cushioned the psychological blow of the German government's sabotage and espionage plots within the United States, but the widely publicized charge that German American communities were inundated with propaganda bred concerns about Teutonic de-Americanization. After all, science and popular stereotypes portrayed Teutons as inherently clannish. To which clan, their adopted or ancestral one, would they ultimately pledge allegiance? American Teutons were not yet outsiders, but the prospect of that trust being broken through underhanded means, be it by German agents or immigrants themselves, facilitated German Americans' supposed slide into Otherness. If editorial opinion is any indication, Anglo-Saxons generally chose to keep German Americans within the American fold throughout the intrigue drama of 1915, with most refusing to believe that foreign propagandists could undo the impact of years living in Anglo-Saxon society. But this embrace would loosen as incessant charges of German propagandizing and disloyalty contributed to Anglo-Saxons' reconception of the German American community as a dangerous and subversive alien threat.

Early in the neutrality period, Americans appear to have remained ambivalent over the potential impact of German propagandizing on Teutonic Americans. While concerns that German American leaders were working to organize and indoctrinate their communities to act to Germany's benefit surfaced in the early months of 1915, many leading publications maintained with certainty that any attempts to sway the Teutonic population would fall on deaf ears. One prominent case was that of the National German American League (NGAL; a separate organization from the NGAA). Shortly after its founding in early February, the NGAL resolved to lobby Congress for a policy of "genuine American neutrality" that would disallow any commercial or financial arrangement with any warring power. Seeing this as a scheme to sever American economic ties to Great Britain, newspapers across the nation accused the delegates of attempting to bind the United States to the interests of autocratic Germany. The Philadelphia *Public Ledger* called the NGAL's resolutions "a pro-German plot"; the New York *Sun* claimed that the United States' tightening relationship with the Allies was "historically, legally, and morally correct," whereas the NGAL's version of neutrality would mean "the enlistment of the American people under the flag of Germany." The editors of the *New York Times* added that "never since the foundation of the Republic has" a group "more completely subservient to a foreign Power and to foreign influence" convened for the purpose of influencing the nation's foreign policy.[24] By contrast, many editors maintained that the Anglo-Saxon United States had nothing to fear from pro-German propaganda. The *Brooklyn Eagle* was confident that "the incorrigible agitators" would not even "find a corporal's guard of followers." The *St. Louis Republic*, published in a city with a very sizable Teutonic population, "refuses to be alarmed" that the NGAL could have any effect on American policy because German American voters were no different from any other true American. Any organized bloc of citizens, it reasonably argued, would "vote together because that is the way they intended to vote anyhow, or they disregard the opinions of their organizations because they think their private judgment is better than that of their lodge brothers."[25]

Even as headlines divulging news of Teutonic intrigue plots became more common and US–German relations grew more strained over U-boat attacks, many prominent publications continued to hold on to the positive prewar disposition toward German American faithfulness. In June, the magazine *World's Work* referenced concerns about the prospect of Teutonic immigrants' complicity in a German conspiracy similar to the intrigue suspected of the NGAL, arguing, "The European war has revealed one conscious movement which Americans had hitherto only faintly comprehended: an imperial determination to use several million Americans of German origin as positive assets of the German Empire." Yet most Teutonic residents continued to embrace their American identity, thus signifying a clear distinction between "the mass of decently living Americans of German origin" and "a few noisy newspapers, a few blatant professors, a small collection of curbstone orators" who openly celebrated their loyalty to Germany.[26] The problem was a few misguided souls, not German Americans writ large.

By the end of 1915, however, stories of German intrigue within the United States, situated alongside apocalyptic preparedness propaganda, had left some white Americans with a sense that a less assimilable, and thus potentially more dangerous, variety of German had invaded their country. In December, a contributor to the *World's Work* offered an explanation for German Americans' apparent lack of allegiance to the United States, arguing that race and nineteenth-century immigration patterns explained the presence of both ardently loyal and ferociously disloyal German Americans. The writer claimed that the most pro-American Teutons migrated prior to the 1870s from southern Germany, "those parts of the present empire which, historians and ethnologists tell us, represent the finer and softer side of the German character." The first batch of German immigrants were very capable of adopting Anglo-Saxon culture, but they were not without their problems. According to the writer, many early immigrants looked to set themselves apart by establishing a nation within a nation, or "a kind of German Quebec," in Wisconsin. But these Teutons were able to redirect their clannish proclivities and "displayed a high grade of Americanism in every regard." Yet after the birth of the German Empire in 1871, a new breed of German immigrant came to the United States. These new immigrants were so unlike the previous immigrants that they "represented almost a different race from those who had come earlier." The difference was that the militaristic Prussians of central and eastern Europe likely made up the majority of the newer German Americans. They were "hard-headed, practical, enterprising men. . . . Pride characterized these immigrants of the 'seventies and 'eighties, just as republican idealism had marked those of the earlier period." At the same time, the Great War had exposed the newer Prussianized German Americans' inborn stubbornness and insularity in that they "still have a certain allegiance to the Fatherland"; consequently, they "presented a more fruitful soil for German agitators."[27] Many American Teutons, then, were alien Others who were possibly incapable of Americanizing and thus easy marks for German propagandists.

How deeply such propaganda had reached into these communities and how receptive German immigrants were to it were open questions during the remainder of American neutrality. Confident pronouncements of Teutonic loyalty suggested that Americans continued to feel at least somewhat assured of German Americans' ability to Americanize. Anglo-Saxons viewed American Teutons in a much different light than more recent immigrants from southern and eastern Europe, who they believed were volatile and largely incapable of adapting to Anglo-Saxon culture. Yet the implication of a vast German propaganda effort raised the issue of whether German Americans shared more in common with those less desirable aliens than previously thought.[28] In the minds of an increasing number of Americans, German propaganda threatened to undermine the Americanization of the largest and most assimilable foreign-born population in the country. If that were to happen, some feared, what would become of the country and white Anglo-Saxon identity?

The question of German American loyalty and its implications for national security inspired a public debate on assimilation that played out in the press. Although many Americanization drives were based in a genuine concern for others, Americanizers also thought of these campaigns as a means of assuaging lingering popular fears that Protestant Anglo-Saxons were losing control of their country to people of different and presumably inferior races.[29] Un-Othering aliens was a way to mitigate that apprehension by homogenizing American society as much as immigrant capabilities allowed. But by 1916 the events of the previous year had led Americanizers to begin doubting the effectiveness of their efforts. Frank Julian Warne, an expert on assimilation, perhaps spoke for most Americans when he said, "With startling sudden-ness the effects flowing out of the war have brought to public attention as-pects of immigration that heretofore have been regarded with unruffled complacency. . . . We have found that our forces for assimilating this foreign element have not been working." Making an implicit reference to increasingly common doubts about the dependability of Teutons, Warne declared that it had become clear that "many of these . . . are not strangers to the hand that stabs in the dark or the lips that betray with a kiss."[30]

Explanations as to why Americanization may have proven unsuccessful varied. Theodore Roosevelt couched presumed immigrant treachery in na-tionalistic terms, claiming, "The politico-racial hyphen is moral treason." All immigrants "bring something of value to our common national life," but their Americanness must be measured by the degree to which they allowed them-selves to be stirred into the nation's racial-cultural melting pot. In short, it was up to immigrants to un-Other themselves.[31] In a January 1916 letter, the pro-gressive journalist Ray Stannard Baker chastised Roosevelt for the absolutism in his anti-hyphen rhetoric. The former president's Americanization strategy of lambasting the immigrant into submission would never breed tolerance, "nor ever arrive at more democracy—for at the very basis of democracy lies understanding and mutual confidence; not mutual suspicion and fear."[32]

Many commentators agreed with Baker that Anglo-Saxon smugness was largely responsible for the prevailing suspicion that foreigners were direct threats to their "American" identity and culture. Novelist Winston Churchill, not to be confused with his British namesake, lamented the impression that Anglo-Saxon culture had "gradually become obscured" during the decades-long transition from a mostly rural to "a complex industrial society." The infusion of immigrants seeking employment and political freedom had led many to believe that the United States was "no longer Anglo-Saxon." Yet the real problem, he maintained, was Anglo-Saxon society's inability to make inclusion into the American in-group attractive to immigrants by offering viable solutions to the inherent inequality of industrial capitalism. Churchill considered himself "in accord with experience and modern opinion" in "that environment is stronger than heredity, and that our immigrants [will] become imbued with our [Anglo-Saxon] racial individualism." But Americans had yet to open up Anglo-Saxon society and culture to modification, and, consequently, immigrants were less inclined to follow Anglo-Saxons' example and allow assimilation to take hold.[33]

Like Churchill, popular novelist Margaret Sherwood maintained that white Americans' negligence had perpetuated the outsider status of the foreign born and could cost them a bit of their own Anglo-Saxonness. Sherwood saw Americanization similarly to how turn-of-the-century imperialists viewed the "white man's burden," advocating that "civilizing" foreign youth by teaching them American and English literature was the key to lasting assimilation. "They [foreign-born and even native-born children] can never be Americans in the truest sense of the word without fuller knowledge of that which is finest and oldest in English race tradition. . . . Possibly in attempting to share it with young aliens we may rewin more of it for ourselves, and learn to know better the genius of the Anglo-Saxon race," a race that had "carried civilization the farthest, in the matter of securing freedom." What made the "English race" civilized and superior, she argued, was its "power of trained emotion, of emotional control." Sherwood then described German Americans as if they were little different from the presumed inferior races of the American overseas empire or radical immigrants from Europe's backward corners. Germans, though the intellectual equals of the Anglo-Saxons, "have managed to train their minds but not their emotions." Instilling the art of "self-mastery" (or civilization) in "all races," Germans implied to be the most urgent case, would un-Other the alien and ensure "the Anglo-Saxon tradition" would rightly "prevail over all others."[34]

The editors of the *World's Work*, by contrast, advanced an even harsher view of Americanization, holding that some foreign races were simply not capable of un-Othering themselves. "We have had ample proof in the last ten or twelve years that the processes of assimilation have not been thoroughly effective," they lamented. "We have large undigested lumps of foreign-born residents who have not acquired either American ways of living or American ideals of government." The failure of Americanization was a racial and legislative issue. The editors proposed a new immigration restriction policy that presaged the 1924 Johnson-Reed National Origins Act by basing immigration limitations on a race's "capacity for genuine Americanization." The immigration of certain foreign peoples would be more thoroughly restricted if their American kinsfolk did not show the ability to Americanize quickly. The downside, however, was that the plan would not restrict the immigration of Germans, a people who had shown the capacity but not always the willingness to Americanize. The editors claimed that German "clannishness . . . is a racial tendency and an admirable one, but it constitutes a danger to a country whose progress depends upon the maintenance of homogeneity." In light of recent suspicions, then, Teutons' ability to Americanize should no longer color Anglo-Saxon impressions of their trustworthiness. With German imperialists trying "everything in their power to make the Germans a political unit here," all that Americans could do was hope that potential German immigrants would stay put in Europe after the war.[35]

Disagreement over why the Americanization of so many immigrant groups had failed likely exacerbated Americans' inability to make sense of where German Americans stood. The assimilation debate made clear that many white Americans, even so-called experts, were finding it increasingly difficult to view American Teutons differently from the less respected and presumably more volatile European races. Accordingly, the confusion and anxiety in the press over pro-German propaganda, German American loyalty, and the seemingly ubiquitous German agent persisted while actual intrigue became less prevalent. The British ambassador, Cecil Spring-Rice, recognized this phenomenon among the general public, informing the Foreign Office in December 1915 of "a great change" in American attitudes toward German Americans that had originated in the press. "The continued publications as to German plots and German outrages have gradually aroused public opinion," he reported, "and the excitement appears to be growing."[36] By the end of 1915, the Othering of the German American was accelerating.

For Woodrow Wilson, that excitement was already near a fever pitch. The president's anxious and frustrated reaction to the discovery of the Rintelen spy ring and smaller alleged plots betrayed his growing impression that

Germany had surreptitiously invaded the United States. "I am sure that the country is honeycombed with German intrigue and infested with German spies," he confided to his close friend and advisor Colonel Edward House in August 1915, before official revelation of the German Embassy's involvement. "The evidence of these things are multiplying every day." House responded to the rattled president by reinforcing his fears, suggesting that pro-German terrorism or an insurrection could be imminent. Responding to Wilson's question as to where the rebellion would begin, House proposed that the German mob would probably target areas where they could do the most damage. "Attempts will likely be made to blow up waterworks, electric lights and gas plants, subways and bridges in cities like New York," he reported. "I do not look for any organized rebellion or outbreak, but merely some degree of frightfulness in order to intimidate the country." House revealed his animosity toward American Teutons, not just the kaiser's regime, by referring to them as if they were unstable foreign radicals and regretting that preparations against terrorism would be unnecessary if the United States did not have such "a mad people to deal with."[37] While Wilson was not so fearful of German intentions that he considered declaring war at this point, his concern over the possibility of a German-led insurrection of the foreign born was indicative of his and his country's growing suspicion of German American Otherness.

The president also contributed to the increasing fear that Spring-Rice referenced, consistently raising doubts about German American loyalty in his public statements. His repeated charges of Teutonic treachery, which he often cast broadly as an issue among the foreign born in general, carried substantial weight with most Americans because of the growing prestige of the office of the president in recent years.[38] Through the emergence of the activist federal state, the public perception of the president's importance to national political life changed considerably from the late nineteenth-century model of president-as-administrator to the Theodore Roosevelt standard of the vigorous "public man" who concentrated his efforts on policies and actions that would benefit the American people at-large.[39] This conversion and the success of many federal progressive reforms resulted in the American people developing greater trust in their president's competency by the time of the Great War, even though the federal state still had little direct impact on most citizens' lives.[40] Consequently, because of Americans' regard for his office, Wilson's public doubts about German American loyalty likely shaped public opinion more than it echoed it.

With it being an election year, the president would have the country's attention for the greater part of 1916, and he chose the specter of the internal enemy Other as one of his chief campaign issues. More specifically, Wilson and his campaign concentrated their rhetoric on a popular charge that could not have portrayed German Americans as any less American and threatening to Anglo-Saxon traditions: their alleged corrupting of American politics and elections on behalf of a foreign government. On June 14, Flag Day, Wilson spoke of his faith in the "vast majority" of loyal foreign-born Americans but also his anxiety over those working "to undermine the influence of the Government of the United States." Wilson likened the alleged conspiracy to a snake that "works underground, but it also shows its ugly head where we can see it." Referring to reports of German agents allegedly bribing congressmen, the president surmised that these serpents were "trying to levy a species of blackmail" on the United States and demand the government "do what [disloyal German Americans] wish in the interest of a foreign sentiment or [they] will wreak [their] vengeance at the polls."[41] For electoral extortion to be possible, American Teutons would have to vote en masse against a patriotic candidate, which would indicate their standing as an unassimilated race who did the bidding of outsiders instead of freely following their individual consciences. Wilson's vision, which his eventual reelection suggests he shared with no small number of Americans, was a far cry from the prewar perception of the freedom-seeking Teuton who could seamlessly absorb into Anglo-Saxon culture and society.

During the campaign, Wilson's advisors and press allies consistently portrayed his Republican opponent, Supreme Court Justice Charles Evans Hughes, as the "Kaiser's candidate," the beneficiary of Teutonic un-Americanness and an instrument of a vast German conspiracy to control American domestic and foreign policy. Democrats even presented evidence they believed supported their portrayals of Hughes as a German sympathizer. In June, Wilson's Chief of Staff Joseph P. Tumulty, a trusted advisor who had been with Wilson since his days as governor of New Jersey, convinced the president to include in the official Democratic platform a stern repudiation of hyphenism and political parties that would curry the favor of disloyal immigrants. The policy statement asserted that the party "condemn[ed] all alliances and combinations of individuals . . . of whatever nationality or descent, who agree and conspire together for the purpose of embarrassing or weakening the Government or of improperly influencing or coercing our public representatives in dealing or negotiating with any foreign power." In an attempt to tie Hughes and the Republican Party to the alleged conspiracy in which German Americans were believed to be a part, the Democrats also "condemn[ed] any political party which in view of the activity of such conspirators, surrenders its integrity or modifies its policy."[42] Samuel G. Blythe of the widely circulated *Saturday Evening Post* endorsed the Wilson campaign's plan of "t[ying] this hyphenated favor to Hughes" as a keen political strategy because, presumably, it was moving public opinion. "The Democrats began the Americanism feeling-out long ago," Blythe reported, "and found it to be popular."[43]

The change to the Democrats' 1916 platform, though, does not seem to have been purely a cynical ploy to fearmonger for votes. Tumulty privately reported to Wilson that he believed Hughes's campaign may have made a Faustian bargain with the kaiser, becoming a participant, willing or unwilling, in a scheme to Germanize the United States. "An effort is under way to debase our politics through the creation of the German voters in the United States as a power," Tumulty charged. "The instrumentality through which this power is to be exerted is the present candidacy of Judge Hughes. It does not need to be established that Justice Hughes is seeking the support of German Americans by un-American commitments, in order to prove that what I have said is true. It is a fact not susceptible of being controverted that there is an organized movement among the Teutonic Americans to deliver their three million or more votes to Mr. Justice Hughes in November."[44] Surprisingly, the Hughes campaign did little to refute Wilson's charges. The Republican candidate did not immediately go out of his way to denounce "un-American" immigrant groups and, despite some embarrassment, openly accepted the support of several prominent and, probably unbeknownst to him, Berlin-funded German American organizations.[45]

Tumulty's indictment of Hughes, along with Wilson's implicit accusations of German American unfaithfulness since the war began, demonstrates that the president's camp saw the existence of a Teutonic conspiracy to be a real possibility or perhaps even an active threat to the United States. Tumulty's estimate of three million Teutonic votes for Hughes—roughly equal to the number of members of the National German American Alliance—also reveals that the White House believed German intrigue was rampant throughout more than just a small portion of the German American population. Although it is impossible to measure the impact that Wilson's anti-hyphenism and Hughes's uncomfortable embrace of immigrant groups had on the election's outcome, the mere fact that the president and his friends banged the drum loudly and often is indicative of their assessment of American public opinion. The Wilson campaign's decision to denounce the "hyphen vote" and alleged foreign influences on the election indicates that he and his political allies assumed many American voters also believed in the existence of an anti-American conspiracy. Their confidence that at least a majority of white Americans had developed a nativist view of the once trusted Teutonic American, along with Wilson's victory at the polls, suggests that nearly a year of continuous news of German intrigue and several more months of anti-German campaign hyperbole had a drastic impact on Anglo-Saxons' feelings toward their German American neighbors.

Wilson, however, did not win decisively, proving victorious by one of the closest margins in presidential election history, nor did his campaign lead white Americans to panic or universally condemn all German Americans.[46] Yet, as the wartime words and actions of Anglo-Saxon Americans would demonstrate, it would be a mistake to conclude that this meant they dismissed the president's suggestions that German immigrants were anti-American Others. In 1916, the anti-German rhetoric of Wilson's campaign and its allies in the press fell on an audience that was concerned, but not overly alarmed, about the possibility of widespread German American perfidy. With the rash of exploding factories and bridges mostly ending by late 1915, the unsolved blasts at Black Tom and Kingsland notwithstanding, and the German government's restriction of its U-boats easing tensions, Germany and American Teutons did not look as threatening as they had months before the election. In other words, although politicians and newspaper editors had given them plenty of reasons to doubt German Americans' devotion to the United States, many Americans had not given up on them.

The events and rhetoric of 1915 and 1916, however, ultimately primed Anglo-Saxon Americans for what was to come in early 1917 and beyond. Because of the return of unrestricted U-boat attacks in January and the revelation of the Zimmermann Telegram in March, most Americans discarded any remaining doubts as to the Germans' penchant for aggression and intrigue. Fearful warnings of a vast Teutonic conspiracy against the United States also appeared less hyperbolic. With war looking increasingly like a foregone conclusion, the question of German American loyalty carried even greater importance. If they were not active agents or at least sympathetic to their fatherland, why had so many German immigrants apparently resisted Americanization and the president's pro-Allied neutrality?

Yet, although anxiety over the possibility of war was at its highest since the *Lusitania* sinking, ambivalence over Teutonic Americans' Otherness persisted in early spring 1917. The pro-Ally *Chicago Tribune*, for instance, poked fun at those "many worthy Americans" who "need[ed] a cold douche of common sense to restore" an even temper. "A German bartender overhearing an argument on the war," for example, would not be privy to anything "for which he would be given a pension by the Imperial German Government." At the same time, the men at a nearby table "are not necessarily emissaries of a foreign foe because they are consuming Hungarian goulash." Other publications, however, saw less reason to keep a cool head. The *Washington Evening Star* claimed that German spy rings established by ejected embassy personnel had yet to be flushed out, while the Philadelphia *North American* argued that "thirty months of ceaseless agitation and intermittent disturbances, ranging from foreign intrigue disguised as pacifism to open violence and terrorism" proved widespread German plotting was and would continue to be a legitimate danger.[47] This tack of assuming that the instances of sabotage and espionage from 1915 were the norm despite the lack of demonstrable evidence would be repeated often while the United States was at war.

Another trend that foreshadowed the paranoia rampant after the war declaration in April was the glut of strange and unsubstantiated reports that reached the Department of Justice and similar federal agencies just before or soon after the release of the Zimmermann Telegram. Generally, the accounts shared a similar theme—Teutonic spies, propagandists, and saboteurs, with the help of German American collaborators, were trying to wreak havoc across the United States on the kaiser's behalf. For example, in late February, Assistant Secretary of Labor Louis F. Post informed the Attorney General that his department had held up the naturalization application of a Hungarian immigrant living in St. Louis because the man allegedly wore "cross flags of Germany and Austria-Hungary" and "portraits on his lapel of the Kaiser and of Emperor Franz Joseph." The suspect also allegedly proclaimed he would be "perfectly satisfied" if Germany "invaded and over-r[a]n the United States."[48] One would assume that this man would have been more circumspect had he been an actual enemy secret agent. On March 10 the publisher of the *Elmira (NY) Daily Advertiser* wrote the War Department about "a rumor prevalent" in town about the arrest and confinement in the federal prison in Atlanta of a young woman spy and a man presumed to be her father. The woman, who allegedly had tried on three separate occasions to enter the country, was believed to have "had papers of an international nature under a wig on her head." The superintendent of the Atlanta prison replied to the letter, explaining that he had no idea to whom the Elmira editor was referring and, besides, Atlanta was a male-only prison.[49]

A day earlier, the chemist L. H. Baekeland of the Navy Consulting Board informed industrialist Howard E. Coffin, who served on the National Council of Defense in Washington, of an article from the *Columbus (OH) Dispatch* claiming that the nephew of Gottlieb von Jagow, the German Foreign Minister, had applied for citizenship. Aside from his blood relation to one of the kaiser's chief advisors, the biggest strike against Jagow the younger's naturalization was that he apparently fit the old template of the alien radical saboteur. Jagow lived near Sulfur, Louisiana, where "a few sticks of dynamite judiciously placed in the power plants, both there and at the Freeport, Texas, sulfur mines, might seriously cripple our munitions industry by destroying our source of sulfuric acid, at least temporarily." Baekeland, though, did not mention whether Jagow actually was the foreign minister's nephew, whether his behavior had been in any way suspect, and, if really a German agent, why he would not have disguised his name to avoid detection.[50] As would often be the case after April 1917, Department of Justice files do not indicate whether these cases were resolved. Yet the accounts, especially the naturalization cases, are indicative of the growing fear in early 1917 that German Americans could not be trusted. The transition from reliable and beneficial Americans to internal enemy Other was near completion.

Rumors such as these had to have begun somewhere. While presumed Teutonic racial traits, the specter of foreign radicals, and indisputable evidence of recent German intrigue directly influenced individuals' perceptions of the truthfulness of the news stories they read and campaign rhetoric they heard, the reliability of a rumor's source often greatly affects its degree of believability in the eyes of beholders. The sources of many alarmist news stories were administration officials and powerful congressmen who, because of the responsibilities of their office, were privy to classified investigations, most of which contained unsubstantiated accounts. Reports of exaggerated spy tales and immigrant disloyalty like the ones just cited, therefore, were self-reinforcing in that their essence, if not their specific details, often informed newspaper and magazine articles on the threat of German spies and German American disloyalty. These, in turn, both reflected and shaped attitudes that led to officials' overreactions and exaggerated rumors of Teutonic malfeasance that patriotic citizens would report to authorities as fact. Citizens' increasing fear and distrust of German Americans after April 1917 would feed this cycle of paranoia until the end of the war and beyond.

Despite the relatively limited size of the federal government in 1917, many Americans appear to have trusted that Wilson, his cabinet, and Congress knew the true extent of the German spy network and German American disloyalty, which implied that press coverage had only scratched the surface. John Price

Jones, a correspondent for the New York *Sun*, assumed the Wilson administration withheld secret information from the public. In his book *America Entangled*, published in March 1917, Jones cited the president's 1916 Flag Day address as proof that Wilson knew that Germany was trying to control American politics through secret agents and its loyal Teutonic American subjects. "When [Wilson] made his charge," Jones wrote, "he had back of him a vast amount of evidence which never has been and never will be made public." Jones concluded that the "aim" of the German agents and their German American and pacifist partners "was to make Congress vote and the President act just as the Emperor of Germany deemed most suitable to the interests of the Fatherland."[51] The *Minneapolis Tribune* professed a similar amount of trust in Congress, quipping that most Americans would presume anyone who would claim that 100,000 foreign spies were at work in the United States was "seeing things" if the assertion had not come from North Carolina Senator Lee Overman, the chairman of the Senate Judiciary Committee. In that capacity, Overman often received "credible reports from secret service men" and the Department of Justice. The editors showed little concern for an Allied propaganda campaign or conspiracy within the United States, claiming that Great Britain and France likely sent a significant number of secret agents but only to tail the "sinister movements on the part of Teuton 'sleuths.'"[52] For Jones, as well as those alarmed by Overman's claims, no actual proof of a broad German conspiracy and Teutonic immigrants' treacherous activities was necessary because the sources were beyond reproach, thus further confirming German Americans' status as likely enemy Others.

Presumably the most dependable source on German plotting and German Americans' well-hidden Otherness was the commander-in-chief. Wilson was genuinely fearful of Teutonic scheming and un-Americanness, and in his address to Congress on April 2, 1917, he established that these factors played a central role in his decision to ask for a declaration of war. "One of the things that has served to convince us that the Prussian autocracy was not and could never be our friend," Wilson claimed, "is that from the very outset of the present war it has filled our unsuspecting communities and even our offices of government with spies and set criminal intrigues everywhere afoot." Suggesting that German Americans had always been outsiders, if not invaders, the president asserted that not only was the plot nationwide, but "it is now evident that its spies were here even before the war began."[53] The president's claim that spies had been plotting within the United States prior to the war's eruption in 1914 indicates that he saw German sabotage, espionage, and propagandizing as more than just an attempt to undermine American assistance to the Allied powers. Instead, with the weight of the moment behind him, he implied these tactics were part of a larger long-term conspiracy targeting the Anglo-Saxon United States directly. That some German Americans were believed to be involved in this plot also suggests that un-Americanized Teutons had been roaming the country for years, making their claims of American patriotism seem hollow and prewar admiration for their racial character misplaced.

With Congress's official declaration of war on April 6, the transition of German Americans from fellow "Anglo-Saxons" into an undemocratic and insidious sleeper cell was complete for a significant number of Americans. Germany was now the obvious enemy of the United States, and after over two years of rhetoric from trusted politicians and in the press about American Teutons' complicity in the kaiser's conspiracy (some of it based in truth, much of it not), Anglo-Saxon Americans had been conditioned to view any suspicious incident as the work of disloyal enemy Others. But enemy agents did not lurk around every corner and were not responsible for every industrial accident, burned bridge, or argument critical of American policy. To many white Americans, however, the internal Teutonic threat was quite familiar because they believed they knew the Germans' "character" and had faced off against similarly dangerous aliens in the past. By spring 1917, with the collective American imagination having forged a new image of the German American based on a reassessment of existing stereotypes, Anglo-Saxon proclamations of Teutonic American trustworthiness were harder to come by. Once the United States was at war, the claims that the internal enemy Other posed an existential threat to the United States quickly replaced Americans' prior respect for or ambivalence toward German Americans. Despite years of peaceful assimilation, the neutrality period from 1914 to 1917 had effectively "Othered" the German American community.

As shapers of public opinion ratcheted up the alarmism during wartime, locally grown rumors sprouted from the rhetoric and from Americans' stereotypes about the German temperament. Consequently, a greatly intensified cycle of anti-foreign and conspiratorial anxiety emerged as some citizens began to act on their growing racial and apocalyptic assumptions that Germany and German Americans sought to undermine their government, their way of life, and Anglo-Saxon identity. While the rumor mill and American propagandists churned out even more menacing visions of hidden Teutonic intrigue, fearful Anglo-Saxons concluded that it was the responsibility of every loyal citizen to stamp out the German threat within.

CHAPTER THREE

The War on the Internal Enemy Other, 1917–1918

Protestations of loyalty do not help, for one of the most influential weeklies of New York has said, "Beware of the German-American who wraps the Stars and Stripes around his German body." . . . When one looks at our comic periodicals it would seem that a campaign of ruthless hate against the American of German descent is an eminently desirable thing.

GERMAN AMERICAN PROFESSOR HERMANN S. FICKE, September 1917

No other one cause contributed so much to the oppression of innocent men as the systematic and indiscriminate agitation against what was claimed to be an all-pervasive system of German espionage.

JOHN LORD O'BRIAN, head of the War Emergency Division of the Department of Justice, 1919

In September 1917, Miss A. D. Mitchell of Sarasota, Florida, did her patriotic duty. Enemy agents were at work in her community, and it was high time someone put a stop to it. Mitchell contacted the Military Intelligence Division (MID, one of the federal government's primary investigatory bodies) about a threat that, if left unchecked, could do great harm to her community.[1] The MID quickly dispatched an investigator, T. S. Marshall, to the scene. According to Mitchell, a man by the name of Bolge, the manager of a bakery in nearby Osprey, was a German American conspirator. Previously, Bolge and his family had received few visitors, but lately, "many automobiles stop at the place." Even more suspicious, Mitchell conjectured to Marshall, was "that due to the nature of the shoreline in this neighborhood it is easy for the German families living at intervals along the shore to convey information to each other in rapid order," and word is "that some such systematic arrangement is had among them to keep themselves posted in this way." Clearly, Bolge was not working alone. Rumors circulated that Bolge was persuading his African American employees "to consider the white Americans as their enemy" and promising that "in the event of German supremacy equal wage scales and social equality will prevail."

According to another citizen of Sarasota who also contacted the MID, Bolge had thrown all caution to the wind. Rumor had it that the enemy agent had been seen wearing German insignia on his clothing, including a badge with an image of both the German kaiser and the recently deposed Russian tsar, the latter being an interesting choice considering Germany and Russia were at war.[2]

The MID and the Department of Justice (DOJ) investigated thousands of similar tales of German intrigue throughout the twenty months of American intervention in the First World War. As in practically all of their investigations, federal agents found no conclusive evidence of a German conspiracy in Osprey or Sarasota. The few German intriguers who remained undetected in the United States after April 1917 had acted as go-betweens and financial agents during neutrality. The most dangerous agents, the saboteurs and spies, had slipped away to Mexico or Europe as war between the United States and Germany loomed near, leaving the remaining facilitators no one to direct. Authorities did not know for certain until long after the war that these agents, which included a horse-poisoning physician and the chief saboteur of the Black Tom facility, and their handlers were able to flee the country without detection.[3] In short, the United States essentially was spy-free while at war with Germany. Yet despite little or no proof that German agents still were at work, fear of an extensive Teutonic espionage, sabotage, and propaganda network was far more intense and pervasive after the declaration of war than it had been when actual German intrigue had been taking place.[4]

This intensified fear was a result of the thorough and rapid Othering of the German American population and many white Americans' persistent sense that the nation was vulnerable to foreign usurpation. After the shared trauma and creeping doubts about Teutonic loyalty during the nearly three years of neutrality, the prewar trust in German Americans had largely vanished. In its place stood a collective fear that un-Americanized Teutons were colluding with the kaiser's agents in an attempt to undermine or supplant Anglo-Saxon dominance in the United States. Popular racial interpretations of the Teuton's close kinship with the Anglo-Saxon suggested that German Americans were fully capable of assimilation, but the widespread assumption by 1917 that they had *chosen* not to Americanize gave extra weight to claims of a deep-seated Teutonic conspiracy. This anxiety over an alleged plot was so extensive and profound that it led Americans at all levels of society—common citizens, educators, the press, politicians, judges—to suspect Teutonic sabotage, propaganda, or subterfuge at the slightest hint of trouble. Anglo-Saxons acted on their paranoia, often taking draconian or unprecedented steps to defend them-selves and their communities from the perceived threat within.[5] In short, German Americans had earned their Other status not by being perceived as a race the Anglo-Saxon should dominate, as is often the case with perceptions of Otherness, but by being perceived as a race that threatened to subordinate white Americans in their own country.

This fear was largely racial and apocalyptic in nature. Many white Ameri-cans asserted that the traits that defined German American Otherness—their clannishness, inquisitiveness, duplicity, and authoritarianism—directly threat-ened Anglo-Saxon identity and power. The growing anxiety over German American disloyalty during neutrality morphed into a widespread conviction after the war declaration that Teutonic plotting and German American de-ceitfulness were part of a coordinated attack on the country. The aim of the alleged conspiracy was to "Germanize" the United States, which would result in the degeneration or destruction of the Anglo-Saxon race as Germans and German culture engulfed and reshaped the country into autocratic Germany's image. While clearly hyperbolic, alarm over Germanization schemes was not entirely unprecedented, as many white Americans for several decades had feared that most immigrant groups could act as an invading horde capable of tearing down Anglo-Saxon culture and institutions. Assumptions in the press and from propagandists that German Americans were responsible for practically every economically harmful fire or explosion suggested to many Americans that the Teutonic race had much more in common with the volatile, uncivilized, and radical immigrant Other than previously thought. With many white Americans now convinced that German Americans were in fact un-American outsiders, applying familiar models to an unfamiliar Other, whether consciously or not, likely helped them move past any remaining uncertainty over the Teuton's trustworthiness. Anxiety over the conquest of the Anglo-Saxon nation from within added a passionate sense of urgency to the country's defense against imagined saboteurs and Germanizing propagandists. That so many white Americans largely drew these racial and millennial conclusions so quickly and completely illustrates the decisive influence such assumptions had on early twentieth-century American culture and the perceived tenuous-ness of Anglo-Saxons' hold on their country.

That Americans' fear of German American Otherness grew into near-mass paranoia after the declaration of war was largely the responsibility of the press, private propaganda associations, and the Wilson administration's Committee on Public Information (CPI), whose messages and style differed significantly from those of the neutrality period. For one, ambivalence toward German Americans was rare as certainty of their Otherness became more widespread, even among propagandists themselves. Therefore, the stories and warnings in wartime propaganda were more urgent and hyperbolic, alerting Americans that the German plots alluded to during neutrality were more expansive and dangerous than they had imagined. At the same time, wartime propagandists attempted to define the aim of the plot—the transformation of the United States into a "Germanized" colony—and the means by which it was being carried out. Consequently, patriotic Americans would know what to look and listen for when confronting suspicious Teutons. As Anglo-Saxons transitioned out of the episodic stress of neutrality to the continuous strain of wartime, those with the power to calm the country's collective anxiety, political leaders and the press, did quite the opposite.

Few press outlets went as far as the popular *Everybody's Magazine*, which from late 1917 into spring 1918 printed a series of articles on intrigue and German American loyalty. The series title, "Invaded America," left little doubt as to the perspective of the author, investigative journalist Samuel Hopkins Adams. Although "ninety-nine per cent of [German Americans] favored the Fatherland" (Germany) prior to April 1917, Adams inaccurately claimed, that "Germans are a passionately patriotic race" should not be grounds "for resentment." Adams asserted that "the best element of our Teutonic citizenship," presumably only 1 percent of the German American population, remained loyal after the declaration of war, but this did not mean they could be trusted, because by then "this country had already been invaded by Teutonic propagandists in various phases." The German-language press ("the voice of Germany in America") and German American societies at the tip of the kaiser's invading spear were pointed at the majority of American Teutons, who were susceptible to being un-Americanized. In fact, their "nation-wide, expert German propaganda ha[d] been in progress for many years," Adams maintained. The enemy conspiracy ran deep; it penetrated the English-language press, spread discontent among African Americans, tried to redirect American anger onto their allies, used German voters to pressure politicians, aimed to "Teutoniz[e] our educational system," and even attempted to spark an armed German American revolution. Therefore, it was a waste of breath "to prate of 'America first' and urge that our men be held in this country, in case the Germans come across and attack us," Adams concluded. "They have already done it. . . . They have brought the war to America." Although he did not want his essays to "be construed as a broadside directed against all German Americans," Adams openly wondered if the indiscretions of German agents ("only a fractional part of what the Secret Service knows") meant that "my country is too tolerant of the alien within its gates."[6] Adams's series in *Everybody's* tapped into Anglo-Saxons' enduring sense that the growing presence of alien peoples and cultures could lead to the subordination of the Anglo-Saxon race in their own country.

As in many examples of press propaganda during the war, whether or not Adams's concerns were sincere or merely an attempt to exploit genuine war-time fear in order to sell magazines is impossible to know. Not every prominent voice with an opinion on the alleged Teutonic conspiracy, though, was bur-dened with the task of selling subscriptions. Liberal theologian Shailer Mathews seconded Adams's claims that Germany aimed to Germanize the United States. The plan had been in the works "for ten years," during which time the kaiser's regime had "been preparing some day to fight America." Critical to the plot, Mathews maintained, was the un-Americanizing of both the Teutonic and Anglo-Saxon populations. The German regime had spent millions in the United States on "Germanistic societies, alliances and as-sociations" as well as underhanded schemes to brainwash American children by including laudatory descriptions of the kaiser in grammar school spelling books. The scheme's objective was the "build[ing] up in America [of] a community more loyal to herself than to the United States." Against such a threat, Mathews concluded, the nation was "fight[ing] for self-protection."[7] Anglo-Saxon American identity itself was in danger.

The Committee on Public Information's warnings that German American Otherness promised ominous consequences for the nation and for Anglo-Saxonism reached a larger audience than either Mathews or Adams and was often couched in such great detail that the authenticity of their tales seemed above reproach. In the case of the pamphlet *Conquest and Kultur*, the goal of CPI director George Creel's publicists was not just to assert that a conspiracy to Germanize the United States was afoot, but to cite what it believed were direct quotes from some of the plotters and German American well-wishers. A key player in the CPI's version of the Teutonic scheme was the Pan-German League, an organization based in Berlin and mentioned often in anti-German propaganda during neutrality. Several quotations within the pamphlet imply that the League's purported quest to unite Germans across the world in order "to sustain a struggle in support of Deutschtum" was shared by American Teutons who wished German cultural imperialism would engulf the Anglo-Saxon United States. In a letter to a German newspaper written in 1902 and cited in the pamphlet, a Teuton living in New York expressed confidence in the trajectory of Germanism in the United States, asserting that "the German-ization of America has gone ahead too far to be interrupted." The process of de-Americanizing the country, though, would take some time. Within the next century, the CPI quoted the man as saying, "the American people will be conquered," not by invading armies but "by the victorious German spirit, so that it will present an enormous German Empire." The pamphlet included a letter from another German, this one merely traveling through the country, supposedly singing a similar tune. All German Americans were responsible for "see[ing] that the future language spoken in America shall be German," the man allegedly claimed. If they did their duty, the "center of German intel-lectual activity" would move from Germany to the United States "in the re-mote future."[8] The sources in *Conquest and Kultur*, the influence of which the pamphlets' authors appear to exaggerate, painted a frightening picture of the Anglo-Saxon United States' fate if the German conspiracy was not crushed.

Considered during neutrality to be the primary vehicle through which Ger-many was conducting this conspiracy, the National German American Alliance came under even closer scrutiny from various kinds of propagandists while the United States was at war. Despite the NGAA's support for Wilson's decision for a diplomatic break with Germany in February 1917 and the willingness of its members to fight for the United States against their Old World cousins, the press presented new and more detailed accusations of NGAA plotting. The press had little or no evidence for their claims, as if they were fitting the NGAA into the accepted model of the conspiratorial Other that they and countless other Americans had created in their minds.[9] That Congress was investigating the NGAA to determine whether to renew its charter gave official sanctioning to the pariah status of its nearly three million members. The organization's threat to the country was portrayed as far more grave than during neutrality, when the crimes with which it was charged were limited to tampering with elections and fomenting disloyalty. The NGAA's complicity went far deeper, wartime propagandists claimed, in that it was the spearhead of Germany's quest to culturally colonize the entire United States by undermining patriotism and brainwashing white American children to love militarism through the teaching of the German language in schools. Such claims about the NGAA tapped into Anglo-Saxons' intensifying anxiety over the perceived precariousness of their racial identity and control over the nation while also deepening their convic-tion that German Americans were in fact dangerous enemy Others.

Representative of propagandists' charges against the NGAA was David Lawrence's June 1918 article in the *Saturday Evening Post*. The evidence against the NGAA "seems unbelievable—a manifest connection between the schemes of Pan-Germanism fostered by Prussian autocracy and the spreading of German propaganda in America through control of the schools." In an attempt to confirm the internal enemy Other's intention to subjugate the United States, Lawrence informed the *Post*'s over two million subscribers that the NGAA had been in partnership with the Pan-German League, the League for Germanism in Foreign Lands, and the kaiser's government for years. Their goal, Lawrence proposed, was conquest through linguistic imperialism. "Indeed the Imperial German Government looked upon the German language as a political instrument wherewith to consolidate Germans everywhere," which would forge them "into a national weapon." The NGAA, Lawrence concluded, was "the medium whereby the bond was to be perpetuated between the German colony in America and the monarchy of the Kaiser."[10] Lawrence's conclusions were based more in hysteria, stereotypes, and an intolerance for cultural pluralism than evidence. Before 1917, the NGAA's leadership, especially its former president Charles Hexamer, proudly extolled German cultural superiority and the benefits of maintaining cultural ties to the Fatherland. But an appreciation for their Old World heritage did not make the NGAA a tool of the German government or German imperialism. The NGAA, however, buckled under constant allegations in the press and the pressure of federal inquiries. It disbanded in April 1918 before Congress could revoke its charter.[11]

Although some Anglo-Saxons were certain that German agents and un-American Teutonic residents were working to undercut the war effort and reshape the United States, few had any valid evidence that this was in fact true. Few cared, either because they were so certain of American Teutons' Otherness or they were confident that most Americans were convinced that a German American conspiracy really was in motion. This did not mean that propagandists ignored the question of proof. Some offered what they believed were rational justifications as to why Americans had not seen the Germanizers coming before the war and had trouble spotting them now. In many instances, these explanations reinforced German Americans' Otherness in that they alluded to such common Teutonic racial stereotypes as thoroughness, stubborn clannishness, and certain physical features, as well as the belief that they were natural detectives.

The kaiser's German American allies apparently were so effective that the absence of evidence of their perfidy was proof enough for many Anglo-Saxons that they, in fact, were active participants in the clandestine invasion of German culture. The inherent clannishness of the internal Teutonic Other was perhaps the most common explanation for the lack of reliable evidence of its treachery as well as its unwillingness to Americanize. Describing the United States as "a country on the defensive," the *Saturday Evening Post* argued that German spies are incredibly difficult to detect because they are "masters in the simple art of conformity," suggesting that they are uniquely talented at feigning clannishness toward one home while remaining loyal to another.[12] Screenwriter Lewis Allen Browne, writing in the May 1918 edition of the *Forum*, warned that German American parents and teachers were attempting to stave off or undo the Americanization of their children behind the closed doors of their homes and parochial schools. At home, parents taught their children "that the Kaiser is the supreme personality on earth and that the United States is a foreign country and a sometime colony of the German Empire." The indoctrination of German American children, Browne contested, continued at their German-only schools, where their teachers "were carrying out their orders to teach the second generation" to love the Fatherland. "This is not a new policy," Browne continued, arguing that it had "originated in Germany in the days of early Prussianism when those veneered barbarians dreamed of 'Der Tag' [The Day]," when the kaiser would reign supreme over the United States.[13]

Editorial cartoonists also believed they understood why scheming Teutons were so difficult to find: they were hiding in plain sight, often under the garb of patriotism and citizenship. Pictorial images of the duplicitous German were quite common in the mainstream press and explicitly referenced the Teutonic physical stereotypes presented by so-called racial experts. The cartoon German American typically had a large square head and a short, stout, even chubby body that, as Edward A. Ross would have said, did not lend itself to agility. To signal the modern Teuton's link to Prussian militarism, German American characters often sported Otto von Bismarck's iconic walrus mustache or a handlebar likely meant to parody Prussian General Paul von Hindenburg's whiskers. Their clannishness was also central to many anti-German political cartoons. In a sketch from the *New York Evening World* from spring 1918, the "Enemy Alien" was a Hindenburg look-alike with a square head and jaw. While Uncle Sam watches the war "Over There" out a window, "Over Here" the double-crossing German peers from behind a curtain, ready to stab Sam in the back with his dagger (fig. 3.1). The previous autumn, James Montgomery Flagg, best known for the celebrated "Uncle Sam Wants You" imitation of an equally famous British wartime poster, similarly played on racial stereotypes in a syndicated cartoon entitled "Camouflage." In the image, a short, rotund, bespectacled, pipe-smoking, Bismarckian-mustachioed German waves an American flag out a window for all to see, denoting his superficial love of the United States. Meanwhile, in the privacy of his home, he holds high a full beer stein and reveres his master with a shout of "Hoch [praise] der Kaiser" (fig. 3.2).[14]

That German Americans hid behind a mask of citizenship to advance the cause of Germanization was not a charge exclusive to the wartime months. A 1913 German statute, the Delbrück Law, that allowed Teutons to retain their German citizenship even if they naturalized elsewhere occasionally arose in anti-German articles and editorials during neutrality. During wartime, with American Teutons having been so thoroughly Othered and fears of a hidden German invasion having grown to such an intensity, the implication that all German immigrants enjoyed dual citizenship was far more alarming. The Delbrück Law, consequently, gained much more attention from prominent Americans and organizations during wartime despite the fact that the law did not apply in the United States. American naturalization laws required aliens to officially renounce all other national allegiances.[15] This was a fact lost on those Americans who were convinced of Teutonic American Otherness. The German statute "is the basis of the German spy system," the Anti-Saloon League maintained. "It encourages and sanctions treason."[16] Although he did not mention the Delbrück Law by name, Shailer Mathews asserted that "a law making it possible for naturalized Germans . . . to maintain citizenship in Germany" buttressed the kaiser's imperialistic plot to politically and culturally dominate the United States by making the breeding of "this attitude of mind official" German policy.[17] Concerned that the Delbrück Law would give the enemy untoward control over American politics through the ballot, Elihu Root privately worried that it was "a plain provision for control of other countries by perjury." Root also implied that it was a sign of German brutishness, saying, "I have never observed anything more shameless and brazen than this law," which "exhibits appalling moral degeneracy."[18]

Wartime propaganda suggesting that German American Otherness was an intentional tactic and a central part of a larger strategy to conquer the United States deepened the anxiety over a possible conspiracy that had arisen during neutrality. But it also reflected white Americans' genuine sense that their country and way of life was vulnerable to subjugation by a foreign element, with the result being the forfeiture of their Anglo-Saxon identity. The reality of war confirmed to many that a dangerous Other was in fact actively trying to bring this about. It also added an urgency to their fears. Many felt compelled to defend themselves, their families, their communities, their country, and their American identity from the apocalyptic threat of Germanization. That

Figure 3.1. "Over There—Over Here," cartoon, *New York Evening Mail*. Reprinted in *Literary Digest*, April 20, 1918.

Figure 3.2. "Camouflage," cartoon, *Literary Digest*, November 24, 1917.

urgency resulted in fearful Americans taking their community's and nation's defense into their own hands by eradicating all things German from the cultural and social landscape.

One of the prime targets was the German language. If the backlash against the teaching of German in school is any indication, the "Kaiser's tongue" was just as menacing to the United States as a foreign anarchist with a stick of dynamite or even an invading army. Across the country, educators and citizens alleged that militarism, autocracy, and deceit were inherent to the German language. According to the California State Board of Education, German was "a language that disseminates the ideals of autocracy, brutality, and hatred" while a politician in Iowa claimed that "ninety percent of all men and women who teach the German language are traitors." By March 1918, the teaching of German had been suspended in 149 schools throughout the country.[19] Connecting the German language directly to autocracy and militarism while also suggesting it had the power to reshape American society in Germany's undemocratic image, an editorial in the *Leipsic (OH) Free Press* wondered, "why compel our children to study German when their autocratic and imperialistic teachings and acts are diametrically opposed to ours?"[20] Referencing figures from three cities (Columbus, Ohio; Fort Wayne, Indiana; and Philadelphia), the National Committee of One Hundred argued that the larger amount of money spent on "teaching German language and literature to Americans" than on "teaching English and citizenship to immigrants" was incontrovertible proof that German agents had infiltrated the nation's school systems. The committee also claimed that German propagandists were working to block the Americanization of other foreigners, saying that low immigrant enrollment in public schools, as opposed to their enrollment in ethnic parochial institutions, was "due partly to anti-American propaganda."[21]

Other concerned citizens joined together to protect American-born children from becoming Germanized by offering solutions or taking direct action. In August 1917, William H. Hobbs, the director of the Geological Laboratory at the University of Michigan and a leading voice on the suppression of the German language, wrote to the National Security League about his plan to issue a loyalty pledge that all teachers of German would have to sign to maintain their employment. The pledge asked the teacher to promise "not to use my opportunities to germanise [*sic*] or de-americanise [*sic*] my students" through the teaching of the German language. Hobbs even singled out, though not by name, an "openly hostile" professor on the faculty at the university, claiming he was "generally believed a spy" and the "head of the

German kultur movement in the state." Presumably Hobbs's plan would result in the decapitation of the supposed Teutonic propaganda machine in Michigan.[22]

To much national acclaim, the Duluth, Minnesota, Board of Education adopted a resolution ending the teaching of German in the city's public schools. Their rationale was one of the clearest expressions of paranoia over the threat of Teutonic Otherness and Germanization during the war. Fearing that the influence of the German language on impressionable Anglo-Saxon youth would undermine their fundamental Americanness, the board resolved: "The German imperial government, by and through the activities of its propaganda for world domination, has insidiously invaded, intrenched and entwined its ideals in the public schools of the United States in which there are about 20,000,000 pupils and about 580,000 teachers." The board concluded, "Our public schools should be purged of every taint of German idealism and influence, and . . . foster, teach and extend true American ideals and doctrines, and . . . give special effort toward the attainment of a full knowledge and understanding of the English language with all it entails."[23] That the superintendent of schools in Kansas City, Missouri, enacted an identical resolution gives some indication as to how broadly this belief was adopted, at least across the German-heavy and traditionally isolationist Midwest.[24]

Anglo-Saxon Americans' paranoia over the power of the internal enemy Other's language to shape individuals also extended to other aspects of German culture. Orchestra and opera houses, including the Metropolitan Opera Company, refused to perform the works of great German composers such as Bach, Brahms, and Beethoven. The American Defense Society, apparently worried that German music could cause aggressive militarism to set in immediately, warned that Teutonic symphony "appeals to the emotions" and could easily "sway an audience as nothing else can," making it "one of the most dangerous forms of German propaganda." In the same vein, towns and streets named after famous Teutons or German cities were changed to more "American" or patriotic-sounding names. Berlin, Iowa, for example, changed its name to Lincoln, while East Germantown, Indiana, became Pershing. German food was treated no differently. Sauerkraut and bratwurst were famously Americanized as "liberty cabbage" and "liberty sausage." At the same time, statues of once-admired Prussians, such as Bismarck and Frederick the Great, were vandalized or removed.[25] Patriotic Anglo-Saxons refused to let their country and institutions be overrun by the osmotic influence of German language or culture, which they believed German Americans had maintained as part of a conspiracy to overpower the Anglo-Saxon's social, political, and cultural hold in the United States.

Considering the wartime mood, popular regard for the racial theory of use-inheritance, and the apparently inherent linkage between race and language, campaigns to end the teaching and reading of German and the influence of Teutonic culture were much more about rescuing Anglo-Saxon school children from potential Teutonization than about Americanizing young Teutons. The underlying theory of the crusaders against German language and culture was that if both were suppressed, German influence would be as well. Erasing the militarizing and undemocratizing impact of German culture from American society was a means of defending Anglo-Saxon identity. The assumption that mere exposure to even the seemingly innocuous aspects of German culture could essentially un-Americanize adults, children, and, consequently, the United States speaks to popular attitudes regarding race formation, the power of the apocalyptic strain in American culture, and Anglo-Saxons' enduring sense of helplessness against the tide of Old World races and cultures, an open emotional wound further infected by real German intrigue during neutrality and wartime propaganda.

Yet not everyone was comfortable with white Americans taking on the internal enemy Other and the threat of Germanization by themselves. Much wartime propaganda regarding enemy agents or German American disloyalty, especially that coming from the CPI, attempted to convince Americans to both rely on the federal government for protection and assist the government in that task. Many progressive publicists hoped this would prevent Americans from lashing out at innocent people and increase citizens' reliance on the progressive state.[26] While propaganda alerting the country of Teutonic un-Americanness, sabotage, and unity-defying lies explained the stakes of the domestic war against Germanization, private and government publicists offered constructive options for how to handle these problems. The evocation of the federal government as the people's defender against what was ostensibly a non-military threat suggested a genuine and broadly shared assumption that the danger un-Americanized Teutons posed was so great that it required national vigilance and the pervasiveness, in some form or another, of federal power.

As a part of the federal wartime state, the CPI was the most likely source to point concerned Americans in the direction of the Department of Justice or another similar agency. In the pamphlet *The German Whisper*, progressive reformer and CPI associate chairman Harvey O'Higgins informed readers that they "are now on the firing line" because Germany "is attacking in every community in the United States" with "a gas attack of poisonous lies and rumors and false reports." O'Higgins claimed that misinformation and the perpetuation of wild rumors were at the center of Germany's conspiracy to undermine every facet of American society. Teutonic intrigue was the source of everything: "class dissension, religious difference, racial prejudice, and political quarrel." Although in some cases German propagandists had fallen short in their mission, O'Higgins argued that several of their false stories had bred apathy and opposition to the war. Yet patriotic Americans could help save their community from dissolution. "Mr. Citizen, if one of these German whisperers starts buzzing in your ear," O'Higgins pleaded, "send his name and address to the Department of Justice" or the CPI.[27]

The CPI often attempted to conscript civilians in the war against German intrigue through visual media, such as "Spies and Lies," which it printed as a poster and a full-page ad in several of the most widely-circulated magazines in the United States. The ad claimed that "German agents are everywhere," and they were "eager to gather scraps of news about our men, our ships, our munitions." Each sliver of information the spies obtained, though "individually harmless," would be quickly communicated to Berlin and meticulously "pieced together into a whole which spells death to American soldiers and danger to American homes." The assumption that spies were "everywhere" implied that any German American could be a secret agent loyal to the kaiser, a conceivable scenario to those who believed in the racial stereotype of the clannish, stubborn, and duplicitous Teuton. Yet after depicting the threat as plausible, ubiquitous, and personal, the poster offered Americans a means of combating the scourge and protecting their families: keep your mouth shut and report those who do not. The poster instructed Americans not to pass on sensitive military information or spread "malicious" and "disheartening rumors." It also encouraged them to "show the Hun that we can beat him at his own game of collecting scattered information and putting it to work" by reporting saboteurs and propagandists to the Department of Justice. To more closely connect the war at home with the fight in Europe, the poster concluded, "You are in contact with the enemy today, just as truly as if you faced him across No Man's Land." Only "discretion and vigilance" could save the American family and soldier.[28]

Propagandists who implored Americans to rely on their government for protection appear to have had an attentive and eager audience. While it is impossible to ascertain exactly how many Americans bought into claims of an internal foreign plot, the number who worried that German Americans and Teutonic agents worked to weaken and conquer the United States was not insignificant. Writing to President Wilson in June 1917, Attorney General Thomas W. Gregory revealed the extent to which the panic over the imagined German conspiracy had overwhelmed Americans. "There have been days when as many as one thousand letters came to my Department purporting to give more or less detailed information as to spies, disloyal citizens and plots to destroy ships, factories, railroad bridges, munitions plants, waterworks, arsenals, etc., etc., etc.," Gregory reported. Although only a small number contained valuable information, it "became necessary to investigate everything called to our attention."[29] In his diary, Navy Secretary Josephus Daniels succinctly described Gregory's thoughts from a cabinet meeting on the public's understanding of the German spy threat, writing "Talk of spies. Greg—thought hysteria."[30] One of Gregory's subordinates, John Lord O'Brian, in charge of the DOJ's War Emergency Division, put the number at five thousand letters per day, with practically all of the charges being unsubstantiated.[31] It is unclear whether these estimates include the large number of letters sent to the MID. If Gregory's or O'Brian's figure is anywhere close to accurate, it would appear that Americans' fear of a perilous Teutonic conspiracy within the nation's borders was very real and widespread during the war.

The thousands of wartime letters the government received revealed the power of propaganda and Americans' certainty of German American Otherness. Propaganda that asked citizens to act as intelligence officers and painted a conceivable vision of the enemy agent—whether based in actual intrigue before the war declaration, racial stereotypes, or the preexisting paradigm of the plotting and volatile foreign Other—served as self-fulfilling prophecies. Vivid descriptions of Teutonic agents and their methods conditioned Americans to seek out particular traits when observing suspicious people, organizations, and activities. Consequently, many letter writers' and some investigators' conceptions of the internal, foreign-born threat closely mirrored the reality of German intrigue during neutrality while also exaggerating descriptions of the German enemy and its nefarious misdeeds portrayed in conspiracy-laden propaganda.

The letters also reveal the often uncontrollable power of rumor, which served to spread racial and apocalyptic fears and anxiety over the German American Other beyond the immediate audience of the propaganda. Sociologists have argued that during times of heightened nervousness, rumor often masquerades as truth, regardless of whether it operates on the local or national level. When a person or community is overcome with acute or generalized anxiety, their ability to make sense of the unknown or the ambiguous becomes compromised. And in times of perceived danger, communities tend to close ranks in order to combat the danger together. The result is a collective construction of the supposed threat.[32] The coming of—even the prospect of—war is clearly an anxiety-inducing circumstance. The transfer of exaggerated tales of the ubiquitous Teutonic agent from the pamphlet, editorial, or poster into the realm of the rumor further aggravated the national mood and the anti-German message of much wartime propaganda, enhancing the effects of both. As an increasing number of nervous Americans sensed that a foreign invader was attacking the United States from the inside, their growing unease overwhelmed their ability to recognize nuances between reality and their assumptions of Teutonic Otherness. Their sense of national, community, and self-preservation demanded that they unite against the imagined internal menace.

That rumor could exacerbate citizens' anxiety was not an alien concept to Anglo-Saxon Americans at the time. Concerns about its dangers, however, were directed toward the spread of German propaganda, not that produced by Americans. At a meeting of leaders of the Department of Educational Propaganda (DEP)—part of the Council of National Defense's Committee on Women's Defense Work—department chair and women's suffrage leader Carrie Chapman Catt argued "that there is not one single woman here who has not aided German propaganda. Ask yourself if you have not heard some rumor, some gossip without any authority, and have passed it on to somebody else." If they had, they had "been passing in all probability German propaganda without any knowledge of it."[33] Members of some of the DEP's local branches held this same concern. The Woman's Committee of the New Hampshire Council of Defense, for instance, worried that "many traitorous rumors" had been "started with malicious intent by pro-German influences" that undermined the people's loyalty and "weaken[ed] the vigor of our nation in fighting for a great ideal."[34]

Unbeknownst to most Anglo-Saxon Americans, the most dangerous rumors originated in American propaganda and their collective notions of the internal enemy Other. Some of the more illuminating examples of how rumor intensified Anglo-Saxons' fears of German plotting occurred in the South, a region historically prone to fashioning innocuous or non-existent conspiracies and racial threats into fears of apocalyptic doom.[35] For white southerners, age-old anxieties about the stability of the black–white racial hierarchy played a key role in the formation of rumors about the equally terrifying menace of Germanization. While some southerners felt assured of black loyalty because they doubted African Americans' ability to comprehend enemy propaganda, most continued to view African Americans as they always had—as untrustworthy and susceptible to outsiders bent on corrupting or overturning the white southern way of life.[36] The caricature of the German agent whispering secret and seditious schemes into African American ears fit seamlessly with the traditional paradigm of the abolitionist or carpetbagger who looked to conquer the South by conspiring with its least trustworthy and most gullible residents.[37] At the same time, rumors that German agents were attempting to foment black uprisings and that an invasion from Mexico by a multiracial army was imminent permeated many areas of the wartime South as well, indicating how word-of-mouth stories can blow up into amazingly tall yet specific tales when fear and anxiety are high.

In some stories that were ginned through the rumor mill and wound up in letters to the Department of Justice's Bureau of Investigation (BI) or the MID, German agents had tried to convince southern African Americans that the successful Germanization of the United States would mean better times were ahead. According to one such story, a German American shopkeeper in Phoebus, Virginia, was trying to convince his black employees "that they would be much better off under German rule than under present conditions."[38] A MID agent reported in April 1918 that a German American baker told an African American doctor in Tuscaloosa, Alabama, that African Americans should not fight for the United States because "the Germans would treat the negroes better tha[n] the Americans," presumably after the conquest was complete.[39] That same month in Pensacola, Florida, rumors spread that German propagandists had told the African American workers at a shop selling ice cream and baked goods that "when the Germans come here they are going to clean up the whites, and establish negroes in their place." If the story was true, the MID agent concluded, the German promises "would have quite an effect upon them, and put them in a state of mind to cooperate to bring this condition about." Allegedly, these workers and some in other parts of the country (Boston is named specifically in the report) did their part by mixing crushed glass into unsuspecting customers' desserts.[40] How this would have helped bring about German domination of the United States is unclear. As to be expected, the investigator found no proof of such propaganda.

Many of the frantic calls for federal help from white southerners revolved around fears of a multiracial force attacking the United States from within or from across the southern border. Such letters began pouring into the BI's and MID's offices from the outset of the war. On April 6, 1917, the day Congress declared war, D. J. Kirton of Cades, South Carolina, reported to the Justice

Department that several black families had told him of rumors that "two very suspicious looking parties," whom they suspected were German, were visiting every African American home in town under the pretext of selling war insurance. Kirton was not fooled. "I fear there is some mischief or plot in this move," he wrote. Unfortunately there was only so much he could do "to find out what these, or any other suspicious looking characters might be after." But because "we country people would be at the mercy of a mob of negroes headed by these Germans," Kirton asserted that "now is the time for us to nip the thing in the bud." He concluded by asking the federal official what he thought the whites of Cades should do to stave off this threat.[41] In a similar case in May, whites in Hampton County, also in South Carolina, believed they had literally dodged a bullet as word spread that German agents had tried to supply local blacks with ammunition for an armed uprising. By the time the federal agent arrived on the scene, however, the local sheriff claimed to have the situation under control, the threat having inexplicably passed.[42] All that is clear is that at some point whites in Cades and Hampton County were fearful enough of a German-backed racial uprising that these South Carolinians, despite their historic antipathy toward the national government, sought the help of federal authorities.

Probably with the details of a genuine conspiracy on their minds, such as the plot described in the Zimmermann Telegram, rumors swirled of an African American rebellion springing out of Mexico as part of a larger Teutonic plan to subjugate the Anglo-Saxon United States.[43] In September 1917, the MID received a report of a spy ring in Yoakum, Texas, where an African American informant tied un-American enemy agents to labor radicals, explaining to an MID agent that "the Germans and these socialists around here . . . are trying to use the negroes and the Mexicans for their selfish ends." He had heard "that in Mexico the Mexicans are organized, and that when the soldiers are taken away from the border to go to France, two thousand Mexicans will invade Texas." The agent, however, made no arrests and could draw no conclusions about the story's authenticity.[44]

Concerns about a multiethnic invasion across the Rio Grande also resonated far away from the border. In early April 1917, authorities in Birmingham, Alabama, arrested a black man and a white man on the charge that they planned to persuade African Americans to flee to Mexico. A rumor circulated that the pro-German perpetrators spread their message while acting as Bible salesmen. In the predominantly black Mississippi Delta, the white sheriff of one small town claimed that German spies were recruiting local blacks to join an invasion force in Mexico. A federal investigator, however, found no reason to believe that local African Americans were "going to leave the Delta for an army in Mexico. But this kind of rumor is all over Mississippi." The alleged German agents, he reported, were probably not spies after all, or even German. They were most likely labor recruiters from Chicago.[45]

Some citizens, African Americans in particular, were not convinced that Teutonic agents were recruiting southern blacks or that southern whites' fear of a German–African American uprising was genuine. In August 1917, Major W. H. Loving of the MID, an African American officer, composed a memo to his white colleagues that looked to explain the feelings of those facing segregation, the constant prospect of violence, and now charges of working with German agents. "It seems . . . certain," he claimed, "that there are adequate reasons for the unrest and dissatisfaction which is at present manifest throughout twelve millions [*sic*] of Americans of Negro descent, and that no assumption of a special propaganda on the part of pro-German sympathizers is necessary to explain this situation."[46]

The African American press went out of its way to proclaim the unflappable loyalty of southern blacks and to cast aspersions on white southerners who claimed otherwise. The editors of the *Boston Guardian* gave no credence to white southerners' reports because they believed the Germans would not undertake such a "far-fetched folly of hoping for success in such an undertaking." African Americans were not prone to falling for unrealistic promises, such as the carving of "a black republic" out of the United States, the editors asserted, because "it is contrary to the mental and physical make-up of colored Americans seriously to undertake that which is beyond hope of accomplishing."[47] The *Baltimore Afro-American* maintained that Germany overestimated the tension within the "family quarrels" between white and black Americans. "Any neighbor who has attempted to butt in and settle a domestic quarrel and has received a black eye from" the embittered kinfolk "for his pains can appreciate the colored people's reception of German propaganda."[48] In the *Crisis*, the official newspaper of the National Association for the Advancement of Colored People, editor W.E.B. DuBois defended southern blacks' loyalty by questioning the motives of southern whites who alleged a German conspiracy was at work in the South. In the face of institutional and social barriers, African Americans in the South were advancing themselves and, most importantly, "migrating slowly but surely to a land of liberty [the North]." Southern whites, though, resented this reality, DuBois argued. Consequently, "any tale or propaganda by which the Bourbon South can get the country to believe the Negro is a menace would" directly benefit "the slave-holders" because the instituting of "martial law" would "stop migration" of black workers out of the South. The professed fears of German intrigue in the South, DuBois concluded, were a convenient excuse for controlling black labor and excluding blacks from whites' definition of Americanism.[49] At the same time, if white concerns were in fact intentionally bogus (some most likely were), their assumption that most other Anglo-Saxons would believe their rumors and accusations speaks to the pervasiveness of anti-German paranoia throughout the country.

Perhaps a greater indication of the power of rumor and the degree to which anxious Americans had bought into the idea of an internal Teutonic conspiracy is that the specter of a German-sponsored black uprising also haunted whites as far away from the southern border as the Atlantic and Pacific coasts. A woman in Seattle, Washington, informed the MID that the African American chef at the Puss 'n Boots bakery told "a friend of hers" that German agents had been providing arms and money to "certain negroes in this county" so they could "start a revolution, acting in conjunction with a force of German reservists which would invade the United States from Mexico." The woman claimed that the kaiser's representative apparently offered African Americans "a part of the conquered territory" in return for their help Germanizing the United States.[50] On the other coast, the MID investigated a report from a Miss Steers about a German plot in the works in Harlem, New York, where African Americans had been purchasing property and furniture at an alarming rate. Her unwelcome neighbors clearly were "acting as agents for German financiers," her proof being that they held a dinner for a "distinguished German" before his alleged departure for Mexico. To make matters worse, "a family of Spaniards" had also moved in nearby, their home acting as headquarters for the hatching of "some kind of Mexican plot." The plot unfolding before Steers's eyes, she deduced, was "indicative of the organization methods of German propaganda."[51] Similar concerns about the complicity of northern blacks in Teutonic plots arose in Philadelphia, Detroit, Washington, DC, and other major cities.[52] As with accusations in the South, federal agents found no solid evidence of a conspiracy in any of these investigations.

African Americans were not the only familiar non-Anglo Other anxious white citizens connected to the Teutonic scheme. After the United States entered the war, the implied conflation of German saboteurs with immigrant radicals many in the press had made during neutrality appears to have solidified in the minds of the significant number of Anglo-Saxon Americans who were becoming increasingly fearful of Germanization and German American

Otherness. This blending of anxieties was clear in the rumors civilians reported to federal agencies about possible German sabotage across the country. With the old trust of American Teutons having been discarded, many Anglo-Saxons and propagandists interpreted nearly every fire or explosion in the context of the alleged German conspiracy and the documented reports of actual sabotage from 1915. In the process, they saw an enemy that was no less volatile and uncivilized than the heavily accented, whiskered, and wild-eyed alien radical ideologue of the popular imagination who had fomented strikes, destroyed employers' property, and generally threatened to overturn the existing social order. As with their alarm over the prospect of black insurrection, this rendering of the enemy was quite recognizable and, consequently, easy to fear.

Just like the investigations of African American collaboration with German provocateurs, BI and MID inquiries into claims that German agents had or had tried to sabotage valuable infrastructure and industrial targets turned up empty. The legitimate evidence trained detectives uncovered, though, contrasted sharply with the anxiety-induced reports in the press and from most civilian informants, which indicates the degree to which assumptions of German American Otherness influenced white citizens' perceptions of local and national events. In June 1918, for instance, the MID received news of an explosion and fire at a railroad depot in tiny Americus, Georgia, that locals "presistantly [*sic*] reported" had been the work of "alien enemies," a common and vague term that could apply to a Teutonic agent or immigrant radical. The depot's proximity to an airfield required an immediate investigation. But after little inspection, the MID agent found there was "no possible connection of [an] alien enemy with this fire or explosion" and concluded that the blaze was the fault of a couple drunken clerks.[53] A lawyer in Fairview, Utah, testified to a MID agent that the destruction of a large dam near the town was the work of German saboteurs. The lawyer's proof was that the giving way of the dam— with the ensuing destruction of crops, coal mines, and several miles of the Denver & Rio Grande railway line—would "result in serious damage to the country." Thus, it had to be the work of saboteurs. According to the MID agent, however, "no traces of the dam being dynamited was found." In fact, "the concrete had not been shattered, and there were no small pieces of concrete lying around." Although the detective concluded that enemy activity was possible, the shabby repairs done to the dam over time and the high water level were the more likely culprits.[54]

Investigators also were forced to deal with Americans' fear that the tools of sabotage could end up in the hands of enemy agents. In May 1917, a Michigan man told investigators that while his community had taken the proper steps to protect its coal mining explosives, about a quarter million pounds of dynamite and half a million pounds of black powder sat unprotected in Terre Haute, Indiana. "Little attention," he claimed, "is placed upon the significance of this matter."[55] It is unclear why the man would have known about the security of someone else's explosives in faraway Terre Haute, but, as in the cases of the depot in Georgia and the dam in Utah, his concern that they could end up in the wrong hands, and that those hands existed and actively sought out dynamite, speaks to the thoroughness with which the image of the bomb-tossing and degenerate alien radical had influenced American perceptions of German residents.

Far more frustrating for federal agents than mistaken and panicky reports of Teutonic plots was working with the DOJ's army of unofficial and untrained civilian detectives, the American Protective League. Founded in Chicago in the early spring of 1917, the APL rapidly grew into a 250,000-man organization that the DOJ called upon to assist its grossly undermanned Bureau of Investigation in scrutinizing the thousands of warnings and complaints from anxious citizens. In fact, the amateur APL accounted for the vast majority of the federal government's investigative capability during the war. Their accounts, however, suggest they suffered from the same siege mentality as those who wrote fearful letters to the government. The APL's federal sanctioning and its members' lack of formal training made its illegal spying and arrests a greater danger to American institutions than any German spy. Equally problematic was that the federal government's recruitment of the APL, like its calls for citizens to act as snitches, was an admission that it was too weak to protect the country on its own. Through the APL, the Department of Justice attempted to wield more power than it officially possessed while avoiding formal responsibility for the amateur investigators' excesses.[56]

Ultimately, the APL was not particularly helpful. The contrast between the reality that federal agents uncovered and the imaginations of nervous APL detectives often was quite stark. Most APL men appear to have fallen victim to the fear that any or all German Americans could be a volatile enemy Other, as evidenced by their consistently entering investigations assuming German sabotage, not accident or bad fortune, was the cause of a fire or explosion.[57] Federally trained investigators in most cases quickly discounted the civilian sleuths' predetermined findings. In August 1918, for instance, an APL agent advised that federal authorities investigate a German American for his part in an explosion at a chemical plant in Marquette, Michigan, where he worked as a watchman. The German seemed dodgy because he "had acted suspiciously in connection with inquiries he had made about the dates of arrival of [a] certain mechanical apparatus which is in no way connected with his work." Although offering no guesses as to what the Teuton planned to do with the contraption, the APL agent proclaimed that the suspect was likely a saboteur. The MID agent who followed up on the case, however, deigned to interview the suspect's employer, who was "absolutely convinced" the German American was "a loyal employee and a loyal citizen." With that, the case was closed.[58] In a similar situation outside Albany, New York, in April of that year, police removed dynamite from an unprotected magazine, the doors of which had been shot at repeatedly. The police had questioned many of the enemy aliens in the immediate area, most of whom were Austrian, and found them to be loyal to the United States. Yet the APL investigator on the scene claimed to have a list of enemy alien males who were unknown to local authorities and, thus, were unaccounted for. At the time of the BI's report, the APL man had yet to complete his investigation or turn over his inventory of unfriendly outsiders, but his assumption that the perpetrators were part of a secretive transient group of conspirators speaks volumes about his mindset.[59]

Equally problematic for federal investigators who operated in the world of facts were the assertions of industrialists, big and small, who tried to exploit the national hysteria by fraudulently blaming the destruction of their property on Teutonic sabotage. In the majority of industrial sabotage claims, DOJ and MID investigators were left to posit that the owner or a hired arsonist set the fires to defraud their insurance company or that the blazes were the result of negligence, incompetence, or bad luck. In an April 1918 letter to Attorney General Gregory, John Lord O'Brian reported that "it is the consensus opinion" of insurance companies and federal fire investigators "that substantially no fire losses of [suspicious] character during the past year have been caused by enemy activities within the country." In fact, "It is safe to say that in 97% of the reports of such instances the complaint is unfounded."[60] The defrauders had judged their stories of Teutonic sabotage to be plausible lies. Moreover, considering the depths of nationwide panic, it is likely that many of the well-meaning people in the remaining 3 percent who reported to the DOJ or MID saw the shadow of the German Other in the charred remains of their factory or mill. Beneath even the counterfeit claims of sabotage was an acknowledgment of Anglo-Saxon Americans' lingering sense of vulnerability to dangerous Others capable of explosive, uncivilized behavior. A large number of plant owners, it appears, were comfortable exploiting the national mood.

Occasionally, trained detectives also had to compete with the press's depiction of the hot-blooded German Americans' sabotage campaign. An interesting example of the contrast between press accounts and investigators' reports is the coverage of a large fire that engulfed the docks and ships at Port Newark, New Jersey, in late January 1918. According to the *New York Times*, the federal government believed the fire added credence to "the widely current report that enemies are again plotting in this country to cripple American war preparation by incendiarism and other forms of violence. This became clear the previous night when" the governor mobilized the state militia, allegedly at the behest of the federal government, to surround the burning facilities.[61] While there is no way to be sure, the alarmist tone of the story suggests that the reporter's "federal" source could have been an untrained and excitable APL agent.

The *Times*'s version of the story, as the two New York City police investigators on the scene at Port Newark found, did not correspond to the facts on the ground. There was no need to call in the cavalry, they concluded, because the tiniest precaution could have saved the port from its fiery destruction. An employee's failure to put out a small fire used to dry sand and that "was supposed to be extinguished every day at 5 P.M." was the likely cause. The reason such a small fire overwhelmed so much of the facility was that "the nearest fire alarm signal [was] about a mile away," and there was inadequate water pressure to extinguish the flames. Although the investigators admitted that "the guarding of this site from the water" was inadequate, noting that it was "possible to gain access to some parts of this pier from the water without detection," this observation did not alter their conclusion as to the source of the blaze.[62]

The wide gap between the reality investigators encountered and the imaginations of propagandists, nervous letter writers, and crusaders against Germanization also played out in Washington. Somewhat surprisingly, top officials at the Military Intelligence Division grappled with this distinction despite the reports its agents had submitted. The MID's 1918 official report on the effect of pro-German and anti-American proselytizing reads like the American propaganda that consumed the civilian population. Although the report claims that to attribute every setback in war mobilization to German intrigue "would be hysterical and ridiculous," the MID's analysis of German propaganda comes close to doing just that, at times reproducing lengthy hyperbolic newspaper and magazine articles as if their authors' conclusions were above reproach or matched those the MID hoped to make on its own but, without evidence, could not. In the chapter entitled "German Propaganda in America," for instance, the report cites the *Saturday Evening Post*, *New York Times*, *New York Tribune*, and Congressional Record extensively, instead of evidence that MID, BI, or APL investigators had compiled. Other common accusations against alleged pro-Germans and disloyal German Americans litter the entire volume. The MID mentions the Delbrück Law, despite the fact it did not apply in the United States; describes Germans as a monolithic people ("The Germans have shown marvelous skill and thoroughness in their schemes" and "are immensely clever" with an "enormous talent for conquest"); claims pacifists, radicals, and socialists were at worst active German agents or at best gave aid and comfort to the enemy; charges that the National German American Alliance was a front for the kaiser's scheme to dominate the Western Hemisphere; and alleges that Americans spread pro-German rumors unconsciously and needed to be more vigilant.[63] The MID's summary appears to suggest one of two conclusions: either it exploited the illusion of an internal German conspiracy for the sake of maintaining the agency's current level of funding, or its leadership and those who prepared the report believed Teutonic plotting ran deep but had yet to find enough of its own evidence to support the theory.

At no time was the contrast between reality and imagination more consequential than in the passing of the Espionage Act on June 15, 1917, the purpose of which was to protect the nation from those guilty of undermining American war mobilization or actively carrying out a pro-German conspiracy against the United States. More specifically, the statute made it illegal to "make or convey false reports or false statements" with the intent of obstructing the work of the military, convincing men to shirk military service, or attempting to infect the military with disloyalty. In practice, the DOJ and federal courts applied the law broadly, prosecuting those whose anti-war rhetoric or labor radicalism could hinder any aspect of war mobilization, be it military, industrial, agricultural, or psychological. Many judges operated under the assumption that if an action could disrupt American war mobilization, it must be actively pro-German and, thus, part of a wider Teutonic plot. To keep Germanizing and anti-American propaganda from reaching the eyes and ears of soldiers and civilians alike—and so the Wilson administration could deny having directly censored the press—the Espionage Act also gave Postmaster General Albert Sidney Burleson the authority to deny mailing privileges to any publication that he deemed radical and pro-German.[64] In a letter to a friend, Burleson described the Espionage Act as a weapon against the presumed German conspiracy, claiming the law "aimed to prevent crimes against our country" and to end "the circulation of other matter containing false and treasonable statements, the intent and effect of all of which is manifestly to create hostility to the government, decrease its efficiency, weaken its military power, lend material aid and comfort to the enemy, and in every way further the cause of Prussianism in our land."[65] The Espionage Act, meant as a means of national self-defense against German American Others and their alien radical allies, reveals the degree to which federal officials shared in the national frenzy over the purported Teutonic plot.[66]

Federal authorities, though, had found no actual German conspirators, German American or otherwise. Instead, federal courts prosecuted hundreds of pacifists, socialists, agrarian populists, and anarchists under the Espionage Act for speeches, newspaper editorials, and pamphlets calling for strikes, resistance to conscription, industrial sabotage, and an immediate end to the war, thus lumping them all under the umbrella of Germany's alleged plot to control the United States. Victor Berger, the German-born socialist politician and editor of the *Milwaukee Leader,* saw the writing on the wall for himself and his newspaper. Writing to Burleson in July 1917, Berger refuted the argument that the Espionage Act made the nation more secure. "Our country is supposed to be a democracy and a democracy cannot exist without healthy opposition," he argued. "We find in history that a strong opposition was permitted in old Rome (so long as the republic really existed) even during the life and death grapple with Carthage—and our republic is surely not fighting for its existence as Rome fought with 'Hannibal ante portas.' As a matter of fact we are not fighting for our existence at all."[67]

Berger's concern for democracy was not unfounded. With Anglo-Saxon Americans feeling as if they were being held under siege by a cunning yet volatile internal Other, many deemed the erosion of individual liberties a price worth paying to secure their nation and identity. And security is exactly what the Espionage Act promised to bring. Former presidential candidate and future Supreme Court Chief Justice Charles Evans Hughes best articulated the predominant wartime legal opinion regarding the statute when he wrote that "self-preservation is the first law of national life and the Constitution itself provides the necessary powers in order to defend and preserve the United States." John Lord O'Brian likewise argued that because it was "the right of the nation in time of grave national danger to protect itself against utterances intended to weaken its power of self-defense," restraints on free speech during wartime were perfectly legal and appropriate. Supreme Court Justice Oliver Wendell Holmes's famous 1919 ruling that seditious speech in wartime constituted a "clear and present danger" when it brought "about the substantive evils Congress has a right to prevent" articulated what legal officials at the time believed was the difference between what was legally protected in wartime as opposed to peacetime.[68]

All of these opinions, however, were awash in the millennial strain of popular American culture in that they were based in the assumption that the United States and Anglo-Saxon democracy were facing an existential danger. This notion may have appeared true when viewed through the lens of hysterical wartime propaganda, but in reality there was nothing "clear" nor "present" about the alleged German conspiracy. Even if Hughes, Holmes, and like-minded officials and legal experts cynically exploited widespread fear in order to justify silencing critics of the government or industrial capitalism, their apparent comfort with employing the apocalyptic anti-German argument is indicative of the degree to which most Anglo-Saxons associated the perils of Teutonic Otherness with the security of their family, community, nation, and race.

In the name of defending the country and its Anglo-Saxon citizens from Teutonic intrigue, many rabid federal judges conducted kangaroo courts, often haranguing defendants on the importance of Americanism and the danger of the imagined German conspiracy during the trial and after handing down a sentence. One well-known example is that of Judge Henry DeLamar Clayton, Jr., who presided over the 1918 sedition trial of Russian Jewish anarchists Jacob Abrams, Mollie Steimer, and four accomplices charged with spreading propaganda against American military intervention in the Russian Civil War. For two hours during the October sentencing hearing, Clayton, wearing a black armband in honor of a brother who had fallen in France, tore into the defendants for their anti-American and alleged pro-German views to justify their stern sentences under the Espionage Act. Because of the "inherent right of self-defense" provided in the Constitution, he argued, the defendants' conviction for spreading "their covert German propaganda stuff" stood on a firm legal basis. Ultimately, Clayton concluded, laws limiting free speech in wartime were critical if the United States were to defeat the "devilish and artful German Kaiser and his military satraps."[69] Although autocratic Germany would be one of the last countries with whom anarchists would ally, Clayton, as many judges would do during wartime, portrayed foreign radicals and German conspirators as being one and the same, thus casting the latest alien Other into the mold of a longer term internal enemy and thus more easily justifying the defendants' sentences.[70]

In hindsight, the dangerous precedent set by the Espionage Act was not worth the cost because it did little to make many Anglo-Saxons feel safer from Germanization. Clearly, the federal government's efforts to convince citizens to rely on the state for protection seems to have had mixed results. Despite its calls for individual citizens to report on any suspicious individuals, rumors, or activities, the size of the BI and the MID, even with the help of the American Protective League, was not adequate for their task. Consequently, the slow pace at which investigators could respond to local distress calls and their inability to prosecute real enemy agents did not match the urgency of white Americans' fears. If German spies and propagandists were everywhere, should not more of them have been arrested? This was bad optics for the federal government in that it appeared as if the Wilson administration was not taking the threat seriously or was incapable of defending the country against Teutonic plotting. In many parts of the country, patriotic Americans did not wait for federal detectives to act because, in many cases, they did not feel they could afford to.

Misgivings about the ability of federal authorities to confront the menace led some Americans to organize locally to defend against Germany's covert invasion or to punish the internal enemy Other and its sympathizers. In a pamphlet advocating the formation of local home defense leagues, the American Defense Society defined "the primary purpose of each League" as "local defense and protection." Members should not be of military age, which the Selective Service Act set at 21 to 31 in 1917 and adjusted to 18 to 45 in September 1918, but still needed to "be physically fit, and of sober habits and cool heads." The ADS, however, appears to have viewed the leagues as local paramilitary organizations. Its plan to militarize home defense volunteers suggested that the threat the community faced—a foreign, anti-American conspiracy—was an imminent danger that might require the use of force. The ADS offered members a detailed list of a dozen tasks home guardsmen must carry out, including "suppress[ing] local disorders"; guarding important infrastructure and public buildings; "patrol[ling] towns, surrounding country, rivers, harbors and sea-coasts"; spying on those of suspicious loyalty; providing arms and uniforms (with insignia) to members; ensuring that men of military age enlist; "register[ing] motors, vehicles," and other machinery "for home defense and military use"; and "act[ing] as an emergency police body."[71] Any community that went to these lengths would have been very afraid of a possible German conspiracy and quite skeptical of the federal government's ability to keep their families safe.

Some citizens rejected the organized and defensive measures of home defense leagues and looked to compensate for the government's inadequacies by going on the offensive against Teutonic plotters. While their motivations were often local, the press and several well-known and well-respected Americans frequently proclaimed the federal government's competence and attentiveness to be wanting. They encouraged vigilant citizens to make up for that deficiency on their own through force. The *Washington Post* was critical of propaganda efforts to convince Americans to act only as snitches while waiting on federal power to confront the German threat. Instead, the newspaper wanted citizens to take the fight to the enemy, declaring in August 1917 that both Wilson and Congress had been "easy-going and generous toward the enemies of the United States." Showing a disdain or indifference to the principles of due process and the presumption of innocence, the editors maintained that one of the most glaring mistakes the government had made was assuming "that all enemy aliens in the United States are harmless unless they attract attention by some overt act." No German Americans, the *Post* implied, could be trusted. Citing an explosion at the Mare Island shipyard near San Francisco, the editors charged the DOJ with being inattentive to the real danger the Teutonic American population posed. If the government was not up to the task of defending the nation from threats within the borders, the *Post* concluded, then citizens must be proactive.[72]

Prominent Americans within and outside the Wilson administration seem to have agreed with the *Post*'s sentiment. Former president Theodore Roosevelt and current Navy Secretary Josephus Daniels, for instance, did not ask audiences to passively call on the federal government to fight local battles for them. Instead, they asked them to directly confront the only enemies within the nation's immediate reach: the disloyal and scheming German American Other. "The Hun within our gates masquerades in many guises," Roosevelt maintained in October 1917. The Teuton "is our dangerous enemy; and he should be hunted down without mercy."[73] Similarly, Daniels directly alluded to the treacherous German American's Otherness, proclaiming that Anglo-Saxons should "put the fear of God into the hearts of those who live among us, and fatten upon us, and are not Americans."[74]

Inspired by calls for aggressive national defense at home (and, in some cases, local animus), mobs of patriotic white Americans punished alleged pro-Germans, which at times included non-Teutons. The Tulsa, Oklahoma, County Council of Defense summed up vigilantes' mood well when it warned that "any person or persons who utter disloyal or unpatriotic statements do so at their own peril and cannot expect the protection of the loyal citizenship of this nation." Vigilantes followed through on this promise by forcing alleged enemies of Americanism to kiss the American flag, banishing them from towns or even states, tarring and feathering them, selling off their private property to buy government war bonds (known as "Liberty Bonds"), painting them yellow, parading or dragging them through the streets wrapped in an American flag, and, in the most extreme cases, lynching (or attempting to lynch) the accused.[75]

Such instances were often intertwined with local anxieties that national fears of foreign plotting and Germanization had exacerbated. One example occurred in Hampton, Iowa, where a MID agent reported in October 1917 that "several prominent lawyers and bankers" considered "tarring and feathering" a German American Lutheran pastor named Bittner because of his alleged attempts to indoctrinate American-born Teutonic children with Prussianism. That the pastor moved to town "about the time wa[r] was declared" and began both a Lutheran church and "a German Lutheran School" smelled of conspiracy, the businessmen charged. That "German children were withdrawn from the public school" to learn solely in the German language in Bittner's school probably did not help his cause, even though it is likely that the German children who attended did so to avoid harassment by native-born public-school students. When the MID agent informed the lawyers and bankers that he would "let [Bittner] understand that his anti-American views did not look well and would not be tolerated . . . and that he" should "keep his mouth shut," the town leaders were apoplectic. Bittner deserved more than a stern talking-to, they asserted. The report does not indicate what, if any, legal or extralegal punishment Bittner faced.[76]

Bittner was relatively lucky. The most infamous incident of wartime mobbing was the April 4, 1918, lynching of Robert Prager in Collinsville, Illinois, not far from St. Louis. Prager, who had tried to enlist in the US Navy but was denied for medical reasons, was a German-born immigrant accused of spreading the un-American gospel of socialism to members of a local miners' union. There was no evidence of his involvement in any scheme to undermine Anglo-Saxon democracy or that Prager was anything less than indifferent to the American cause.[77] Whatever the mob's motives—a knee-jerk reaction to fears of Teutonic intrigue, a personal vendetta, or some other incentive—the fact that they asked Prager before his hanging whether or not he was an enemy agent suggests that their belief in the mere possibility of a campaign to Germanize the United States gave them a justification for murder.

Prager's death made national headlines, with most leading politicians and newspapers denouncing mob violence. But some in the press saw a patriotic silver lining in the murder. The *Washington Post* declared that "in spite of excesses such as lynching," Prager's murder was a sign of "a healthful and wholesome awakening" in the traditionally isolationist Midwest.[78] While the editors of *Everybody's* found "the lynching of a disloyalist in Illinois" to be "crude and regrettable," it was also "high time" Americans stopped showering the German American enemy with love and sympathy. In case the American people had forgotten, the nation was at war.[79]

For Attorney General Gregory, Prager's death further highlighted the distance between the press's and public's imagination and the near complete lack of evidence his trained detectives had found in their investigations. Responding to a friend who had commented on the public criticism that the government was soft on spies, Gregory crassly joked, "If you will kindly box up and send me from one to a dozen I will pay you very handsomely for your trouble. We are looking for them constantly, but it is a little difficult to shoot them until they have been found." Gregory also expressed frustration over the discrepancy between what he read about German intrigue in newspapers, which often inspired vigilantism, and the reports he received from his men in the field. Most news stories on German espionage made greatly "exaggerated statements . . . to the effect that spies are being constantly caught and not prosecuted, or are being paroled or released without trial, or that the Government is taking no adequate steps to discover and prosecute spies and disloyal citizens." The truth was that "scores of thousands of men are under constant observation throughout the country," and a significant number had been prosecuted under the Espionage Act. This, Gregory lamented, was not enough to overcome the impact of hyperbolic tales of a vast and ongoing German conspiracy.[80] A. Bruce Bielaski, wartime head of the BI, also complained of the same problem to Gregory in January 1918, which indicates that charges in the press of DOJ lenience toward spies and disloyalty had frustrated the attorney general and other department higher-ups for quite some time before the Prager incident.[81]

To combat public criticism leveled at the government, Congress and the Wilson administration amended the Espionage Act on May 16, 1918. Under the newly expanded law, known as the Sedition Act, the defendant's words or actions, not their intent, was all that mattered, making prosecutions for allegedly disloyal rhetoric or actions far easier for judges and juries. Although he deflected any blame for Prager's murder, Gregory publicly defended the DOJ and conveyed the need for a tougher sedition law soon after the German American's death. "While the lynching of Prager is to be deplored," he said, "it cannot be condemned. The department of justice has repeatedly called upon congress for the necessary laws to prevent just such a thing as happened in the Illinois town." Despite his knowledge that most reports of German intrigue were bogus, Gregory claimed that the mob (none of whom were prosecuted) was not responsible for Prager's killing. Instead, he blamed German propaganda, anger over the disloyalty it generated, and Congress for the weak federal laws that frustrated citizens and prevented the DOJ from protecting the American people from the enemy within.[82] In reality, the revising of the Espionage Act into the Sedition Act occurred because of the perception that the government was not reacting to the people's sense of dread and urgency over the danger of the supposed German conspiracy. Anglo-Saxon Americans' sense of vulnerability and fear of German American Otherness were real, and, in their minds and in the messages of wartime propagandists, the internal menace was an existential threat that must be confronted at all levels.

Propaganda presenting German Americans as conspirators hoping to undermine Anglo-Saxon power and identity, along with the federal government's slow and inconclusive responses to citizens' fears, helped create the conditions in which vigilantism became acceptable. Yet the collectively shaped image of the internal enemy Other and the Anglo-Saxon American identity it was purported to threaten formed out of a variety of sources. Apocalyptic and Darwinian understandings of the struggle with the German American Other on the home front informed many vigilantes' fears, suggesting that these factors were deep-seated and transcended wartime propaganda. Most cases of vigilantism were not only attempts to protect one's physical home and community from untrustworthy outsiders. They were also a means of defending one's identity, considered malleable yet deeply ingrained, from being subordinated to another's, which was a consistent fear that influenced Anglo-Saxon identity formation and their perception of the various alien Others in their midst.

Despite the episodic but glaring instances of lawlessness, Gregory remarked in a 1919 speech to the North Carolina Bar Association that the federal government had kept domestic peace and order during wartime. He proclaimed proudly that he "doubt[ed] if any country ha[d] ever been so thoroughly and intelligently policed in the history of the world" as the United States had been during the First World War. At the same time, Gregory characterized the United States as having been under siege from within. The nation contained "about four million un-naturalized alien enemies" in 1917, and "there were many communities in which they constituted a majority of the population, and some in which the German language was almost exclusively spoken." With the army mobilizing to fight in Europe, it was difficult "to protect a thousand vital points on our coast, and in the interior" against "at least a substantial part of the 4,000,000 [who] were intensely hostile to our country, and would be glad to take advantage of any favorable opportunity to cripple our resources, impede the organization of our armies and furnish information to our enemies."[83]

Such heavy policing would not have seemed so necessary had German Americans not been Othered so quickly and completely by the time the United States entered the Great War. Within his self-congratulatory speech, Gregory reflected the pervasive wartime belief that American Teutons were a ticking time bomb awaiting word from Berlin on when to detonate. Before the war began in 1914, few Anglo-Saxons would have drawn this conclusion about their Teutonic cousins, whom they had trusted, due to their close cultural and racial kinship, to become fully assimilated and patriotic Americans. Germans were believed to be naturally stubborn, efficient, secretive, parochial, patient, and inquisitive, traits that before the war carried positive connotations. Yet by the time the United States entered the fray in April 1917, many had concluded that these traits signified the Teuton's natural penchant for intrigue, unwillingness (not inability) to Americanize, and desire to thoughtlessly serve the interests of their kaiser and Fatherland. To many Anglo-Saxon Americans, their German neighbors were not who they had thought they were, and the speed with which they reached this collectively construed version of reality added a sense of shock to their feelings of betrayal.

For those who viewed German Americans in such a way, the stakes could not have been higher. White Americans' new assessment of German residents evoked long-held racial and apocalyptic anxieties regarding the durability of Anglo-Saxon identity and control over the United States. That angst was transferred onto the suddenly less familiar German American, with the new internal enemy Other often being viewed in the same fearful manner as many foreign peoples and ideologies had been in recent decades. As a result, the words, fists, and imaginations of patriotic Americans ran wild during the war, and they directed most of their vitriol and violence at the supposedly unassimilated foreigners they presumed had come to destroy their country and way of life. An internal war of national self-defense was at hand. Yet to those Americans who subscribed to such a view, Germany's surreptitious invasion through immigration, propaganda, and acculturation was only half the battle, as the kaiser and his minions sought to finalize their conquest of the United States, and ultimately the whole world, through blunt force.

CHAPTER FOUR

Resisting Regressive Militarism, 1917–1918

A victory for Germany—that is, a conclusive victory and a "German peace"—
would mean that . . . the United States would be first a defeated nation and then
a conquered nation. It would take orders from Potsdam—promptly. Eventually
it would parade at the goose-step. At its head, on horseback, would be not an
American President but a German Kaiser.

NOVELIST BOOTH TARKINGTON, 1917

If we had not gone into the war on the occasion which we have . . . if we had sat
by submissive while wrong was enthroned and militarism made the rule of life
of the rest of the world outside of the borders of our own republic, the spirit of
Washington would have wept as it watched, and the people of the United States
would have been called upon in a very short time to exchange the peaceful avo-
cations which have made their civilization great for a civilization armed to the
teeth and ready to expect an attack which would not have been long delayed.

SECRETARY OF WAR NEWTON D. BAKER, July 4, 1918

"The Prussian is cruel by birth; civilization will make him ferocious," the
great German intellectual Johann Wolfgang von Goethe was reported to have
asserted well over a century before the First World War. Samuel Harden
Church, president of the Carnegie Institution in 1918, could not have agreed
more as he applied Goethe's claim to the German people as a whole. "When
we seek a phrase to express our abhorrence of these people we must go back
to a spiritual and intellectual Germany that is dead and gone," Church asserted. In place of the old refined Germany stood a backward, militaristic
nation and a people bent on conquest and the destruction of western civilization. Goethe's phrase was particularly fitting, Church asserted, because the
basis of the German "ogre's conception of frightfulness" was the defilement
of young women in occupied Belgium, which they carried out with a "beastly
and degenerate ferocity." It was this "spirit of the German people to conquer,
destroy, ravish, and kill everything that is not German" that bonded the

United States and the Allies together in their war against this new, regressed Germany. If this backward-sliding nation won the war in Europe, there was no guarantee its people would not ravage the United States with the same beastly ferocity.[1]

Such descriptions of the German enemy in Europe and the threat it posed to the Anglo-Saxon United States were ubiquitous after the April 1917 declaration of war. Many white Americans were already convinced from German intrigue—both of the real and imagined variety—that Germany was no ordinary foe. When they looked across the Atlantic at the European Teuton, however, they saw a somewhat different adversary. While Anglo-Saxon imaginations conceived of both the "Prussianized" German and the disloyal German American as volatile, manipulative, and pursuing the Germanization of the world, the actions of the kaiser's armies made European Germans appear particularly degraded, aggressive, calculating, brutal, and complicit in their government's aggressive global conspiracy. Comparisons between the sabotage and intrigue on the home front and German atrocities in Belgium were extremely rare, which suggests that most Americans viewed German Americans and their European brethren differently.

The words and actions of European Germans in the years before and during the war signaled to American propagandists and many in their target audience that a drastic cultural (and, thus, racial) shift had occurred within Germany since its unification in 1871, and the militaristic and autocratic Prussian monarchy was to blame. Propagandists maintained that the dominance of the racially and culturally backward Prussians of Eastern Europe forced the Teutonic cousin of the Anglo-Saxon to take a sharp U-turn on the path of continued progress. While some white Americans worried during neutrality that urban life and luxury had overcivilized and softened the Anglo-Saxon to the point of regression, wartime propagandists argued that Prussian militarism had brought on a racial-cultural decline within the Teutonic race in Europe as well. In the German case, however, the deterioration was much more extreme and took on a much different character. Militarism did not make the German weak. On the contrary, as Goethe suggested, the ultimate consequence of their degeneration was hyper-aggression and barbarism. To many Americans, the European Germans' territorial avarice and atrocities in Belgium betrayed its racial-cultural regression, leaving their "whiteness" in doubt. In an era when a nation's actions and culture often were seen as expressions of its people's racial traits and development, the militarized, or Prussianized, German overseas easily fit the role of the dangerous enemy Other.

American politicians, commentators, and propagandists asserted that the German people's alleged degeneration posed a direct threat not only to Europe but to the United States; they offered persistent warnings that the Prussianized Teuton exhibited an unquenchable thirst for conquest and destruction. Using a style of argument that would later prove effective during the Cold War and the War on Terror, they declared that the Allies would have to win "over there" in Europe so Americans would not have to fight German militarism "over here" in the United States.[2] If not defeated in Europe, the kaiser's hordes would likely attempt to bring their depravity and brutality to American shores, defiling American communities, homes, and women in the same way they reportedly had in occupied Belgium and northern France. To prevent a victorious Germany from spreading its bestial Prussianism to the United States, Anglo-Saxon Americans may have to forsake progress and democracy, and revert to a militarist state. In either scenario, an Allied defeat in Europe would lead to the disintegration of Anglo-Saxon identity, due to life under the German jackboot or to mandated militarism for the sake of national defense. Americans would have to risk degenerating themselves in order to protect their families and nation from the enemy Other overseas. Victory meant a millennial peace, prosperity, and the expansion of democracy across the globe. Defeat meant insecurity, the destruction of democracy, and, quite possibly, brutal foreign rule. The conflict in Europe, like the war waged against Germanization inside the United States, was a battle for the soul of the Anglo-Saxon nation.

In that sense, the difference between Americans' understanding of their enemies within American borders and those in Europe was one of scale, with the Prussianized German seemingly the more dangerous. The origins of both fears, though, appear to have been the same. Oversimplified, racialized, and apocalyptic depictions of the overseas enemy worked because they echoed the bases of many white Americans' apprehension over the perceived impact that the demographic, economic, and cultural shocks of recent decades, most notably immigration, could have on Anglo-Saxon culture. Many white Americans asserted that the millions of white, yet supposedly inferior, ethnicities from the back corners of Europe challenged the Anglo-Saxon race's hold on American society and politics. Depictions of European Germans as a brutal, bestial, and aggressive people bent on conquering the United States undoubtedly resonated with Americans to whom these were merely passing concerns as well as with those who saw the teeming alien masses as a throng of potentially violent trespassers. Although propaganda portraying the internal and external Teutonic threats as two sides of the same coin were not as common as one would think, the fear of spies and an apocalyptic invasion both reflected the same sense of Anglo-Saxon doom that had often arisen in the years before the war began. Like the war against the internal enemy, the nation's war in Europe became an extension of the decades-long battles they and their parents' generation had been waging over the fate of their racial, cultural, and national identity. In this do-or-die war of self-defense against a plotting, barbaric, deceptive, and aggressive Teutonic enemy, nothing less than Anglo-Saxon American identity was at stake.

At the same time, white Americans expressed their fears of immigrant hordes and Prussianized European Germans through the symbols and language of imperialism. Aliens from the underdeveloped areas of Europe as well as those races subject to imperial rule by the United States or a European Great Power were said to be backwards, barbaric, and in desperate need of the civilizing influence of an advanced people who had long since passed out of the subordinate races' present state of incivility. Propaganda portraying Teutonic soldiers, or the entire German nation, as regressed, salivating beasts utilized these words and concepts, thus offering Anglo-Saxons and other Americans a familiar and effective means through which to understand their enemy overseas as a dangerous racial Other. A poster depicting a Teutonic soldier as a bloodthirsty ape or a speech suggesting years of militarism had made German culture more medieval than modern would have immediately resonated with most audiences, and warnings that such decivilized brutes soon could be headed toward American shores certainly added an additional inducement for wartime sacrifice.

When attempting to understand what made European Teutons so brutal and dangerous to "American" identity, some followed the lead of many anthropologists and other scientists who referenced pseudosciences and Darwinian use-inheritance. During the war, several well-known professional and amateur scientists hypothesized that phrenology—the theory that the shape, size, and texture of the skull denoted racial characteristics—held the key to understanding "the Prussian Ferocity in War," as paleontologist Henry Fairfield Osborn called it. Osborn, who greatly influenced Theodore Roosevelt's thoughts on race, cited Prussians' supposedly rounded skulls as evidence that they had little in common biologically with the advanced Teutons in northern Europe. Prussian round-headedness, he claimed, corresponded to that of the Tartars of Asian Russia and "the Most Ancient Savages." Real Teutons, who Osborn claimed made up only 10 percent of the German population, had long, "gentle" skulls similar to those of other civilized races, such as the Anglo-Saxons.[3]

Similarly, William S. Sadler found that round-headed and racially degenerate "Alpines" had almost completely replaced the long-headed and thus racially superior "Nordics" who had once resided in Germany. Only a small cabal of Nordics (about "ten to twelve percent," mirroring Osborn's assumption) remained in Germany and exerted control over the brutal and highly impressionable Alpines who were committing atrocities on land and sea. This situation would not have been a problem, Sadler suggested, if the long-headed German leadership had chosen to follow their fellow Nordics, such as the Anglo-Saxons, in their "march toward democracy and liberalization of human thought." But they did not. "The German conundrum of today is due to the fact that the ten percent Nordic long-headed, ruling class that dominates the Germanic peoples has sacrificed its intelligence, its conscience, and its largely superior culture to its inherent ambition, love of leadership, and dominating tendency to conquer, exploit, and rule—traits not at all new in the Nordic race, but tendencies which have been, in later years, suppressed and held down in behalf of the higher, more noble civilized culture which characterizes the white nations of today," Sadler explained.[4] Presumably, Germany was no longer a white nation.

Propagandists were not ignorant of such theories. Assuming George Creel needed to be made aware of his findings about "the present-day German people," Sadler offered to send a copy of his book for use in CPI propaganda. Sadler worried that most Americans were unaware of "what we were up against in the present organization and racial constituency of the so-called German people," but he had "found this presentation of the war" to be useful in educating "troubled and perplexed" Americans. Creel, who often was quick to turn down unsolicited propaganda suggestions he believed were based in falsehoods, must have thought Sadler's findings to be credible, or at least he assumed most Americans would be easily convinced. He replied several days later, thanking Sadler for his offer and promising to forward Sadler's materials to the CPI's pamphlet editor.[5]

Most in the scientific community, however, found theories like phrenology repugnant. A reviewer in a prominent scientific journal, for instance, eviscerated Sadler's book, calling it "devoid of merit" and "potentially mischievous" because it could contribute to the wave of anti-German sentiment "and thereby arouse racial prejudice among the laity."[6] If CPI propaganda and Creel's welcoming response to Sadler's offer is any indication, the reviewer was right to be worried. The explanation of racial degeneration that Osborn, Sadler, and like-minded pseudoscientists offered resonated with many Americans whose knowledge of the latest racial science was nil or, at best, limited. At the same time, many likely found racialized explanations of the war convincing because they had shown themselves to be inclined to understand progress and conflict in such a manner. What else could explain the once-enlightened European German's apparent regression into barbarism? Descriptions of their evident racial decline in Darwinian terms, as being the result of years of exposure to the overwhelming and primitive environment of round-headed Prussian autocracy and militarism, fit contemporary understandings of race and helped mold the enemy Other into a form deserving of Americans' fear.

Many leading Americans and propagandists couched their assumption that European Germans' degeneration threatened world progress and the United States in the familiar imperialist terms of racial development. Secretary of War Newton Baker, speaking to Civil War veterans in early 1918, described the United States and the Allies as being at the forefront of civilization and the Germans as lagging behind the evolutionary curve. On the Western Front in France, the "civilized and free powers of the world" were "facing the last remaining vestige of medievalism, autocracy, and despotism; facing an adversary who has brought back into the art of war the cruelties of the savage which as civilized men we scorned many years ago to use and emulate."[7] Interior Secretary Franklin K. Lane also suggested that Germany had reverted to a more primitive time. "Let Germany be feudal if she will," he declared. "But she must not spread her system over a world that has outgrown it."[8] Elihu Root wrote to a confidant that "during the past fifty years Germany has been demoralized by Prussian influence exerted with the same thoroughness of method which characterizes Prussian military organization." The kaiser had made an "incessant appeal to the lower motives for more than a generation" of Germans, which "has debased the standards of life, of morals, of art, of literature."[9] In short, all-encompassing militarism had stripped the German people of all that had made them great, Root concluded, leaving them more brutal and less civilized.

The National Security League and the CPI also both explicitly and subtly asserted that the once-great Teutonic Other's evolutionary step backward endangered the United States and civilization at large. According to Robert McNutt McElroy, chairman of the NSL's Committee on Patriotism through Education, "if Germany wins" the United States "will be ruled arbitrarily from Berlin." In such an event, the Prussian warlords would degenerate the American people just as they had their own citizens in Germany. "We will become inert; supine; in short, slaves and servitors to a revivified rule of the Dark Ages," McElroy concluded.[10] In an NSL leaflet, the novelist Robert Herrick employed imperialist imagery specifically, warning that if Germany achieved even a partial success in Europe the civilized world would degenerate into the most primeval of environments, and Prussian militarism would "become the moral law of all the world—the jungle law!" Presumably, this would not benefit mankind the same way it had Tarzan, instead forcing civilized societies to regress or die. "In order to survive," Herrick warned, "we must all accept this law of the jungle."[11] While often more restrained than the NSL, the CPI also supported the notion that Prussian dominance over Germany had decivilized the Teutonic race. In *Conquest and Kultur*, Guy Stanton Ford and the popular pamphlet's editors quoted hundreds of German political, military, and social leaders to claim that a backward "medievally minded group" of Prussians controlled Germany. According to Ford, who wrote the pamphlet's foreword, the Wilhelmine regime and Prussian culture had decivilized the German people into a "misshapen image . . . leering with bloodstained visage over the ruins of civilization."[12]

Perhaps the most overtly racial explanation for German aggression and cruelty came from Elmer Ellsworth Rittenhouse of the Committee for Patriotic Education in his widely circulated pamphlet entitled *Know Your Enemy*. As the CPI had done, Rittenhouse included short quotations of prominent and powerful Germans without providing context. These Teutonic self-incriminations proved that "the Prussianized Germans have two distinct natures; the human and the beast. . . . It is the beast that confronts us now." The animalistic side of the decivilized Teuton, Rittenhouse argued, was evident in the head shape and facial features of "the idol of the German people, [Paul] von Hindenburg." Below a portrait of the Prussian Field Marshal, Rittenhouse included a caption that reads "The Law of the Jungle." He then asks readers to "study this face" that "typifies the 'Blond Beast' in the Prussian nature," a reference to philosopher Friedrich Nietzsche's famous description of Prussians. There was not a hint of civilization to be found. "Any 'milk of human kindness' there?" Rittenhouse asks. "Any tolerance, compassion, sympathy for 'inferiors,' or the weak and oppressed? Or do you find arrogance, cunning, hate, cruelty in the cold, fierce glint of the eyes and in the lowering scowl of command? Could you ask for a more striking suggestion of Brute Force and pitiless cruelty—the low dome, the square head, the latent ferocity in the gaze, the bull neck, the powerful, beast-like jowls and mouth? How naturally would the savage slogan of the Blond Beast come hissing from those Jaws." Rittenhouse also found Germans' decivilized nature in their actions. "This reversion to barbarism" manifested as more than "the desire to conquer weak peoples but to deport and to destroy non-combatants in large groups, tribes or nations in order to secure their land

and property for colonization." Prussian belief in and practice of the cruelest form of Darwinism would likely find its way to American shores. "If the enemy wins this war he will dominate our country and 'frightfulness' will be our lot if we resist."[13]

The popular press also consistently offered racially tinged explanations of the European Teuton's regression into the Other and of how that degeneration gave meaning to the American war effort. When referring to reported atrocities in Belgium, Irvin Cobb of the *Saturday Evening Post* argued that the German's "mental docility" and "his willingness to accept an order unquestionably and mechanically to obey it, may be a virtue, as we reckon racial traits of a people among their virtues." But "in war this same trait becomes a vice." Cobb, however, drew a clear line between European Germans and German Americans, contending that for Teutons in the United States this tendency to obey robotically and possibly violently was mitigated by their eagerness to "readily conform to [their] physical and metaphysical surroundings here," which also led their children to "amalgamate with our fused and conglomerate stock." This same principle held true in Germany as well, Cobb claimed. Living "in conformity with the exact and rigorous demands of . . . Prussianism" had reduced the European Teuton into a man who "may, at will, be transformed from" a brave and level-headed soldier into a "relentless, ruthless" killer. The degenerative impact of Prussian *kultur* on the German people, Cobb concluded, was the "very menace which must confront our people at home in the event that the enemy shall get near enough to our coasts to bombard our shore cities, as undoubtedly he would seek to do; or should he succeed in landing an expeditionary force upon American soil."[14]

Cartoons and posters could more easily and immediately transmit the ideas of race, civilization, and apocalyptic doom that were ubiquitous in oral and print propaganda because they generally were simple and lurid, and they appealed to common values through symbols that would have been instantly familiar to most Americans who would have encountered them.[15] During the First World War, the symbols were often racial and millennial in nature and associated Prussianized Germans with more easily identifiable models of savagery, duplicitousness, and Anglo-Saxon fear. For instance, in December 1917, Oliver Herford of the satirical magazine *Life* offered a phrenological explanation of German cruelty of which Osborn and Sadler would have been proud. Herford's cartoon pinpoints the areas of the kaiser's brain that were responsible for the Prussianized German's cruelty. The *Lusitania* sinking, for instance, symbolizes his "humanity" while the impaling of an infant on a

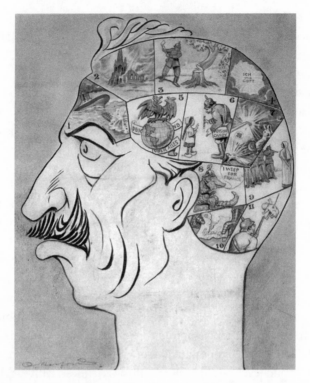

Figure 4.1. "Frenzylogical Chart," cartoon, *Life*, December 6, 1917.

bayonet (a regularly repeated charge in both American and British propaganda) represents his "love of children" (fig. 4.1).[16]

Artists also suggested that the European German had more in common with the primitive ape than with the historic Teuton or Anglo-Saxon. To explain the inherently degenerative quality of Prussian militarism and its danger to the world, the *Columbus (OH) Dispatch* depicted the European Teuton as a gorilla donning the infamous Prussian spiked helmet (a symbol of militarism in posters and cartoons) alongside a quote from Wilson's December 1917 annual address to Congress in which he claimed the German government lacked any "capacity for covenanted peace." In one arm, the German beast clutches a mostly naked white woman labeled "civilization"—her torn clothes suggesting the ape's brutality went beyond mere military aggression—while his left hand holds a rock, marked "kultur," that he is prepared to hurl at the remainder of the civilized world.[17]

Government-produced posters alluding to the German atrocities in Belgium recounted in the famously exaggerated Bryce Report, in particular the

Figure 4.2. "Hun or Home?," poster. Library of Congress, Prints & Photographs Division, WWI Posters, LC-USZC2-654.

raping of women and the destruction of homes, highlighted Prussianized Germans' devolution from whiteness through their uncivilized actions. As with wartime propaganda warning of German American spies, most Americans were aware that many of the depictions of Teutonic atrocities described in the report were at least partially true. In their pictorial renderings of German outrages, propagandists exploited this by applying a racial and apocalyptic glaze to what were familiar stories. Artists commonly depicted the "Hun" as morally depraved or less than human—often hunched over, with long arms and long hands, similar to a gorilla. One of the most striking Belgium-inspired posters appeared as part of a campaign in 1918 to raise money for the war effort through "Liberty Loans." In "Hun or Home?," Henry Patrick Raleigh's referencing of the Germans' primeval behavior required little interpretation. His Hun was a silhouette of an ape-like, knuckle-dragging figure, hunched forward and seeming to use his hands to walk while bearing down on a young woman carrying her child (fig. 4.2). With "Remember Belgium," which may be the most disturbing poster on this theme, Ellsworth Young steered clear of literal animalistic depictions of the German, instead conveying the Hun's bestial nature solely through his actions. The poster depicts a Prussian-helmeted, mustachioed German soldier dragging a very young girl away as a burning village silhouettes their image. "Halt the Hun," also a 1918 Raleigh creation, played on the same idea by portraying a large, ogre-like German (thick body, long hands and arms) standing over another helpless woman and child in front of their burning home or town. In this poster, however, Raleigh provided a male contrast to the degenerated Hun—a tall, sturdy, and chivalric Anglo-Saxon soldier coming to the woman's rescue. The Prussianized German in the latter two examples was not only a rapist but an arsonist as well, bent on defiling the young and destroying the family and home unless he was stopped, perhaps by a robust and gallant Anglo-Saxon doughboy supported by Liberty Bonds.[18]

As the atrocity scenes were meant to indicate, the fate of civilization and democracy hung in the balance and would be decided in the present conflict. Perhaps the most famous example of this was a poster printed before the United States had entered the war. In 1916, H. R. Hopps created "Destroy This Mad Brute," which depicted a giant gorilla with a blond mustache and a spiked helmet labeled "militarism" brandishing a bloodied club marked "kultur." Along with the obvious allusion to Teutonic racial degeneration, the most significant aspects of the poster are that the wild-eyed, salivating beast carries a bare-chested damsel in distress (denoting his defilement of civilized culture), that he has left Europe in ruins behind him, and that he is standing on the shore of "America," where the brute presumably would turn his attention after he had finished his decimation of the Old World (fig. 4.3).[19]

While the Prussianized Teuton in these cartoons and posters was a demolisher of all things civilized and virtuous, the implications of the images went beyond mere demonization of the enemy. The effectiveness of such renderings likely was enhanced by their tacit referencing of the supposed interconnectedness of rape and racial degeneracy, which was often used as justification for white violence against African Americans. In the late nineteenth century, Anglo-Saxon Americans, especially in the South, began to grow increasingly nervous about the perceived regression of African American men, who they believed had grown more bestial without the civilizing discipline of slavery. Their decline, many whites asserted, manifested most dangerously in their alleged inability to control their most primal urges, which created a propensity to force themselves sexually on white women. Rape charges, al-

Figure 4.3. "Destroy This Mad Brute," poster. Library of Congress, Prints & Photographs Division, WWI Posters, LC-DIG-ds-03216.

though unfounded in the vast majority of cases, often resulted in the alleged perpetrator's lynching as white southern men sought ways to maintain their social authority and the racial hierarchy. Not unlike nativist fears outside of the region, white southerners' anxious response to their assumptions of black inferiority and depravity was also a reaction to the rapid economic, social, and political changes that had rocked the former Confederacy in the decades after the Civil War. Black freedom, voting rights, office holding, and relative economic independence were very clear indications that the continuation of white supremacy in the South was not guaranteed.[20]

Yet the pervasive themes of civilization and regression, which formed the underlying rationale for imperialism, allowed Americans all across the United States to attach a variety of meanings to the image of the primordial beast who stripped innocent and virtuous white women of their purity. The addition of women and young girls as victims, for instance, was not always a literal allusion to rape. German aggression was a crime against civilization itself. Wartime propaganda from both sides of the Atlantic consistently employed women (often bare-chested) as symbolic representations of civilization— Columbia, Joan of Arc, the Statue of Liberty, the executed British nurse Edith Cavell, or the victimized Belgian. The sanctity and protection of the home and nation, of which women were the purveyors, were central to contemporary notions of progress, masculinity, and Anglo-Saxon supremacy. German disregard for the purity of women, the nation, and the home denoted their descent from true whiteness and the threat they posed to Anglo-Saxons if they set foot on American soil. When viewed within the context of the pamphlets, editorials, speeches, and other forms of propaganda meant to explain the threat that the degenerate Teuton posed to the country, these and similar images suggested that the apish European Germans would commit similar atrocities if they invaded the United States, violating the sacredness of both the civilized nation and its women.[21]

Although many argued that European Teutons had regressed, it also was clear that their degeneration did not diminish their intellectual or military capabilities. Like Tarzan in the jungle, Prussianized German soldiers had come from good stock, had developed physically and psychologically in a primordial (militaristic) environment, and had not lost touch with the tools of modernity. In wartime propaganda, the combination of their regressed, more primitive character with modern science and military technology transformed the German soldier not into a warrior befitting a great race, as preparedness advocates had hoped for Anglo-Saxon men, but a dangerous "superman," an almost unstoppable enemy whose primeval disposition left him incapable of compassion. The conflation of the German enemy with the imagined black rapist was not complete in that most whites found it impossible to accept African Americans as their intellectual equals. The German enemy, therefore, was far more dangerous.[22]

Presbyterian minister Charles Wadsworth, Jr., recognized the combination of German progress and Prussian regression and believed it to be lethal. "The savages that confront us have explored the recesses of creation, discovered laws of Nature, threaded the labyrinth of matter, and mastered the forces of the universe." They "stand upon the very pinnacles of science." At the same time, "the savages confronting us are dehumanized monsters, embodiments of 'schrecklichkeit' [terrorism]. With all their amazing abilities, and with all their towering attainments, they have dug themselves into a pit immeasurably more degraded than that in which primeval savages grovelled [*sic*]." Prussianized Germans, Wadsworth concluded, borrowing a term from Nietzsche, "are super-men." Their "climbing of the ages" had been redirected toward "an abyss of demonism and depravity. The great process of evolution has in them taken an appalling turn . . . and has brought forth a beastly insanity which is the menace of the world."[23] In summer 1917 the *Dayton (OH) News* simplified Wadsworth's point with an illustration of a Prussianized German caveman (as opposed to an ape) wielding a club, sword, whip, and imperial flag while wading through the ocean toward the United States. An invading fleet also sails at his back while German bombers fly above his head. The caption, "Win the War on the Other Side or We Shall Have to Fight It on This Side of the Atlantic," and the conflation of autocracy and militarism with primitiveness suggested not only that the once proud German nation had regressed, but that its regression caused it to be a direct threat to the United States. At the same time, the mixing of the modern (the planes and navy) with the prehistoric figure implied that although the Prussianized Teutons had degenerated, they retained many of the intellectual capabilities that allowed them to become civilized in the first place (fig. 4.4).

Unlike most political cartoons, practically all posters, even those that did not threaten a Teutonic invasion or the demise of democracy, offered specific actions Americans could take to win the war and prevent German savagery from engulfing the Anglo-Saxon United States. While Hopps's 1916 work asked men to defend against the "mad brute" by enlisting in the army, the most frequently requested activity in wartime posters depicting or alluding to invasion and German brutality was the purchasing of Liberty Bonds or War Savings Stamps. Portrayals of the German as a degenerated savage with its eyes set on the United States did not become a common sight on posters until the third Liberty Loan campaign in April 1918 and the drive to sell War Savings Stamps that same year.[24] Before, artists emphasized the threat autocracy posed to democracy by making common use of the Statue of Liberty, which would resolutely or nervously tell viewers to purchase a bond "Lest I [liberty, or civilization] Perish."[25] Events on the battlefront likely affected the shift in poster art toward the more apocalyptic and racially fueled, although such arguments were nothing new by spring 1918. After redeploying roughly one million soldiers from their victorious war in Eastern Europe against Russia, the German army began what they hoped would be a series of war-winning offensives on the Western Front in late March. Germany's renewed strength and the tactical

Figure 4.4. "An Ounce of Prevention Is Worth a Pound of Cure," cartoon, *Dayton (OH) News*. Reprinted in *Review of Reviews*, July 1917.

successes of their first attempts to break the Allied line sent waves of alarm through Paris and London and panicky dispatches to Washington begging for more American men and resources before it was too late.[26]

The fearful consequences for the United States if Germany's offensive proved successful were clearly evident in Liberty Loan and War Savings Stamp poster art produced in 1918. The posters' messages were far from subtle. Reminiscent of Raleigh's ogres and Hopps's mad brute, the contribution of artist Adolph Treidler to the National War Savings Committee, entitled "Help Stop This," presented the bloody, dagger-wielding German soldier as apish, with a thick neck, large hands and feet, long arms, and a slightly humped back. The monster gazes upon the apocalyptic remnants of a town with apparent approval while stepping on (or over) a bleeding female, presumably his stabbing victim. Below the scene, viewers are asked to "Buy W.S.S. [War Savings Stamps] & Keep Him Out of America" (fig. 4.5). Fred Strothmann took a somewhat similar

Figure 4.5. (left) "Help Stop This," poster. Library of Congress, Prints & Photographs Division, WWI Posters, LC-USZC4-9928. *Figure 4.6. (right)* "Beat Back the Hun," poster. Library of Congress, Prints & Photographs Division, WWI Posters, LC-USZC4-2950.

approach in his "Beat Back the Hun" poster, which depicted the German soldier as a dark, zombie-like figure with bloody finger tips, bloody bayonet, and bright green eyes staring ominously across the ocean, presumably toward the United States, over the ruins of a devastated Europe (fig. 4.6). Such broadsides were not merely predecessors to the modern horror film poster meant to excite viewers in the short term. Their warnings that the full force of Prussianized German Otherness—its depravity, brutality, and drive for absolute destruction— would reach American shores and devour Anglo-Saxon democracy if the people did not make sacrifices now were part of a much larger movement to awaken the nation to the possible dangers of apathy.

The push to convince Americans that the United States entered the war to both defend itself and safeguard civilization, though, predated the 1918 work of poster artists. This concept began to circulate from a variety of sources immediately after the declaration of war. Such appeals quickly drowned out Wilson's and other progressives' more idealistic calls to service. The *New York*

Tribune in early May warned that if the United States did not send troops, food, and industrial resources to its Allies quickly, "the collapse of France and the withdrawal of Italy," along with a possible "crisis in British food supply," could force them into an unfavorable peace with Germany that would allow it "to renew her attack upon civilization." That renewed attack would inevitably fall on the United States. "If Germany escapes today, the danger for us tomorrow will be beyond present estimation," the editors predicted. The United States will fall prey to Prussian autocracy, "unless we are prepared to fight . . . for our own existence, calling for our best effort and our ultimate strength."[27] Viewing the war with a Darwinian apocalypticism, the *Kansas City (MO) Times* noted in July that "The world has become too small for democracy and autocracy to live in it together and one of them must perish." If the American people devote themselves fully to this "death grapple there can never be a question" that democracy would come out on top.[28]

Early on, key members of Wilson's cabinet (and, quite often, the president himself) were among those undermining the progressive and idealistic definition of the nation's cause, instead espousing the idea that a German victory would prove disastrous for the United States, democracy, and American identity. On the day before the first draft registration, June 4, Secretary of the Interior Lane said in a speech that the nation was engaged in "a war of self-defense." The start of the war in 1914 was the beginning of a figurative "invasion of the United States by slow, steady, logical steps," of which the German offensive against Belgium was the first. If the United States and the Allies lost the war, Lane maintained, "no man will live in America without paying toll to [Germany], in manhood and money." At the same time, "a defeated and navyless England," which he referred to as the historic source of "the inherent love of liberty which we call Anglo-Saxon civilization," could be required to cede Canada to Germany. This would force Americans to "live, as France has lived for over forty years, in haunting terror" of imminent attack by Prussian militarism, which Lane referred to as "this old spirit of evil."[29] Similarly, Agriculture Secretary David F. Houston portrayed the war as part of a historic and racial mission. "If Prussian militarism should be permitted to dominate," he proclaimed, "then the Anglo-Saxon fight for free institutions and liberty, . . . its fight against the absolute rights of kings and barons, with its Magna Carta, its Bill of Rights, its Declaration of Independence . . . would have been in vain."[30] Additionally, Robert Lansing, the secretary of state, claimed that in the war "the future of the United States is at stake." The nation's chief diplomat was "firmly convinced that the independence of no nation is safe, that the liberty of no individual is sure until" Prussian militarism "has been made harmless and impotent forever." The American people, Lansing concluded, must be prepared to fight the war to its ultimate conclusion.[31]

Soon after its creation in April 1917, the Committee on Public Information proved itself capable of painting an even more vivid picture than politicians did of why the enemy Other forced the United States to fight a defensive war. In late May 1917, the CPI began riling up their Four Minute Men, its army of patriotic orators, with stories of impending doom that mirrored neutrality period preparedness propaganda while explaining the importance of convincing Americans to purchase Liberty Bonds. It would take more than "waving flags and singing the Star-Spangled Banner . . . to protect our country and our homes," free Europe from the mailed fist of German militarism, and "protect Democracy all over the world," the director wrote in a message to all Four Minute Men. In an attempt to persuade his speakers and, by extension, their future audiences of the present peril, he explained the apocalyptic cost of apathy. "Who is going to win this war?" he asked. "If we are, we must fight to the last dollar, to the last man, and to the last heart beat. Are you going to stand by and suffer defeat? Are you going to look timidly at long processions of conquering troops tramping down our streets? For either we shall walk down the kaiser's streets or his soldiers will goose-step along Pennsylvania Avenue and sign the Treaty of Peace under the dome of our Capitol in Washington, or in the same room where Lincoln signed the Emancipation Proclamation." The speakers were instructed to frame the issue as a choice between two possible futures. They could "buy Government bonds and get [their] money back with 3 ½ per cent interest" or, if defeated, "pay the Kaiser, not two billions [*sic*] of indemnity, but ten billions [*sic*] . . . just as the poor Belgians had to pay."[32]

Unlike the CPI, the National Security League gained plenty of experience during the preparedness debate describing American involvement in the war in Darwinian or black-and-white terms. Those who contributed to NSL propaganda provided specific explanations as to why Teutonic regression threatened the country's existence and Anglo-Saxon identity. For example, the progressive theologian Shailer Mathews spoke at an NSL convention about the long-term threat decivilized Germany posed to the United States. "We are not conducting a crusade of democracy to make Germany democratic," Mathews argued, contrary to Wilson's claim in his war address. Instead, Mathews affirmed that Americans were "fighting for our national life, for the international morality upon which our national life depends, for the preservation of the civilized world." German brutality in Belgium was a "deliberate attempt . . . to ruin a nation by" pilfering its food, razing its villages and cathedrals, poisoning its water supply, and treating "women and children" in a manner "beyond description." In the event of German victory in the war, "The United States could expect no other treatment."[33]

After the first few months of the war, self-defense arguments became more complicated and nuanced, offering deeper and multifaceted explanations of Germany's conspiracy, its soldiers' brutality, and the dangerous consequences of the German Other winning in Europe. Many Americans had been concerned that the purpose of apparent Teutonic backstabbing and intrigue within the United States was to Germanize the nation and weaken the nation's defenses in advance of a Teutonic military invasion. At the same time, propagandists looked at previous German wars, immigration patterns, and German activities in the Western Hemisphere from the vantage point of the present conflict and believed they had found evidence from even before the current kaiser ascended to the throne in 1888 that the German government had been planning and embarking on its war for world conquest. According to many influential Americans, Germany fought to gain control of the Eurasian landmass, an area that German imperialists referred to as *Mitteleuropa*, in the present war in order to achieve an overwhelming manpower and material resource advantage from which to carry out the North American piece of its plan to crush civilization.

The most complete summary of the German conspiracy to overtake the United States may have come from a July 1918 speech by CPI chairman George Creel, which Woodrow Wilson carefully edited. "The world cannot be safe for democracy," Creel asserted, "while an unorganized autocracy—its people as yet believing it victorious—is intrenched in the centre of Europe, leading 10,000,000 armed men and possessing the resources of 170,000,000 people in the world's central position for all seas and all continents." Even without this *Mitteleuropa*, Germany's plotting against the United States had been quite aggressive. "From the day when it attacked our possession of Samoa by the insidious plot which cost the lives of our sailors in 1889, to the present period when it has filled our land with spies, has slain our citizens on land and sea, and set them at variance by fomenting racial strife, Germany has been our enemy in peace as she is our foe in war." Creel then went on to mention a brief encounter between the US and German fleets near Manila Bay, the kaiser's alleged "plans to control Santo Domingo and Venezuela," Germany's efforts to unite Europe against the 1898 American war in Cuba, and, finally, the attempt to court Mexico and Japan to attack the United States as part of

the Zimmermann Plan as evidence that autocratic Germany had been conspiring for decades to overtake the United States. The CPI chief also declared that
the Teutons' recent attempts to foment disloyalty within the United States began
with the visit of the kaiser's brother, Prince Henry, to Washington in 1902. The
prince's "visit began the campaign to divide our loyal citizens of German birth
and descent so as to render this nation impotent in the defense of its own
security and of the democracies of the world," a plot only deepened by the 1913
Delbrück dual-citizenship law. All of this, Creel (and by extension Wilson)
argued, was "the cause of our entering the present war, as for every other
country at war with the Imperial German Government." Because of its brutally
underhanded ways, German "autocracy endangers our safety and challenges
our freedom."[34] Wilson gave the speech his seal of approval after informing
Creel that he "ha[d] taken the liberty of making some alterations in this paper.
I think you will see in each instance why. As altered, I think it is all right."[35]
With the coming of the Great War, the designs of which Creel spoke appeared
more evident to politicians, private citizens, the CPI, and privately-funded
propaganda agencies who repeated the charges ad nauseum to convince the
American people that the conflict was a war for the preservation of the Anglo-
Saxon nation and all it stood for.

Wilson's assistance with Creel's speech and his various wartime statements
about Germany's quest for global conquest suggest the president viewed the
Teutonic Other's supposed hyper-aggressiveness as apocalyptically as propa-
gandists portrayed it—as a direct threat to the United States now and possibly
in the future. A year before Creel's speech, Wilson asserted in his June 14, 1917,
Flag Day address that the source of a triumphant Germany's postwar power
would be their firm hold on central Europe, western Asia, and the Middle
East—or *Mitteleuropa.* "The so-called Central Powers [Germany, Austria-
Hungary, Bulgaria, and Ottoman Turkey] are in fact but a single Power. . . .
From Hamburg to the Persian Gulf the net is spread," and an Allied defeat
guaranteed that autocracy and militarism would continue to reign there and
ultimately threaten the world.[36]

Wilson's understanding of degenerated Germany as an existential threat to
the United States, Americanism, and western civilization had a decisive impact
on CPI propaganda. In the pamphlet *Why America Fights Germany*, Stanford
University professor John S. P. Tatlock followed the president's lead by arguing
that the kaiser's domination of his Central European and Turkish partners,
along with the lands his armies had conquered from the Allies, would give
Germany "a vast commercial advantage in peace, and a vast wealth and military

and naval advantage in war." Contrary to pacifists' and isolationists' arguments, Tatlock claimed, Germany's acquisition of an intercontinental empire was dangerous to the United States because the German government had been quite open about its hatred for American democracy and plans "for an invasion of America." The latter is likely a reference to a meeting between Wilhelm and the US ambassador to Germany, James Gerard, in which the kaiser reportedly issued a vague warning to Gerard that "America had better look out after this war." The choice was clear, Tatlock concluded. To avoid a brutal German invasion, Americans "must fight Germany in Europe with help" so "that we may not have to fight her in America without help."[37]

For their audience to fully grasp the urgency of the nation's predicament if a triumphant and more powerful German Other arose out of the European cataclysm, propagandists found creative ways to describe, often in vivid detail, how the conquest of the United States would look and feel. A German invasion, they hoped to show, would reduce the United States to a charred, post-apocalyptic landscape. As they had in Belgium and northern France, Prussianized German soldiers would raze American homes, defile American women, murder American children, and seize the reins of American government. Consequently, the great Anglo-Saxon race, its dignity and democracy all but dead, would experience a sharp decline as its Teutonic masters would relegate it to forced servitude. The last beacon of hope for civilization would have been extinguished. While obviously grossly exaggerated, such a future was not beyond the realm of possibilities to many Americans because in many ways it fit the wartime construction of the German Other's capabilities and ambitions. Anglo-Saxon Americans' tendency to view perceived foreign threats in apocalyptic terms, their understanding of racial development, and the real yet exaggerated stories of German invasions and atrocities against civilians helped make the intellectual leap between reality and hyperbole less difficult to overcome.

Perhaps no one more vividly illustrated the Prussian threat to the Anglo-Saxon United States and the apocalyptic consequences of defeat than Joseph Pennell in his 1918 poster "That Liberty Shall Not Perish from the Earth." In Pennell's representation of what would happen if Americans did not purchase Liberty Bonds, Armageddon has descended upon New York City like a thief in the night, leveling divine (or Darwinian) justice on a presumably apathetic and unworthy people by engulfing its wealthiest city in flames. German bombers fly past each side of a torchless and decapitated Statue of Liberty—its head resting at the base of Liberty Island, which also supports the wreckage of a

Figure 4.7. "That Liberty Shall Not Perish," poster. Library of Congress, Prints & Photographs Division, WWI Posters, LC-DIG-ppmsca-18343.

warship—while enemy ships presumably carrying the invasion force steam toward the inferno. Two million copies of the poster were printed (fig. 4.7).[38] Pennell's poster hit on several key themes of wartime invasion propaganda. The cataclysmic attack targets civilians and burns the city to the ground, much like depictions of the German army's atrocities in Belgium and northern France. The beheaded Statue of Liberty suggests that a German victory in Europe would spell the downfall of civilization, democracy, and Anglo-Saxon identity. The all-encompassing inferno touches on millennial understandings of the war in that it is reminiscent of biblical prophecies of death and devastation on or near the Day of Judgment. The most modern of weapons, the airplane, delivers the fiery death, suggesting that Germans' technological advancement combined with their primitive inability to control their aggression made them a particularly grave threat to the country. Finally, through this poster Pennell attempted to convey the frequently repeated claim that Americans had to defeat the

Teutons in Europe so they would not have to fight them in their own backyard.

Pennell's poster also reveals the depths in which wartime propagandists understood and were willing to exploit their fellow citizens' fears and perceived vulnerabilities. After the war, Pennell admitted as much in a short book describing how he created this particular work. He maintained that a poster, "like the old religious painting, must appeal to the people—the people gorged with comics, and stuffed with movies, and fattened on photographs." The most effective posters, of which he argued there were only a few, were successful "because the subjects of those designs . . . are known to and understood by the people and by all the people—whether they are unlettered or whether they are cultured." The alarming consequences of a brutal German invasion that he depicted in his poster, Pennell believed, was self-evident.[39]

The women of the Department of Educational Propaganda, however, did not take Americans' understanding of the consequences of defeat and their fear of the primitive German superman for granted. DEP speakers attempted to drum up support for the war by invoking images of a world whose progress had been reversed under the reign of a decivilized Germany. "If America loses," one speaker declared, "the great evolution of humanity, which has struggled through thousands of years to the point it has reached today, would have to be thrown back to the autocratic rule, which every nation of [the] highest advancement has passed out of into [a] democratic regime long ago." German soldiers, if landed on American soil, would leave "our homes ablaze, our women ravished, our children butchered," actions that made up "the unutterable horrors which always mark the wake of a German army of invasion!" The Anglo-Saxon United States, the bulwark of human progress, must "give her all . . . every drop of her strength unto death," the speaker concluded, in order to ensure the kaiser's forces could not spread their "frightfulness" across the Atlantic. But there was even more at stake. "To lose the war," she warned, "would mean a turning back of the wheels of progress for many centuries."[40] Equally lurid is a DEP speech on the Liberty Loan delivered on behalf of the state Council of Defense in Nebraska, a state as far away as possible from a decivilized foreign invader. "To save your home from the flames destroying France, your babies from the sword that murdered infants in Poland, your daughters from the hordes that ravished Belgian women even as they fled through the streets," the speaker declared, "American men are making the supreme sacrifice. What sacrifice will you make to help equip these defenders of your country? What will you give up that you may help finance the struggle to save American freedom?"[41]

Not to be outdone, the National Security League also sketched out various nightmare scenarios of an invasion of degenerated German soldiers and its consequences for American identity. Orders to do so probably came straight from the top. NSL President S. Stanwood Menken wrote to Elihu Root in September 1917 that he felt "that the bringing of knowledge to the people is the most important thing that can be done in America . . . and that the people must be made to realize that . . . victory [is] essential to National life."[42] The NSL did its part by distributing a series of leaflets in 1917 written by well-known American writers and, occasionally, a prominent individual from an Allied country. Author and acclaimed dog breeder Albert Payson Terhune believed the "alarmists" were correct in proclaiming that a German victory would mark "the setback of humanity, democracy, civilization, rights of man, etc. But, to America, it would mean infinitely more"; the nation would lose its self-respect because it did not do enough to restore the world to the path of progress.[43] Agnes Repplier explicitly linked the war on disloyalty at home with the American war of self-defense in Europe. If Americans did not "crush the traitors at home, and defeat the enemy abroad," she contended, "a bitter future awaits us." That fate would be "see[ing] in our land the blazing homes, the ravished women, the butchered children, the unutterable shame and horror which mark the wake of a German army of invasion."[44] To football legend Walter Camp, the danger to the nation's children was long-term and degenerative. The brutal "defeat and subjugation" the nation could suffer at the hands of a victorious Germany would "very probably produce a suicidal mania" and racial degeneration, especially among children. "Perhaps there are nations and races meant for slavery," Camp considered, but white Americans were not among them. Camp implied that German conquest of the United States would ultimately degrade the youngest generations from their Anglo-Saxon American identity. "Spiritually," defeat and enslavement would transform "our American Youth from thoroughbred racers . . . to dreary draft oxen, struggling with a hopeless load."[45]

Camp was not the only commentator to worry about how a German victory could affect the development of future generations and endanger Anglo-Saxon democratic identity. Some propagandists and politicians argued that an Allied defeat meant the country would have to, at the very least, maintain its current war footing or, at worst, adopt a very Prussian-like militarism until the Teutonic scourge was finally eradicated or had conquered the United States.[46] They claimed, however, that the greatest cost of sustaining the nation's current level of military readiness was not financial but cultural and racial. As much as preparedness advocates longed for a nation of strong fighters who kept their ancestors' more primitive traits within arm's reach, the incessant German craving for aggressive warfare was believed to be so great that the degree of militarization necessary for national defense would dissolve, not strengthen, Anglo-Saxon democracy and identity. After April 1917, some suggested that militarizing American society after the war in order to confront a triumphant Germany would itself Prussianize the country. As had occurred in Germany, the racial and cultural progress of a great people would be reversed by an outmoded social structure. Victory in the current war, therefore, would prevent Anglo-Saxon Americans from having to Other themselves for the sake of their long-term self-defense.

Such an outcome, that the consequences of German Otherness could force Americans to Germanize themselves through militarization, was not lost on Woodrow Wilson and his administration. For the president, these concerns merely became more urgent after the United States entered the war. In his Flag Day address, Wilson made his concerns public, concluding, "If they [the kaiser's regime] succeed, America will fall within the menace," and the United States, along with the remainder of the freedom-loving world, "must remain armed, as [Germany] will remain, and must make ready for the next step in their aggression."[47] Assistant Secretary of the Navy Franklin Delano Roosevelt expanded on his boss's fear for the future but was more directly concerned about the long-term degeneration of the nation's youth. Roosevelt appealed to his audience in a July 1917 speech "to go home not only with the spirit of sacrifice, and of service, but with the spirit of realization of what this war means . . . in its ultimate end." To FDR, that end was clear. "If by any chance the present power of Germany should be left in such a position at the end of the war that it could carry on its policy of before the war [its disregard for international law]," he argued, "then, not only will the world not be safe for democracy, but the United States will not be safe for us or for our children." For the man who would lead the United States in a far greater world war, this was the central point of American belligerency in 1917. "That is the reason why today we must put every ounce of strength into what we are doing," he concluded. "It is only in that way . . . that we have made the United States of America safe, a safe republic, a safe democracy for us in our old age, and for our children and grandchildren, and having done that we shall have made the world safe for democracy."[48]

Creel's CPI borrowed directly from the president, printing nearly seven million copies of Wilson's Flag Day speech as a pamphlet that included footnotes by several university professors that further expounded on the deeper meaning of Wilson's dystopic prophecy of a militarized United States. The crux of the scholars' argument was that incidents of sabotage and espionage, along with sinkings by German U-boats, revealed that "America no longer occupies a position of charmed isolation." The consequences of not destroying the spy network and of losing the war in Europe were twofold. Either "the war may be brought within our borders," or American society would have to become militarized like its Prussianized nemesis, forcing citizens to "shoulder a burden of military preparedness in time of peace such as America has never known."[49] Navy Secretary Daniels and Secretary of War Baker, both technically members of the CPI, also forecast the possible militarization of American society. Daniels told the Alliance for Labor and Democracy that if Germany were to "triumph in Europe," the American people would have to "inevitably" commit "to defensive preparations that will command every effort in the interest of our military strength." In this case, the heaviest burden would be placed on the workingman. Every year more "men will have to be withdrawn from peaceful pursuits to fill the army" and navy "in order that our coasts may be protected from raid and invasion."[50] According to Baker, the world would become Germanized if the kaiser's forces won the war in Europe because "every other nation . . . would either have to be a slave of Germany or an imitator of Germany. We would either have to be weak and subservient to Germany, or else we would have to imitate her military program, and devote the nation to military enterprise to the end that all rights shall be determined by force." Individual rights and liberties, Baker suggested, would have no place in such a world.[51] In a letter to a *New York World* reporter, Interior Secretary Lane worried that the measures the United States would have to take to protect the nation would cause the American people to regress to the level of the savage Teuton. "The war will degrade us . . . make sheer brutes out of us," he wrote, "because we will have to descend to the methods that the Germans employ."[52]

The press also inundated the American public with warnings that defeat in Europe now meant possible degeneration of Anglo-Saxon identity in the future. For example, the editors of the Charleston (SC) *News and Courier* feared that American democracy would be destroyed, not necessarily by a direct German attack immediately after the war but by the lengths to which the nation would have to go to prevent or resist an assault upon its shores in the indefinite future. If the United States and the Allies lost in Europe, they warned, "the America that we know will disappear" because "we would have to abolish it ourselves for our own safety." National defense would demand

Figure 4.8. "Either We Must Win the War, Or—," cartoon, *St. Louis Republic*. Reprinted in *Literary Digest*, March 16, 1918.

that the country "transform this free democratic America into just such a fantastic militarism as Germany is to-day."[53] The *St. Louis Republic* made the horrors of such a development very clear in a spring 1918 cartoon that channeled FDR's concerns. A toddler struggles to hold up a rifle labeled "The Fight for Liberty" while the bayonet at the end of the gun drips blood to the ground. Its caption, "Either We Must Win the War, Or—," indicated that the consequences of defeat were truly unspeakable (fig. 4.8). American boys, for the sake of national defense, would become slaves to the same militarism that had decivilized the European Teuton, a fate the cartoonist hoped the American people would fight and sacrifice to avoid.

Propagandists' descriptions of European Germans' Otherness and the apocalyptic and regressive consequences of a Teutonic victory shaped the manner in which many Americans understood the country's stake in the war. The impact of this propaganda on the American mindset is evident in federal investigative reports and letters to the president, George Creel, and others in the Wilson administration from average and prominent Americans alike. Whether they were concerned about Teutonic agents laying the groundwork for invasion or other citizens' ignorance of the German peril, the officers, investigators, and civilians who composed fearful letters and reports regularly recited the same arguments or reconstructed the same images found in wartime propaganda. Their regurgitation of propagandists' themes and messages reflects the seriousness with which they and likely many silent Americans took arguments that the degenerated and war-hungry German Other posed an existential threat to the Anglo-Saxon American way of life.

Specialists in military matters and some federal investigators appear to have been particularly susceptible to this argument. Their assumptions along these lines reflected the emotions and imagination of a wartime propagandist more than the analytical assessment of an inquiring or strategic-minded official. One of the greatest concerns of military experts inside and outside of government was the German threat to the 1823 Monroe Doctrine, which declared that the United States would consider any European attempt to colonize or interfere with the internal politics of any nation in the Western Hemisphere as an unfriendly act. If propaganda describing the look and feel of a German invasion was true, and many feared that it was, then the German Other's breaching of the metaphorical wall around the Americas would have dire consequences for the United States and its Latin American neighbors. Writing to an American acquaintance in South America in March 1918, former War Secretary Elihu Root said he "wish[ed] Uruguay and Argentina could make up their minds to formally join the list of the nations who are engaged in fighting against the domination of Germany." Keeping the Americas free and democratic, Root implied, was the responsibility of all the republics because "if Germany wins this war, we shall all be dominated by her, and her domination over other countries is practical and oppressive." The Prussianized Germans would rule "in the most cruel and offensive way" because, unlike the peaceful and freedom-loving Americans, "that is [their] nature and . . . purpose." The fight against German imperialism must be decided in Europe before it spreads to the New World. "There will be no such thing as national freedom anywhere under the overlordship of Germany," Root concluded, "unless she is beaten now."[54]

Such paranoia over what a German victory would mean for the security of the United States was even evident among high-ranking officials and agents in the Department of Justice and Military Intelligence Division, who, from the first months of belligerency, investigated the possibility that Germans were trying to weaken American defenses through espionage within the United States. As with wartime investigations of possible intrigue discussed in chapter 3, these conspiracy theories proved difficult to verify. In early May 1917, a Bureau of Investigation agent in Boston reported that an Army cook at the American base defending the Panama Canal, Frank Kump, was "in service [of the] German Government" and had "supplied photographs and plans of forts and harbor defenses in New England" while his company was stationed at Portsmouth Harbor. The BI agent surreptitiously "annexed" the photos from the apparently pro-German attorney for whom Kump worked. BI chief A. Bruce Bielaski then sought the assistance of the MID, whose headman, Ralph Van Deman, ordered one of his officers to watch Kump and report any suspicious activity. After six weeks of investigation, Van Deman reported to Bielaski that Kump was not in Panama nor was he likely to have ever been there. In fact, no one in his alleged company had ever heard of the man, and enlistment records showed that no one by the name Frank Kump had joined the army in the past two years. At this point, the investigation seems to have ended with the BI having not revealed why the lawyer had photos of the canal defenses in the first place.[55]

Fears that covert German agents were working to open the United States to a military invasion reached as far as the Pacific Northwest. In mid-April 1917, a Department of Labor inspector reported to the local DOJ agent in Seattle that an alleged "Austrian Count," who had posed as an English officer in the Canadian Army, had been given detailed descriptions of the coastal defenses at Puget Sound. The "Count" was believed to have convinced a recruiting officer that he was interested in enlisting in the Navy, which apparently was all it took for the officer to give specific details as to the location of mines and coastal artillery to the supposed spy. That a recruiter may have had such critical insight on the Sound's defenses probably should have stirred immediate doubts as to the story's authenticity.[56]

Anxiety over a German conspiracy to militarily dominate the United States was most often expressed independently of concerns over domestic spy activity. In Seattle, Robert Bridges, the president of the port commission, claimed in a July 4, 1917, speech that Germany had the entire nation in its sights. Bridges cited a book that allegedly detailed German plans to invade the United States and attain world power status; the book included a "map of North America" that had written on it "in great bold type the word 'Germania,' the 'A' covering the capital of our country the 'G' being located approximately *where Seattle now stands*. This has been the dream of German autocracy, and for years and years they had been preparing to bring their dream to an actuality."[57] With the German army fighting desperately on multiple fronts in Europe and its surface navy having been bottled up in the North Sea since the Battle of Jutland in spring 1916, the chances of the Germans invading the East Coast, let alone Seattle, were beyond slim. But wartime warnings of an imminent attack clearly had an impact on citizens' nerves.

Americans on the East Coast were even more on edge over the prospect of a German invasion. In July 1918, a lack of coordination between civilian defense volunteers and law enforcement led to a brief but intense panic among residents in the Bronx. "The Bronx today had all the thrills of an air raid," the *Chicago Tribune* reported, "but suffered none of the bombs, when a siren whistle, to be blown in case German airplanes should soar above the skyscrapers of the city, was tested without the police being notified." The sound of the alarm drove mothers to hurry their children into cellars as businesses immediately locked their doors, presumably so the proprietors could find cover.[58] The actual Teutonic air fleet, however, was thousands of miles away and wholly incapable of doing any damage to an American city. The incident is indicative of the acute sense of vulnerability many felt during wartime, which was undoubtedly exacerbated by the continuous stream of apocalyptic invasion propaganda.

Concerns about foreign invasion were widespread enough that advertisers felt free to exploit the general sentiment. In November 1917, *Everybody's Magazine* ran an ad for Iver Johnson's Arms & Cycle Works pitching the importance of its new line of revolvers in "Home Defense." At a time when "defense is the issue of the hour in every city, town, and hamlet in America," it was a man's "duty to defend [his family] from the aggression of treacherous foes that prowl the night." The sketch of a soldier carrying the revolver—rather than a policeman or a husband in civilian clothing—implies that the aggressive and "treacherous foes" who threatened the respectable middle-class neighborhood in the background included more than just the common burglar.[59]

As much as propaganda warning Americans that German barbarity could one day meet them at their doorstep stirred up many Americans into a nervous frenzy, it also failed to move a sizable number. As the CPI admitted in a June 1917 edition of the *Four Minute Men Bulletin*, "The fact that the country is really at war has not as yet come home to the American people. They know it, of course, but they do not feel it."[60] This concern was not unfounded. For a number of reasons, many Americans in the working classes or living in rural areas were immune to the emotional pressure propagandists hoped to bring to bear. For some, such as poorly educated native-born workers and farmers or immigrants who did not understand English, language stood as a barrier between them and most propaganda. Moreover, many people cared little about the war or were ignorant of it because they were mostly isolated from propaganda or the city newspapers that printed it. Others felt as they had before April 1917, that the war was not their fight. Finally, many believed that they actually did "feel" the war, but not in the way propagandists hoped. To supporters of populism and socialism—most of whom were poor farmers, sharecroppers, or unskilled factory workers who had not shared in wartime wage and price increases—American belligerency was not a response to a German plot but was the result of a conspiracy between the federal government and big business to further weaken and subordinate the producing classes. They "felt" the war when their own, a family member's, or a neighbor's draft number was called; when their paychecks did not keep pace with wartime inflation; or when rumors spread of the huge profits that war industries and crop speculators made off of war mobilization.[61] To pro-war Americans, though, these attitudes were dangerous, considering the apocalyptic stakes for the country in the war.

In early 1918, the Kansas Council of Defense hoped to bust through these obstacles with rhetorical blunt force. The council's leaders were concerned "that many of our communities have not had brought home to them the reason why the *local community* . . . should mobilize all its forces to win the war." That pretext was the German Other's unrelenting aggression. The council's solution was a speaking campaign that would simplify the war's meaning and focus on six points regarding the consequences of German Otherness for predominantly rural Kansans: Germany aimed to destroy democracy; it "sought to spread rule of Force and Deception over [the] world"; its "Plan for World Empire included the United States, therefore this community"; the nation was fighting "to Protect this community"; the community was part of the nation and "must face fearlessly the present war status"; and the community could act locally to help fend off the danger.[62] In short, the council hoped to overcome rural parochialism by making the war a direct local concern. A speech from the Kansas campaign hit on all six points while also tapping into nearly all of the most prevalent arguments in wartime propaganda. The speaker quoted prominent Germans, recounted the German conspiracy, demonized German actions in Belgium, warned about an imminent invasion if the Allies lost, and even went so far as to say that "the free and happy and neighborly community life that *you have been enjoying here* will be forever extinct" if the Germans "ever become rulers of the world."[63]

Prominent citizens at times commiserated on how to reverse the apparent disinterestedness of many Americans throughout the country. Some blamed the German Other and its propensity to scheme and destroy. The editor of the *Christian Science Monitor*, Frederick Dixon, agreed with Grosvenor Clarkson, head of the Council of National Defense, that squelching German propaganda would solve the apathy problem. "The country is not awake, and this is largely, in my opinion, because of the enormous German element that has impregnated the political outlook very largely with a belief . . . that Germans, at all events, are no worse than anybody else." This, Dixon maintained, was a false assumption. Instead, he combined German actions with their supposed racial traits, explaining that the German people had "deliberately adopted and assimilated the policy of 'kultur'" because of "the element of domination in the German character."[64]

A more frequent concern of nervous Anglo-Saxons, however, was the presumed provincialism and dim-wittedness of the lower classes and immigrants. While complaining about the masses' apathy or ignorance as to why the degenerated Teuton was a threat, patriotic Americans often parroted the messages in invasion propaganda on the consequences of a German victory for the United States. Carrie Chapman Catt pleaded with state and local branches of the Women's Committee of the Council of National Defense "to form classes for the study of current topics and the vital questions of the war" in schools, including courses on why the country was fighting and "what winning or losing it will mean to this country and to civilization." Catt's urgency was palpable. These classes, she hoped, would "do much to counteract" the German and pacifist propaganda pervasive throughout the country and inspire Americans "to give whole-hearted, loyal support to the Government and the cause that MUST BE WON."[65]

The problem, though, was not just apathy but also the common people's general ignorance and lack of education. Catt later lamented to her colleagues in the Department of Educational Propaganda that indifference was the result of most pro-war propaganda being "too difficult for many of the simple minded people to understand" because, as she claimed, "ninety-five percent of our population have not gone beyond the eighth grade." While it was clear to the educated classes that if Germany won, "the United States would have to pay an indemnity," Catt asserted that "half the people . . . can never understand this word." All propaganda issued by the DEP, then, needed to be dumbed down to the point that "the simplest person can understand."[66]

From the South, where isolationism mostly reigned and education generally lagged, Francis H. Weston, a US district attorney in South Carolina, wrote Attorney General Thomas Gregory that the lack of awareness of or interest in the war among uneducated and insular southerners was alarming. "You have no conception of how ignorant the average man is of the causes that compel the United States to enter the war," Weston claimed. "I think it is very necessary that the people be educated."[67] The well-known farmers' advocate Mrs. G. H. Mathis of Alabama echoed Weston's concern that rural southerners opposed the war because "as a rule, [they] are ignorant" and "do not know the facts." Her solution, in a letter to the CPI, was a month-long speaking campaign—which would be the most effective strategy because of the South's high illiteracy rates—conducted by women's organizations, "in which the issues of the war should be clearly outlined and the inevitable results if Germany wins should be clearly set before the people."[68]

Some believed the problem of mass ignorance of the German threat was worthy of the president's attention. In July 1917, a Chicago architect and member of the Union League Club, Allen Bartlit Pond, wrote to Wilson that he and his cohorts saw "that a very large number of people in this country are still puzzled as to why America" entered the conflict in Europe. Pond grumbled that the masses were "quite at sea with regard to any obligations resting on America" to combat the "deep rooted ambition of the German ruling class and the resultant effect upon permanent peace for America in a settlement of what seem to the uninitiated to be purely local European matters." He suggested that the CPI should further distribute its propaganda "throughout the length of the country" and explain to indifferent citizens why, if premature peace were made, "America cannot, as you have wisely said, hope to keep out of future wars, no matter where started or by what caused."[69] In October, businessman Richard H. Edmonds wrote President Wilson from Baltimore about the continued "need for a great awakening of many of our people as to the realities of the war and the reasons for the war." According to Edmonds, "comparatively few" Americans "understood the deliberate plan of Germany, made many years ago, to enrich itself by war at the expense of other countries." Rural Americans needed to understand the consequences of defeat, he argued, because "there is a need for food conservation in order to save the Allies and thus ourselves."[70]

Those in a position to reduce the masses' ignorance also were seeking advice from the Wilson administration. The president's friend Frank Cobb, editor of the *New York World*, wrote to Wilson in August 1917 to inquire about the authenticity of an alleged State Department dispatch "showing that Germany planned to make war against the United States after crushing France and Great Britain." According to Cobb, Secretary of State Lansing had "confirmed . . .

that there had been such a plot." Assuming the information would be solid gold for propagandists and newspaper editors because it would prove "a policy of settled hostility to the United States on the part of Germany," Cobb advised that this proverbial smoking gun "ought to [be] printed as soon as possible." In his reply, Wilson expressed his own disappointment that he could not confirm Cobb's story, which perhaps speaks to his conviction that the CPI's Othering of the European German was grounded in truth. "Unfortunately, there are no documents in the State Department which could be said to establish" the German scheme. To the president's chagrin, "no conclusion, however well founded in inference, can be established by evidence. I wish it could be."[71]

Lesser-known citizens also feared the dire consequences if their fellow countrymen did not care about or comprehend the Prussianized German Other's true danger to the country. Many wrote to George Creel and others tied to the CPI with suggestions on how to educate the ill-informed and apathetic. The impact of wartime propaganda on these Americans' interpretations of the enemy's regression are clearly evident in their letters' content and urgency. In a March 1918 letter to the CPI chairman, a lawyer and part-time Four Minute Man from Cleveland, Ohio, rejected Wilson's initial idealism as too highfalutin and missing the point of the war. "No more about making the world safe for democracy," the lawyer wrote, "for it goes over the heads of the people we want to reach." A more intense publicity campaign was necessary, he argued, because Creel's publicists faced stiff competition from enemy propagandists. The lawyer estimated that current efforts "d[id] not reach 20% of the American people," while "the Germans are reaching by organized efforts over 80% of the population." Presumably a dutiful reader of his *Four Minute Men Bulletin*, the lawyer concluded that the threats of disloyalty and indifference were of paramount importance because "if this war does not end with a guarantee of security for the Allies we shall have to fight our own battles with Germanism . . . and every thinking man knows it." The unthinking 80 percent, apparently duped by pro-German and anti-war propaganda, required the CPI's attention.[72]

Some suggested to Creel and the CPI that visual proof of Prussianized Germans' Otherness was the only way to grab the attention of the unenlightened. Placing photographic evidence of the most vicious German atrocities in newspapers and on posters throughout the country could awaken Americans from their indifference, undermine pro-German propaganda, and possibly convince redeemable German Americans of the justice of the Allied cause. Apparently the posters already in circulation were not gruesome or terrifying enough. A Cleveland, Ohio, man who claimed to have seen photographs and heard lectures by witnesses of German atrocities in Belgium complained to Creel, "Only a comparative few . . . ha[d] the time or opportunity . . . to hear and see what Prussianism means." To convince the uninitiated, the man suggested the CPI "show reproductions from the Manual of German Military Tactics, pages from German diaries, pictures of atrocities, and *prove to everybody* that [German brutality] is the result of an actual, premeditated policy."[73] Likely hoping for a scoop, Fulton Oursler, a reporter for the *Baltimore American* and later a prolific novelist and playwright, wrote to Secretary Baker about "aggressive skepticism" toward stories in the press describing bestial German behavior in Belgium. Oursler declared with the utmost confidence that authorities had comprehensively validated tales of Germans "cutting off of the hands of Belgian children, and other outrages." Sharing the photographic evidence (which, unbeknownst to him, did not exist) with the public would quiet the skeptics and rile up Americans' hatred toward "our barbaric enemies."[74] Enclosing a clipping from a sensationalized newspaper account as evidence, a man from DeLand, Florida, angrily wrote Creel that the CPI had not included in its pamphlet *German War Practices* "concrete instances" of "young Belgian women or girls hav[ing] had their breasts cut off and the young men with their right hand hacked off." While such actions were likely "sporadic and done without authorization," he argued, they "nevertheless show the individual spirit of the average Hun" and must be made known to the wider public.[75] While not explicitly indicating a fear that German invaders would commit the same atrocities in the United States, such letters suggest that British and American propaganda regarding Belgium, which had inundated the United States since 1914, had successfully Othered the Teutonic enemy with supposed evidence of its regression.

Yet, having facilitated the creation of the German enemy Other through dramatic, familiar, and easily understandable words and images, letters such as these put Creel and the CPI in an uncomfortable position. Citizens were asking for clear evidence of German Otherness, not because they did not believe it, but because they feared a significant portion of the country had yet to fully grasp the apparent truth the CPI claimed to present. Creel, though, had no evidence to provide. In response to a letter from Pennsylvania lawyer Orr Buffington suggesting the CPI import maimed Belgian children and display them in public, Creel asserted that "never as yet have we been able to substantiate the charge that the hands of children have been cut off." He reported that even Brand Whitlock, the US ambassador to Belgium, "states flatly that he has never yet seen any such case of mutilation."[76] The mere fact that Creel, the man most identified with wartime propaganda, at times attempted to correct correspondents' misconceptions of German atrocities in Belgium is indicative of how little control those delivering the messages actually wielded over the imaginations of their intended audience.

They had such little control because wartime invasion propaganda reflected, more than it shaped, contemporary Anglo-Saxon anxieties over the destructive impact that foreign peoples and influences could have on American society. Calling a people "bestial" or "uncivilized" had very specific connotations in the age of imperialism, an era in which the United States and Europe couched their colonial ambitions in terms of bringing "civilization" to the "savage" peoples of Latin America, Africa, and Asia. Thus, the racial implications of such words, as well as images of the decivilized Hun, would not have been lost on those Americans, Anglo-Saxon or not, who viewed the world through such a lens. In short, one reason the European Germans were so easily Othered was that Anglo-Saxon Americans so readily employed the familiar language of Othering when searching for meaning in the Great War. Propagandists described Prussian militarism as the antithesis of democracy and thus the antithesis of progress and an expression of a primitive racial character. The image of an army of decivilized Teutonic soldiers leveling American cities to further an autocratic world conspiracy echoed and tapped into those old fears of virtual foreign invasion, subjugation, and Anglo-Saxon decline.

CHAPTER FIVE

Toward the Democratic Millennium,
1914–1918

In paganism the poor serve the rich, the weak serve the strong, the ignorant serve the wise. In the kingdom of God the rich serve the poor, the strong serve the weak, the wise serve the ignorant. This is the divine order; and the Son of God himself illustrates this order by his own life and death. The ideal of autocracy is organized paganism. The ideal of democracy is organized Christianity.

LYMAN ABBOTT, May 2, 1917

We are in the midst of a crisis that carries in its issue the world's fundamental reconstruction or possible dissolution. . . . It is not possible to exaggerate, it is impossible that we yet comprehend or encompass, the height and the depth and the reach of the question now before us. If ever there was a war between good and evil, it is now.

Editorial, *Current Opinion*, June 1917

"Some have called this war the breakdown of Christianity," Dr. L. O. Bricker informed his First Christian congregation in Atlanta, Georgia, in early May 1917. Those same pessimists also "regard the entrance of America, the last great Christian nation, into the conflict as proof of the utter breakdown of Christianity." What they failed to realize, Bricker preached, was that war is a fundamental aspect of the Christian faith. "With the coming of Jesus the good was arrayed against every form of evil." Thus, "every man and woman who espouses the call of Christ becomes a soldier" on the side of Christian morality. A month before, the United States had entered a war against a foe who allegedly epitomized the oppression and hypocrisy against which Jesus fought during his time. Accordingly, when Bricker heard of Kaiser Wilhelm II or German ministers invoking God's name, he could not help but get "the impression that they must mean the devil when they say 'God.' For the only supernatural power that could aid the aims and purposes and bless the monstrous men and deeds of Prussian militarism is the power that I call 'the devil.'"[1]

To Bricker, the Great War was a struggle between good and evil. Although he did not refer to the war as a final showdown, or Armageddon, Bricker's millennial worldview was clearly evident in his assertion that war was essential to Christianity and that Germans, consciously or not, worshiped Satan. The eruption of war in 1914 and the United States' entry in 1917 raised deep moral and philosophical questions that propagandists, theologians, and ministers like Bricker attempted to answer. Was the war proof that Christianity had failed? Or had the Christian nations of Europe failed Christ? At the same time, German U-boat sinkings and atrocities in Belgium and France raised question about Germans' religious beliefs. Were the kaiser's minions really Christians, like the Anglo-Saxons? Or did their actions reveal them to be pagans, atheists, or even tools of the Antichrist?

In many ways, the First World War certainly looked like Armageddon, or something close to it. Fifty years earlier, many Protestants, especially in the North, had interpreted the destruction and massive loss of life in the Civil War as apocalyptic and the emancipation of millions of slaves as emblematic of the United States' moral and spiritual progress. The cataclysm in Europe, though, was something else entirely. The Great War had produced millions, not hundreds of thousands, of dead bodies. The German army appeared to be waging war against Christianity and civilization as its soldiers stripped helpless Belgian and French girls of their innocence and leveled churches, cathedrals, libraries, and homes. In Transcaucasia, Muslim Turks had slaughtered or left for dead roughly one million Christian Armenians. In late 1917, the British reclaimed the holy city of Jerusalem for Christendom from the Islamic Ottoman Empire. For Bricker and others, the demarcation between good and evil in the war was clear, and white American Christians were called to fulfill the United States' mission to lift the world out of the darkness and spread Anglo-Saxon democracy.

Two strands of millennial thought, pre- and postmillennialism, competed for the attention of Anglo-Saxon Protestants as they tried to understand their German foe and the United States' role in the Great War. In Christian theology, the "millennium" refers to the prophecy in Revelation 20 that Satan would be defeated and Christ would rule on earth for a thousand years. The basic difference between pre- and postmillennialists came down to the timing of Christ's return. According to premillennialists' interpretation of Scripture, the years leading up to the second coming will be marked by severe social, political, and spiritual decay, which will allow the Antichrist to achieve global domination and sink the world into a period called the "tribulation." Christ, however, will return in time to defeat the Antichrist before establishing His millennial reign. To premillennialists, the Great War was not Armageddon but a possible presage to a series of larger conflicts that could bring on the second coming. At the same time, their strict reading of Scripture and its prophecies led most premillennialists to be skeptical of non-biblical sources of earthly authority, such as the modern progressive state and evolutionary science (but not racism). Instead of signs of progress, premillennialist denominations viewed these as evidence of the world's moral decline and rejection of biblical principles.[2]

Postmillennialists, however, believe that Christ will return after Christians have established the millennium through their spreading of the faith. To post-millennialists, also known in the early twentieth century as Christian liberals or modernists, God's presence is evident in human progress, and every step forward (be it religious, cultural, social, technological, or scientific) brought mankind ever closer to Christ's earthly kingdom. Just as Christ was a crusader against sin, postmillennialists optimistically looked to spread the faith across the world. Although much of this could be done through missionary work by the church, postmillennialists also put their faith in the state to uplift the downtrodden through social reform or, in its darkest incarnation, forcing heathens to hear the Gospel through war and imperialism.[3]

World War I, however, divided Christian liberals into two camps: those who saw American entry into the conflict as detrimental to the prospects of international peace and those who viewed the war as an epic spiritual struggle between autocratic wickedness and democratic righteousness.[4] In terms of wartime propaganda, it appears the latter group of postmillennialists won out. Although the mass death resulting from the war led many Americans to lose faith in postmillennial progress and join premillennialist denominations, the common depictions of the Germans as Satanic or pagan and of the war as a chance to spread Christian democracy across the world indicate that pro-war postmillennialists produced the lion's share of Christian-based wartime propaganda. Even secular, non-ordained writers and propagandists provided interpretations of the war and the enemy that were steeped in a postmillennial conception of progress and conflict.

Religious-based propaganda and racialized descriptions of the enemy Other, however, were not mutually exclusive. While much propaganda suggested that the racially regressive impact of Prussianism on European Germans accounted for their aggression and atrocities, some also portrayed the Teutonic Other's allegedly misplaced or mistaken religious convictions as a byproduct of this same racial degeneration. Ministers and propagandists frequently defined German religion as arrogant, materialistic, and backward. From a postmillennial perspective, Teutons' supposed veneration of war, themselves, and pagan gods signified their rejection of or incapacity for Christianity and, thus, civilization and democracy. At the same time, arguments that the German people had been duped into crusading for a false prophet—be it Beelzebub, a pagan god, or their own specifically German god—implied they were docile and dimwitted.

Not surprisingly, renderings of Germans' faith contrasted sharply with that of the Anglo-Saxon. Democracy and service to others were said to epitomize the teachings of Christ, unlike the self-idolatry, violence, and avarice of German religion. That Anglo-Saxon democracy was altruistic was evidenced by American soldiers, who followed Christ's example by giving their lives in Europe's trenches for the sake of humanity. Ministers and secular propagandists asserted that the Anglo-Saxons' supposedly inherent selflessness and self-restraint, which were signs of their civilized nature and devotion to Christian love, were completely lacking in the German Other. In this context, the Great War looked as if it was a struggle between righteous progress and wicked regression. The Teutonic Other's faithlessness threatened more than just the physical well-being of the United States and the world. It was an obstacle to the realization of God's postmillennial plan.

Christianity, especially the crusading type, has been among the most enduring aspects of American identity formation from colonial times to the present. Since John Winthrop famously declared the Puritan community in Massachusetts to be a "city upon a hill" in 1630, the conviction that the English colonies and, later, the United States had been chosen to lead the world toward the realization of the Kingdom of God has been integral to the nation's political, cultural, and geographical development. Yet, while the principle that the New World could passively redeem the Old through its example has stood the test of time, a more militant understanding of God's mission for the nation often has run parallel to it. In the 1780s, politicians and ministers preached that God had freed the American colonies to become His "New Israel," the chosen instrument of God's will and a template for the world. The United States' status as "chosen" also was a critical spur to westward expansion. While largely propelled by those seeking economic independence, most whites justified their conquest of the American West as the Anglo-Saxon's Manifest Destiny to spread Christianity, progress, and democracy, through violence if necessary, across the "untamed" continent.[5]

Yet the United States could not be expected to shine as a beacon of democracy and morality if its light were dimmed by the sinfulness of its people. Running parallel to expansionism in the nineteenth century was the explosion of populist revivalism of the second Great Awakening. This more emotional and urgent brand of Protestantism inspired a surge of conversions and reform movements in the antebellum period, such as abolitionism and temperance, that sought to move the United States closer to the realization of the millennium by exhorting individuals to forsake and modify their wicked behavior. As the Old Testament made clear, those who disobeyed God's commands could expect to lose his divine favor. The pressure to eradicate sin, be it slavery, prostitution, or the "demon rum," was palpable for antebellum millennial reformers. Yet with God's earthly kingdom seemingly on the horizon, few activists saw the federal government as fully sovereign and put little trust in its institutions to assist in their task.[6]

To northern Protestants in the late nineteenth century, however, the cleansing of the national sin of slavery through war and legal emancipation indicated that the state could act as a vehicle for earthly perfection and inspired attempts to utilize government power to enforce dominant Anglo-Saxon notions of morality.[7] The Protestant ethos of redemption, a key component of Great Awakening revivalism, held such a tight grip on American culture by the dawn of the twentieth century that it had a clear impact on secular progressive reformers' motivations for reshaping society through government action. Many progressive crusaders viewed greed, immigrant assimilation, urban sanitation, alcoholism, and sexual depravity as humanitarian, economic, racial, or public health questions with clear black-and-white answers. Their belief in redemption, social perfectibility, and the state's capacity to assist in the realization of these positive aims was just as powerful as the explicitly faith-based motivations of postmillennialist ministers and reformers before them.[8]

The surge of Christian liberalism and the desire for overseas colonies in the late nineteenth century also informed the nation's millennial mission during the Great War in that both were often connected to ideas of Darwinian struggle and Anglo-Saxon superiority. To postmillennialist reformers, the overwhelming number of downtrodden and immoral immigrants, along with native-born whites' greed, prejudice, and distrust of the state, stood as obstacles to the realization of God's kingdom. The continued progress of the Anglo-Saxon nation and the world was not possible without the engagement and physical vigor of white Protestant men, which, some ministers (just like some military preparedness advocates) feared was waning. Many Protestant clergymen in the late nineteenth century looked to increase sagging male church attendance by restoring a "muscular Christianity" that focused on developing men's physical strength through exercise and sport. Men must be hardy and fit in order to spread Christian righteousness to the willfully and unwittingly ignorant masses in the United States and beyond. In the March 1915 edition of the *Forum*, California politician Henry W. Wright echoed the masculine and religious rationale for Anglo-Saxon Christian imperialism, remarking that American democracy and progress were synonymous with Christianity and entailed "real sacrifice . . . the endurance of pain, privation, and even death itself." Those who served and died for the sake of the democratic "spiritual community" became "the great moral teachers and heroes of the race." Democratic crusaders had a partner in their fight for Christian democracy. "The immanence and efficacy of God," Wright concluded, was the "guiding spirit in social progress" as He "strives and suffers with us in the cause of universal evolution."[9] When applied to the First World War, this message implored Anglo-Saxon soldiers and those supporting them at home to confront the crusade with the same strength and courage that Christ showed during the crucifixion. With Christ on the side of democracy, why should anyone be afraid?

Though muscular in terms of its military might, Europe in 1914 seemed in need of the righteousness that liberal Protestants in the United States were selling. "Now Armageddon has a real meaning," intoned the editors of *Collier's* in August 1914. "If this be not Armageddon, we shall never suffer that final death grip of the nations."[10] Despite the three-thousand-mile distance between the United States and the Western Front, the realization that the Great War would be long and costly raised many moral and religious questions among Americans, most notably whether the failure of Christianity was responsible for what some surmised could be the apocalypse. Those who viewed the war as an opportunity to advance Christianity, however, chided such pessimistic talk throughout 1914 and 1915. In December 1914, the *Outlook*, the popular social gospel periodical founded by the prominent Congregationalist minister Lyman Abbott, described the European crisis as the "failure of nations to practice Christianity in international relations." Using what they considered the United States' compassionate dealings with non-white peoples over the last half century as examples, the editors claimed, "Wherever Christianity has been tried it has vindicated its claims not only as the highest law of life but as a working principle." The war, then, was not indicative of the failure of Christianity but "an awful vindication of a God who has said in countless ways, 'The wages of sin is death.'"[11]

Europe's apparent disregard for Christian practices in international relations did not prevent some commentators during American neutrality, especially preparedness advocates, from espousing Christianity as an inherently strong, forceful, and crusading religion. In December 1914, Garet Garrett of the secular *Everybody's Magazine* cited statistics and history to show that the weaknesses of European Christianity could not be blamed for the slaughter. Together, the populations of the six primary belligerents were "97.1 per cent. Christian," and that figure was trending upward. Although Christianity had not stopped aggressive wars from happening in the past, that was not a slight to the religion as much as to "errant man," who "during nearly two thousand years" had not "collectively practiced true Christianity." Real Christianity meant a willingness to battle for what was right. "War in a righteous cause was not inconsistent with Christianity," a Jesuit scholar told Garrett in what could be construed as an implicit justification for military preparedness and previous imperialist and expansionist wars.[12]

The following month in the *Atlantic Monthly*, Agnes Repplier, also Catholic, tacitly advocated for preparedness while explaining that professed Christians, not Christianity, were responsible for the war. Like Garrett's Jesuit source, Repplier drew a stark distinction between military aggression and Christianity. "To prate about the wickedness of war without drawing a clear demarcation between aggressive and defensive warfare," she claimed in reference to pacifist churches, "is to lose our mental balance, to substitute sentiment for truth." That sentiment was cowardice. "The very wrongness of [aggressive warfare] implies logically the rightness of the other," she opined. "And whatever is morally right is in accord with Christianity. To speak loosely of war as unchristian is to ignore not only the Christian right, but the Christian duty, which rests with every nation and with every man to protect that of which nation and men are lawful protectors."[13]

To pro-Allied Christians who asserted during neutrality that Christianity at its core was a manly and actively militant religion, turning the other cheek, the *modus operandi* of Christian pacifists, was not appropriate when malicious forces threatened others.[14] The *Outlook*, for example, affirmed that "nothing in this teaching nor in any other teaching of Jesus Christ" justified "the assumption that we are to suffer others to be injured and stand by unresisting." Rage and conflict could be virtuous and an expression of love for one's fellow man. Jesus displayed "terrible anger" on occasion in the New Testament, the most revealing being "his attack upon the corruptionists" when he overturned the tables of those who stole from the poor and made "the temple of God into a den of thieves." Placed in the context of the war, the editors argued that anger derived from love of peace and hatred of oppression would inspire "Christian heroism." Those who shirked this duty did so out of "either unintelligence or carelessness or cowardice."[15]

In October 1915, the *Outlook*'s editors published an exposé on Christian duty laced with military terminology. Their militant language, however, was not a metaphorical call for domestic reform or spreading the social gospel. Identifying the cross as "the battle-flag of Christianity," the editors presented their religion as one primarily of gallant self-sacrifice. "Christianity is a call to enlist in a long campaign against the forces of sensuality and selfishness in the individual and in the community," they contended. For a man or nation to fear such a sacrifice was blasphemous. "The fear of war is not the same as the love of peace," the article concluded. "It may be simply the crime of cowardice on a national scale," a crime some Christians hoped to prevent the American people from committing.[16] The war, it seemed, had intensified muscular Christianity into an even more militaristic conception of Anglo-Saxons' Christian duty.

A letter to the editor of *McClure's Magazine* published in March 1916 implied that at least some Americans endorsed the idea of a militant crusading Christianity and an end to neutrality in the name of Christ. The letter's author argued that the mistaken notion "that the smaller the army and the smaller the navy we possess, the smaller will be the incentive for war" was "a misconception of Christian principles." Kindness and altruism could not "protect this Republic from foreign aggression." Peace would only come once "America ceased crowding the indulgence of Providence." Reiterating the messages of many pro-preparedness editors, the author concluded that God only helped those who helped themselves; thus, only by actively pursuing peace through preparedness could the American people feel safe from external threats.[17] This letter, with its warning of foreign attack, by U-boat or invasion, suggests that this *McClure's* reader made the connection between preparedness and Christian duty on his own.

As was the case with the virility of the Anglo-Saxon male, the nation's collective religious muscularity was of paramount importance because Germany's offenses, affronts, and threats indicated that it, more so than the other warring nations in Europe, failed to apply Christian principles to international relations. Propagandists commonly portrayed Germany's actions in diplomacy, on the battlefield, and under the surface of the Atlantic as evidence that the European Teutons had degenerated to the stage of their brutish Prussian overlords. Some also argued that this racial regression was evident in the Germans' religious faith, suggesting that the kaiser and his people prayed to a different god than their Christian enemies did. If to extend Anglo-Saxonism to savage lands was to spread Christianity, democracy, and civilization—the prime jus-tifications for American imperialism—nations that denied individual liberty could not be truly Christian and, by extension, revealed their backwardness. By this metric, the Prussianized Teutons of autocratic Germany were not followers of Christ.

If Christians no longer populated the land of Martin Luther, the monk responsible for the Protestant Reformation, who or what did Germans wor-ship? The Othering of the European German on religious grounds began very early in the war, long before the United States entered the conflict. In Janu-ary 1915, Randolph H. McKim, the well-known spokesman for the southern Lost Cause myth and reverend of the Church of the Epiphany in Washington, DC, railed against the idea that Christianity had betrayed the world. It was, in fact, "the cold mathematical godlessness of militarism that has broken down; it is the brutal and cynical philosophy that 'Might makes right' that has failed." Germans, he concluded, had turned away from Christianity to worship militarism, which McKim referred to as "the deification of force." A perverse version of Christianity thrived in Germany, and the aggressive tendencies it evoked could not be allowed to spread. "With good conscience and without violating the principles of the religion of Christ," a man could "defend his home and his country from unprovoked attack." Responsibility for the war, therefore, lay with the aggressive German autocracy and its denial of Christian values and morally justified warfare.[18]

That German faith had become overly militaristic stood in stark contrast to the courageous yet peace-loving image of Jesus Christ. In May 1915, the month of the *Lusitania* sinking, *Literary Digest* claimed that to Germans the war was a religious crusade and warned of a "New Spirituality" taking shape in Ger-many that focused on the destruction of "eternal peace." According to the editors' source, the London-based *Christian World*, German religious doctrine declared that a world without war had "no moral meaning," making it "a realm of the devil." With such a perspective, the article concluded, Germany clearly fought against the dawning of Christ's earthly kingdom.[19] In a similar vein, Congregationalist theologian William Jewett Tucker argued that militarism, not Christianity, had become Germans' hollow and craven religion. In the June 1915 *Atlantic Monthly*, Tucker maintained that the "mock heroics of mili-tarism" in Germany had little to teach the valiant crusaders of Christ. Unlike Prussian militarism and its cowardly tactics of killing unarmed innocents while concealed under the ocean surface, Christianity was "a religion which was born in the supreme act of courage." With the *Lusitania* clearly on his mind, Tucker pushed for the end of neutrality on the basis that continued inaction was "no guaranty [*sic*] of righteousness," the furthering of which was the object of Christianity. Germany, then, was the enemy of Christian virtue. Only when American peace advocates "pass[ed] into the stage of moral militancy" would the United States "develop its own type of heroism." In short, through militant Christianity and the waging of righteous warfare, the United States could live up to its divine calling and defeat German militarism, the greatest obstacle to permanent peace.[20]

With the declaration of war on April 6, 1917, giving American men the chance to finally act on their courageous Christianity and help fulfill the nation's millennial mission, it became even more important to explain exactly what the Christian United States was up against, both at home and abroad. Condemnations in propaganda and the press of German Lutheranism as inherently evil or misguided, however, were rare, likely because German Americans were far from the only subgroup of Americans to attend Lutheran services. For instance, in response to the Nebraska State Council of Defense's blanket allegations of Lutheran disloyalty in July 1917, the Norwegian Lutheran Church of America pointed out that Lutheran synods had "3,774,774 baptized members" and spoke "the Gospel in seventeen different languages" throughout the United States.[21] Moreover, that Martin Luther's sixteenth-century protest was the reason why most Americans' Protestant denominations (and, to some degree, the United States) were founded was impossible to ignore. Propagandists in the press, the Committee on Public Information, and patriotic societies, as well as federal investigators, rarely questioned Luther or Lutheranism and only raised suspicions about the motives and loyalty of German American Lutherans in the context of German-language parochial schools, which Lutheran churches often funded and operated.[22]

The lack of verbal vitriol did not prevent some skittish Americans from treating Lutherans as agents of Germanization. Along with pacifist Christians, German American Lutherans at various times and places faced the wrath of an untrusting populace. By the time the United States had joined the conflict, many German Lutheran churches, the vast majority situated in the Midwest, had already painted themselves into a corner. Not only were services often conducted in the German language, but many pastors and parishioners also openly supported the German war effort and defended the sinking of the *Lusitania* because it had carried arms meant to kill their Old World relatives.

Although most German Lutheran churches professed their loyalty to the United States after it entered the war, Anglo-Saxon anxiety about Germany's imperial designs for the country did not always leave room for tolerance.[23] Vandals targeted German Lutheran synods, especially in the Midwest, busting out windows and splattering yellow paint on church walls. Mobs of angry and anxious Americans also tarred and feathered or beat German American ministers for allegedly spreading pro-German propaganda, obstructing Liberty Bond drives, or openly advocating disloyalty.[24]

While overzealous citizens occasionally tagged German American Lutherans as spies or propagandists, Anglo-Saxons found the faith of the Teutons in Prussianized Germany to be far more threatening, despite their distance from the United States. Propagandists and ministers effectively Othered the Teuton's spirituality through a variety of overlapping charges, all of which were meant to portray Germans' faith and national character as degenerate and the binary opposites of those of the United States and its allies. They often cited the enemy Other's alleged rejection of Christianity and worshipping of false idols, be it Satan, premodern pagan gods, or even themselves. Portrayals of Germans' misguided religious devotion consistently referenced their alleged racial-cultural degeneration as the likely cause. By contrast, as with the editorials regarding Christian courage, preachers and secular propagandists referred to the New Testament to argue for the holiness of the United States' millennial mission to defeat regressive anti-Christian militarism and spread democracy.

The Teuton's idol worship apparently had been present since the start of the war. Having been stuck in Europe in the opening months of the war in 1914, Irvin S. Cobb of the *Saturday Evening Post* claimed to have had various conversations with German officers and was surprised that he never heard "any one of them, openly invok[e] the aid of the Creator." In a May 1917 article, Cobb professed to have learned upon encountering "civilian Germany" that the soldiers' apparent reluctance to call on God's assistance was, in fact, an expression of their faith. The German home front had "remodel[ed] its conceptions of Deity to be purely and solely a German deity." Cobb found that "any Christian race, going to war in what it esteems to be a righteous cause, prays to God to bless its campaigns with victory and to sustain its arms with fortitude. It had remained for this Christian race to assume that the God to whom they addressed their petitions was their own peculiar God, and that his Kingdom on Earth was Germany and Germany only; and that his chosen people now and forevermore would be Germans and Germans only." In short, to German civilians and soldiers it was self-evident that God had graced their nation and wartime mission. Although Cobb argued that German blasphemy was the result of indoctrination by a fearful regime surrounded by enemies—Russia to the east, France to the west—his characterization of Prussianized Germany's religious faith also conveyed that the German people followed a false idol: themselves.[25]

During American intervention, the press regularly damned European Germans' alleged worshipping of a false idol. The editor of the *Providence Journal* reported that "Germany's God is a reflection of herself—merciless, conscience-less, a blasphemous negation of all that the Christian era has laboriously taught mankind." Similarly, according to *Current Opinion*, the German God was "not the God of the rest of the world." Basing part of their argument on the work of a Danish minister and an English writer, the magazine's editors asserted that "Germany . . . is worshipping a false God—a God of wrath and cruelty, of unbridled egotism." It could not be allowed back "into the fellowship of the nations" until their "false God" was "dethroned." The Germans' misplaced faith also brought into question their character and temperament, both understood at the time to be inheritable traits. *Current Opinion* called upon a philosophy professor from the University of Wisconsin to psychoanalyze the impact of the Germans' mistaken beliefs on their psyche. Their religion, he contended, exposed an "incipient insanity," illustrated by "delusions of grandeur and the mania of persecution" that was evident in the character of Germans as well as the "criminally insane." In line with the popular perception that criminality can be a biological trait, the professor concluded that "the disease is incurable."[26]

Postmillennialist arguments concluding that German religion was narcissistic and misguided often suggested that the kaiser, the brainwasher-in-chief, and his people had fallen under the sway of a false prophet, who, posing as the Christian God, directed them toward evil ends. To some, such an understanding appeared to fit with the prophecy that the Antichrist would claim to be anointed with God's spirit and be chosen to create the Kingdom of Heaven on earth. For example, adventure novelist Cyrus Townsend Brady, writing for the National Security League, made a clear connection between Germany's false god and the Antichrist. If Germany proved victorious in the war, "a premium would be put on murder; rape would become a praiseworthy action . . . and Hell would take the place of Heaven with the so-called German God in Satan's place."[27] At the very least, Germans' alleged spiritual egotism and the German army's and navy's brutal acts against civilians indicated that the kaiser and the German people were not worshiping the same god as the Anglo-Saxons. Also writing for the NSL, author Joseph C. Lincoln described the "Prussian god" as self-referential, "sporting an upturned mustache above a von Hindenburg jaw." The Teuton, it seemed, was its own false god. The Germans' misplaced faith, Lincoln worried, could lead to the triumph of evil over the world. "The gentle Jesus in our churches," he warned, "would be replaced by an idol 'made in Germany.'"[28] Such characterizations of the enemy revealed propagandists' astute understanding of how to court Christians to support the war and their knowledge of biblical prophecy while also showing the profound impact of millennial Christianity on Americans' understanding of the conflict.

While propagandists' claims that German actions were evidence of false idol worship or a possible alliance with the Antichrist resonated with many Americans, political cartoons further simplified these arguments. Editorial artists portrayed Germany or the kaiser as bloodthirsty, the pal of Satan or Death, and their religious faith as un-Christian, evil, or confused. Devilish depictions of the kaiser and his people were most prevalent after the beginning of Germany's series of massive offensives on the Western Front that nearly won the war for the Central Powers in March 1918. These battles resulted in some of the highest casualty rates of the war. Previously, most wartime cartoonists had depicted Wilhelm as a sadistic murderer of the weak, but at this stage in the conflict they also began rendering him as Satan's willing partner and as an agent of mass death.[29]

A cartoon from the *Providence Journal* entitled "His God" revealed the presumed source of Germany's sadism and which supernatural being had actually chosen Germany as a partner. The kaiser, in full military dress and holding a bloodied saber, stands over a slain woman and child as Satan, almost twice the size of the brawny kaiser, points ahead and says to Wilhelm, "Forward with God to Fresh Deeds and Fresh Victories!" The message, of course, was that Germany followed the guidance of Satan, in this case undisguised. The woman and child are clear reminders of the alleged German affinity for cruelty evident during the Germans' "rape" of Belgium and the sinking of the *Lusitania*.[30]

A disturbing image from the *Chicago Herald* furthered the theme of the kaiser's partnership with the Antichrist by depicting the raising of a German war "monument." The marker is a gigantic cross covered with dozens of faceless and genderless bodies hung as if crucified. The kaiser, standing proud and tall with the slouching Austrian emperor to his left and the crouching Ottoman

Figure 5.1. "Raising Their Monument," cartoon, *Chicago Herald*. Reprinted in *New York Times Current History*, April 1918.

sultan to his right, watches as his soldiers pull the cross upright in its final resting place in the middle of the Atlantic Ocean. The artist casts Wilhelm in a role similar to that of Pontius Pilate, the Roman official who sentenced Jesus to death nineteen hundred years earlier. By sanctioning the strategy of unrestricted U-boat warfare, the cartoonist suggests, the kaiser had in essence condemned the innocent victims of his submarines to a similarly unjust death. Placing the Catholic emperor of Austria-Hungary and the Muslim sultan of the Ottoman Empire next to the kaiser, both in obvious subservience, implicated them in the atrocities as well and spoke to the kaiser's confusion over which god he actually served (fig. 5.1).

Pastor William E. Barton of the First Congregational Church in Oak Park, Illinois, preached in July 1918 that hating German autocracy was fine even though "there is no merit or sure proof of patriotism in consigning the Kaiser to hell." Besides, "it is superfluous," Barton argued, because "he is in hell now."[31] Some cartoonists agreed, continuing to depict the kaiser alongside Satan, his supposed lord and partner. That summer the *Newark News* printed a cartoon of a joyous encounter between the emperor of Germany and the Prince of

Figure 5.2. (left) "Sardonic Humor," cartoon, *Newark News*. Reprinted in *New York Times Current History*, August 1918. *Figure 5.3. (right)* "The Kaiser's War Council," cartoon, *Washington Times*. Reprinted in *New York Times Current History*, September 1918.

Darkness. The grinning kaiser, seemingly in the subservient role of cabinet minister, presents to his sovereign the front page of a newspaper with a head-line quoting him as asking, "What have I not done to preserve the world from these horrors?" Beelzebub, with a boulder for a throne and sporting a similarly upturned mustache as the kaiser, finds the lie hysterically funny. The rocky and dark setting gives the impression that the meeting takes place in the nether region (fig. 5.2). Perhaps meant as a slight to the Germans' alleged belief that God was their partner in the war, the *Washington Times* in September 1918 portrayed Satan and Death as the kaiser's collaborators and Hell as the meeting place of their "war council." Wilhelm sits in front of a map holding a quill pen. Flanking his right is the Angel of Death, who, with his boney hand, orders the kaiser to mark a particular spot on the map. To Wilhelm's left, the Devil smiles, looking on with great interest at the newest battle plan. Most significant, though, is the kaiser's expression, which exudes both depression and resigna-tion (fig. 5.3). The artist's message seems to have been that Wilhelm had become almost zombie-like in his obedience to these dark forces, or that the kaiser regretted his infernal alliance with the false prophet.

Some propagandists and ministers tried a different approach, suggesting that German racial degeneration and backwardness left them susceptible to Satan's charms, and this, in turn, could have dire consequences for the world.

Francis J. Oppenheimer, writing on behalf of the National Security League, contended that Germany's worshiping of a false god indicated that the Teutonic race's progress had been stunted. He alleged that the kaiser's "court pastor" preached that "Germany is the center of God's plan for the world." Oppenheimer's response to Prussian egotism and misunderstanding of God was to exclaim, "Poor savages! Too frail for the mad sport of thinking." The day of "universal love and peace of God will never be while the Lords of Murder and Might darken the earth with shadows from hell."[32]

Satan was not the only possible false god corrupting the deteriorating German mind. Propagandists and clergymen often characterized the German Others as uncivilized pagans who worshiped themselves, warfare, and ancient Norse gods. In terms of their faith, the kaiser and his subjects were portrayed as having stepped back in time to an age before Christ's lessons of love and peace had reached Central Europe. According to Lyman Abbott of the *Outlook*, Prussianized Teutons' denial of self-government indicated their primitive nature, that they had not advanced to the same stage of human progress as the Anglo-Saxons or that they had regressed. "The reverence demanded [by the kaiser] is for a God who is the ally of the military power," Abbott claimed. "The worship is of a God who is by Odin [chief god in Norse paganism], not by Jesus Christ." The United States declared war on "this pagan Power," he concluded, in order to "maintain for all humanity" the principles of democracy and "personal comradeship with the heavenly Father."[33]

Perhaps the most elaborate explanation of German racial and spiritual degeneration came from Carl Krusada in the February 1918 issue of the *Forum*. "Has Christ and His glorious message passed the German, uncomprehended, even unchallenged?" he asked. "To be sure, the German makes the gesture of Christianity, but in his heart has he remained a pagan?" The answer to both questions, Krusada predictably answered, was yes. Teutons and Anglo-Saxons viewed God much differently. "Anglo-Saxon piety" and "the equality in meekness before the Lord" that characterized Christianity in the United States and Great Britain were lost on the German, whom Krusada consistently depicted as self-centered and religiously backward. "The Germanic mind in its simple form accepts God as semi-anthropomorphic" or as a "superkinsman" who acts as an equal partner instead of master. To explain why the German people were not Christians, Krusada argued that Teutons accepted the wrathful God of the Old Testament while showing little interest in the divinity of Christ. At the same time, indifference to Christ also was part of Germans' ancient heritage. Because of the militarism inherent in this "race of nomadic barbarians . . .

that had considered death on the battlefield the sole key to Walhalla [the hall where fallen soldiers live for eternity with Odin]," Germans saw Christ's teachings as less attractive than those of the Norse war god. The German people, therefore, had worshiped war gods for centuries. Only the most courageous soldiers were welcomed into Odin's Walhalla. Heaven to a German, Krusada suggested, was "to spend the hereafter at the round-table, in company of bearded, battle-scarred warriors, presided over by the mighty Wotan [Odin in German], entertained by recitals of terrific combats, forever feasting on barbecues and vast quantities of mead, forever welcoming new arrivals, mortally wounded warriors picked up from the battle-grounds by the Walkyre," which are female figures in Norse mythology who choose who will die in battle. Krusada concluded, "It was but natural that these lusty barbarians accepted Christ with misgivings, under inward protest."[34]

While most religious-centered explanations of the war and the enemy were of the postmillennial variety, arguments seemingly based in premillennialist beliefs were not uncommon and often shared much in common with modernists' views. Both viewed German militarism as the root of the Teuton's moral decline and the threat the race posed to civilization. Premillennialists, however, understood autocratic militarism as the result of Germans' rejection of biblical teachings and, more importantly, their embrace of state power and Darwinian natural selection. Believing that the Bible was the primary authority on truth and appropriate earthly behavior, premillennialists of the early twentieth century saw autocratic government, modernism, and Darwin's theory of evolution as direct challenges to God's word and authority. Therefore, German militarism and its "Might Makes Right" philosophy were absolute evils.[35]

Mainstream sources of premillennialist anti-German propaganda consistently identified the Darwinian teachings of the Prussian philosopher Friedrich Nietzsche as a key source of Germans' sinful modernism. Then and now, Nietzsche is best known for his statement that "God is dead" and the concept of the "supermen," who fill the vacuum God left by establishing a new morality devoid of notions of good or evil. Elmer Rittenhouse, in his racially tinged pamphlet, *Know Your Enemy*, argued that Germans had replaced God with "a religion of war" and the Darwinian ethos of the "survival of the 'fit.'" The strong were "of course the Germans, who charge themselves with the duty of eliminating 'unfit' nations." In other words, the Germans ultimately worshiped themselves, the supermen of Nietzsche's work. Self-idolatry, Rittenhouse contended, was at the center of Germany's bid for world domination and its brutal treatment of non-combatants. Atrocities in the name of Nietzschean ideals were a "reversion to barbarism" and the antithesis to Christianity.[36] The *Outlook*, the most popular postmillennial publication in the United States, took a somewhat premillennialist stance in an article that identified Nietzsche as the source of Germans' self-centered religion. The writer portrayed Nietzsche's theory about a race of "supermen" as a misguided mixture of natural selection and eugenics (the theory that regulating human breeding can limit the incidence of undesirable traits). Nietzsche and the German people believed that "supermen will have world control" and "will replace God" after weaker races that could not contribute to the new un-Christian code of morality died off. The Teuton would be left only with itself to worship. The destruction of Christianity and the breeding of supermen, the *Outlook* concluded, was the aim of the German war effort. "The war of the Huns against civilization" was "Nietzsche in action."[37]

Although he did not cite German vanity or physical traits, Henry A. Wise Wood, the chairman of the secular Conference Committee on National Preparedness, found German religion to be simultaneously backward and modern. Wood described the war as a Darwinian struggle "for mastery" between "a civilization that is the legitimate outgrowth of Christianity, expressive of kindliness, good faith, and democratic tolerance" on one side and "a reincarnation of ancient barbarism, weaponed stealthily by modern science behind a mask of Christ, which has sprung suddenly to the world's conquest" on the other side. Put more simply, "the old morality" ("the barbaric conception of rule by force alone") was again challenging "the new" ("the spiritual power enthroned by Christ"). Christendom faced a "modern crusade" to disarm the destructive infidel, Wood proclaimed. His description of the postwar world, however, alluded to both the postmillennial Kingdom of God and premillennial distrust for modernism and evolution. Victory, he concluded, meant "humanity will ascend to undreamed-of heights of opportunity and freedom." But defeat would bring the rule of "soulless scientific barbarism" that "blasphemously feign[ed] the approval of God to palsy a trustful Christendom."[38]

Few spoke of Germany's apparently evil aims and actions as apocalyptically and with as much vitriol as the professional-baseball-player-turned-revivalist-preacher Billy Sunday. Sunday was a premillennialist and the most popular minister in the United States. According to one biographer, "Sunday likened the Second Coming to the imminent but unpredictable arrival of a 'Bank Inspector'" because "nothing else does so much to 'keep us right.'"[39] The timing of Christ's return was not the only disagreement Sunday had with Christian liberals. Christianity was not about "godless social service nonsense," he preached, but about saving individual souls and a literal interpretation of the Bible.[40] Through his theology, crusades against alcohol, and flamboyant preaching style, Sunday had become easily the most well-known religious figure in the United States, his popularity peaking during a long revival in New York City in April and May of 1917.[41] Peter Clark MacFarlane of *Everybody's Magazine* wrote that Sunday drew much larger crowds than Woodrow Wilson or Theodore Roosevelt did, arguably the two most prominent Americans of the time.[42]

Like most Midwesterners, Sunday, a native Iowan, had little use for the war prior to April 1917, rarely discussing it in his sermons except to rejoice that the United States was not involved. Yet once Congress declared war, he began defining the conflict as a battle of good versus evil. Sunday became as much a propagandist as a preacher, consistently portraying the conflict as an opportunity to wage holy war against the forces of wickedness.[43] For Sunday and his followers, the war was not holy because it would usher in the Kingdom of God. Instead, the war was Satan's way of testing the nation's faith and, thus, a chance to prove that Anglo-Saxons were, in fact, God's chosen people and that the United States personified Christ's teaching. Despite pronouncing early on that the United States was fighting Prussian autocracy and not the German people, for most of the conflict Sunday offered no redemption to the German nation. "All this talk about not fighting the German people is a lot of bunk," Sunday exhorted in a February 1918 sermon. They had rejected Christianity and become the Devil's minions. For Sunday, the war was very black and white. "I tell you it is [kaiser] Bill against Woodrow, Germany against America, Hell against Heaven," he explained. "Germany lost out when she turned from Christ to Krupp [a major German arms manufacturer] and from the Cross of Calvary to the Iron Cross." Sunday even quipped that "if you turn hell upside down you will find 'Made in Germany' stamped on the bottom." The revivalist also occasionally revealed a tinge of racial nationalism in his invective, once referring to the German people as a "weazen-eyed, low-lived, bull-neck, low-down gang of cut-throats of the Kaiser." Sunday went so far as to suggest the Spanish influenza outbreak in 1918 was the work of the Satanic German nation while simultaneously citing the possibility of a German conquest of the United States. The epidemic "started over there in Spain when they scattered germs around," Sunday charged. "If they can do this to us 3,000 miles away, think of what the bunch would do if they were walking our streets."[44]

Billy Sunday's significance lies in the immense popularity that allowed him to share his staunch Christian nationalism with extremely large numbers of

Americans. Sunday's demonization of the kaiser and the German people, while similar to that of postmillennialists in its absolutist portrayal of each side's faith, was much harsher and unforgiving. Those who followed him on the "sawdust trail" likely left his sermons angry and more fearful of German victory than inspired by the chance to serve God. Sunday's stance, however, appears to have fit the national mood during the war more closely than postmillennial calls for a Kingdom of God that left room for a German nation that had the potential to progress beyond its paganism or Satanism.

The devilish depictions of the enemy Other emanating from newspapers, magazines, politicians, and pastors like Sunday notwithstanding, the point of most religious-based arguments was not to instill fear but to mitigate it. The muscular courage Christ exhibited while on earth was the model. Unlike pacifists and the cowardly, the argument went, Jesus did not back down when evil reared its head. When attacked, Christ stood his ground, forgiving his oppressors for whatever punishment they doled out. At the same time, nothing raised Jesus's ire more than attacks upon the innocent. Ministers and propagandists challenged Anglo-Saxons to do as the New Testament demanded and imitate the teachings and actions of Christ. Many believed that only those who subscribed to this definition of Christian courage, both for the individual and nation, would achieve victory over evil. The German Other, with its religious attachment to militarism, resembled the forces against which Christ fought during his lifetime. To oppose such an autocratic and spiritually backward force was to crusade in the name of God. The conflict in Europe did not mark the failure of Christianity. It signified its triumph.

When making their calls for muscular Christian courage, politicians, ministers, and propagandists presented the United States in much the same way as Germans depicted themselves: as the God-ordained liberator of a spiritually wayward world. No race was as fit for democracy and leading the world toward the millennium as the naturally freedom-loving Anglo-Saxon. While other advanced races also were capable of self-government, Christian nationalists, modernists, and premillennialists alike conceived of American democracy as the epitome of Christ's teaching. Framing Anglo-Saxon faith and mission as the binary opposites of those of the German, however, was indicative of a deep lack of self-awareness. Americans often used declarations of divine favor to justify a level of duplicity and brutality against Native Americans and imperial subjects that far outpaced that of German cruelty in Belgium and northern France. At the same time, during the Great War, Anglo-Saxons treated German claims to be God's chosen people as threatening to their own identity as Christ's torchbearers. In short, propagandists and ministers described competing notions of Manifest Destiny, one based in familiar and positive myths of the American past, present, and future, the other created from Anglo-Saxon fears and misconceptions of the German enemy Other.

Anglo-Saxon Americans began casting themselves as soldiers of the Almighty and the war as a postmillennial crusade from the very beginning of American belligerency. On the night of Wilson's call to arms on April 2, 1917, pastors opened both the Senate and House sessions with prayers that defined the soon-to-be-declared war in such terms. In the Senate, the pastor pleaded for God to give them the "wisdom and grace to . . . advocate the cause of righteousness . . . and seek the accomplishment of Thy purpose and the enlargement of Thy kingdom on earth." The prayer in the House session was similar. Wilson touched on the same themes in a more secular tone that evening in his war address. The United States was going to war "to vindicate the principles of peace and justice in the life of the world as against selfish and autocratic power." The American people would "fight for the things which we have always carried nearest our hearts—for democracy . . . for a universal dominion of right by such a concert of free peoples as shall bring peace and safety to all nations and make the world itself at last free." The next day, Treasury Secretary William Gibbs McAdoo wrote to the president, his father-in-law, to congratulate him for having "done a great thing nobly!" "I firmly believe it is God's will," McAdoo continued, "that America should do its transcendent service for humanity throughout the world and that you are [H]is chosen instrument." Similarly, Interior Secretary Franklin K. Lane claimed that the United States and the Allies represented "the world of Christ." Postmillennial visions also clearly affected many of the senators and representatives who voted for war on April 6, which, perhaps not coincidentally, happened to be Good Friday. For instance, Murray Hulbert, a congressman from New York, maintained that "Christ gave his life upon the cross that mankind might gain the Kingdom of Heaven, while to-night we shall solemnly decree the sublimest sacrifice ever made by a nation for the salvation of humanity, the institution of world-wide liberty and freedom."[45]

That God was allied with the United States was clear to many Anglo-Saxons outside of Washington. The best-selling novelist Harold Bell Wright proclaimed in the February 1918 issue of the popular *American Magazine*, "This, our nation, is a Christian nation. We, the people, are a Christian people." Wright described the holy war raging in Europe as Armageddon, as a "world-struggle for the divine rights of humanity" that threatened democracy, which he described as "the Christian principles of government, to which we owe our very national existence." Although Wright did not explicitly state that Germany followed Satan or the prodding of a false prophet, he suggested as much. The forces opposed to Christian democracy showed themselves to be "the enemies of humanity" through their bestial acts on land and sea. Teutons carried out their wicked exploits "with the same spirit that nailed the world's Saviour to a guide post where the roads to heaven, earth and hell corner" and were "fighting now to extinguish the fire [Jesus's] teaching kindled." The crusading United States, by contrast, had been spreading "the gospel of freedom and the divine right of humanity" across the world. Considering that Christ died to free humanity of its sins, it seemed natural that one could "see the man of Galillee in the trenches, shoulder to shoulder with his comrades who have drawn the sword of human liberty." In the ultimate struggle between Christian democracy and devilish militarism, Wright concluded, "the sword of America is the sword of Christ," the Anglo-Saxon's brother-in-arms.[46] White Americans' conception of God could be just as self-referential as that of the Germans.

Comparisons between the Anglo-Saxon's divine mission and the Teuton's pursuit of a false prophet's wicked ends resounded from pulpits across the United States as well. Presbyterian minister John H. Boyd of Portland, Oregon, claimed that before the country entered the war it had been clear to most Americans "that the real German . . . carried with him an atmosphere of intense self-esteem." Yet, since April 1917, Germany had been "unmasked." Unlike Anglo-Saxon egotism, which Boyd, to his credit, admitted was a problem, the German variety "strikes deeper" and "carries with it the sense of mission and destiny . . . that is to be realized by force if need be." Perhaps because they did not know that the United States had already been chosen for this purpose, the Prussian regime exploited Teutons' narcissism by instilling the belief "that they were the elect nation upon whom God had put the responsibility of the world's advancement and control." Because of the success of Prussian brainwashing, Boyd concluded, the kaiser and his subjects "ha[d] become a solidified, inseparable mass of purpose," thus implicating the entire German nation in the Prussians' apocalyptic drive for world domination.[47] A Presbyterian minister in Philadelphia saw the current conflict between democracy and autocracy as "a large factor for the bringing about [of] 'peace on earth among men of good will.'" It was the duty of the Christian warrior to ensure this progress toward the millennium was not stunted: "Woe betide the man or men who seek to establish the doctrine of 'might over right,' tyranny over liberty, and frightfulness over humanity." At the same time, Americans must be

sympathetic toward German soldiers because they could not be held responsible for their actions. "Let not our soldiers be misled . . . that they are only
fighting 'flesh and blood' enemies," the minister claimed. The rape, pillaging,
and plunder were "the works of the *devil in the Germans.*" The real fight was
against Satan, whom one could "resist with faith and prayer" as their only weapons.[48] That American soldiers had treated non-white Native Americans and
imperial subjects similarly was either ignored or conveniently forgotten.

In the *Outlook*, Lyman Abbott established one of the clearest dichotomies
between Anglo-Saxon and German spirituality in an April 1918 editorial in
which he argued that each nation's faith directly corresponded to its government. "Democracy" is more than a "mere form of government. It is a religious
faith . . . in a word, it is human brotherhood." The four tenets of democracy—
religious, industrial, educational, and political liberty—correlated with Scripture and were nowhere to be found in autocratic Germany. In the kaiser's
kingdom, individual freedoms were squashed, feudalism thrived, indoctrination trumped education, and the religion forced upon the German people was
"of a God imagined by Odin, not Jesus Christ." The United States was at war,
Abbott concluded, "in order to establish for humanity the right."[49] In an earlier
article, Abbott made a connection between Germans' egotism and their faith
in a false prophet while also neatly explaining the moral superiority of the
American cause. The editor-minister cleverly employed the most iconic figures
of Anglo-Saxon democracy and German autocracy to demonstrate the stark
difference in each nation's faith. First, Abbott cited an exchange between a
clergyman and Abraham Lincoln during the Civil War in which the minister
said that he hoped God was on the side of the Union. Lincoln reportedly replied, "That does not concern me; what concerns me is that we should be on
the Lord's side." Yet Kaiser Wilhelm, Abbott maintained, did not exhibit such
humility. In his Christmas 1917 speech to his troops, Wilhelm declared, "The
year 1917, with its great battles, has proved that the German people has in the
Lord of Creation above an unconditional and avowed ally on whom it can
absolutely rely." God, the Kaiser mistakenly believed, had chosen Germany, not
the other way around. Thus, "the difference between Abraham Lincoln and the
Kaiser is the difference between true and false religion, true and false faith."[50]

Although lacking the credibility of the clergy on matters of faith, the secular,
non-ordained propagandists of the Committee on Public Information offered
similar explanations of Germans' sense of Manifest Destiny while also ignoring
the double standard. In the pamphlet *Why America Fights Germany*, John S. P.
Tatlock wrote that "from the Kaiser on down, the Germans talk much of God

being with them; but it is not the God of the New Testament, nor the God of the Hebrew prophets." War itself, Tatlock claimed, was the primary object of Germany's devotion.[51] In another widely distributed CPI pamphlet, *Conquest and Kultur*, its editor, Guy Stanton Ford, similarly maintained that Germans worshipped a "war god to whom they have offered up their reason and their humanity." One example Ford offered for its apparent irony was a University of Berlin philosophy professor who touched on Germans' belief that they were God's true crusaders. "As for us we are truthful, our characteristics are humanity, gentleness, conscientiousness, the virtues of Christ," the professor maintained in language similar to Anglo-Saxon claims to Christian righteousness. "In a world of wickedness we represent love, and God is with us." Ford's interpretation of a German poet took a more direct tack, insinuating that Germans followed a false idol with an apocalyptic calling. "We execute God Almighty's will, and the edicts of His justice we will fulfill . . . in vengeance upon the ungodly," the poet allegedly wrote. "God calls us to murderous battles, even if worlds should thereby fall to ruins."[52] In an ad entitled "This Is Kultur," which was printed in several popular magazines, the CPI cited German atrocities as proof that the American war effort should be "a Crusade, not merely to win back the tomb of Christ [Muslim Turks had controlled the Holy Land prior to 1917], but to bring back to earth the rule of right, the peace, goodwill to men and gentleness He taught."[53]

The contrast between Germany's worship of a false prophet and the divine blessing of Anglo-Saxon democracy suggested to some Americans, pastors and laity alike, that the war in Europe could be Armageddon or at least a precursor to it. In an apocalyptic speech for the Liberty Loan in Madison, Wisconsin, former mayor Charles Elbert Whelan claimed the link between Anglo-Saxon democracy and Christianity was self-evident. Since God created Adam, "it was His ideal and purpose to make man equal before the law, His law," which had been reaffirmed in "that venerable document, the Declaration of Independence." But in Europe "the fight for God and Humanity is on" against the un-Christian forces of Germany, whose autocratic government did not acknowledge "God's cause: the liberty and equality of the peoples of the earth." Making the world safe for democracy would establish God's law in Europe, thus paving the way for the millennium. "For God and Humanity!" Whelan exclaimed. "Could the Stars and Stripes ever be carried on a holier mission?"[54] Pastor David James Burrell of the Collegiate Church in New York claimed that the conflict would bring "a more serious type of manhood and womanhood; a larger patriotism, measured by the brotherhood of man." Because of the war, "The gates are opening. The roads which Caesar builds for his advancing legions will furnish a highway for the Prince of Peace. Then onward, Christian soldiers, to the Golden Age!"[55] Philosopher and novelist Edgar Saltus saw the war through a more explicitly racial and millennial lens. Victory over Prussian autocracy, "as every white man hopes," would ensure "the beasts are crushed back into their sty" and "the joy of Christendom will be such that it may induce the Second Advent."[56] Germans, it would seem, were non-white obstacles to the realization of Christ's earthly reign.

As in most wars, peace through victory was the ultimate end for the European nations locked in mortal combat. Yet for the Christian United States, according to many editors, politicians, and ministers, peace was not the goal, but the means to an even greater end. Representatives of the League to Enforce Peace (LEP) professed their hope that the end of the Great War could spell the beginning of the millennium. The war must be won "at whatever cost of years or treasure or life," claimed Charles S. Medbury while speaking at an LEP conference in Philadelphia in May 1918. Victory would allow "the sum total of human interests [to] be advanced, war be beaten out of the world's life, and a new civilization established in harmony with the pattern shown us on the Mount." Allied and American soldiers risked and gave their lives on the Western Front, he concluded, "for the redemption of the world."[57]

Woodrow Wilson, however, did not immediately support the idea that the United States' war was a muscular crusade for Christian imperialism. His repeated calls before and after American intervention for a negotiated peace based on the concept of "peace without victory" posed a problem for those who viewed the war as a campaign to spread democratic Christianity and crush sinful German autocracy. Wilson's Presbyterian upbringing and belief in a covenant between God and His people accounted for his view that the Almighty and the United States shared a special bond. But before April 1917, Wilson did not see this relationship as a reason for entering the war. Instead, he argued that his country could best serve God and the world by remaining neutral and forging a just peace agreeable to all. But events would prove to Wilson that the passive Winthrop-like tactic of inspiring through example would not be enough to protect the United States or redeem the world in its darkest hour. Only after numerous German offenses, affronts, and U-boat attacks did he view neutrality and, much later, his hope for a resolution based in forgiveness as untenable.[58]

When given the chance to set the terms of the postwar world at Versailles during the Paris Peace Conference in 1919, Wilson displayed his activist postmillennial worldview to the world. Although making concessions to the French, British, and Italians to the detriment of his postwar agenda, which he famously listed in "Fourteen Points," the president would not budge on his desire for a League of Nations on which "nothing less than the liberation and salvation of the world" depended.[59] On his postwar tour of the Midwest and West to gain popular support for the ratification of the peace treaty and American membership in the League, Wilson explained to his audiences that freedom and Christianity had been synonymous since the beginning of time, even as autocrats battled against God's plan for mankind. The president said in a September 1919 speech in Oakland, California, that "when you look into the history not of our free and fortunate continent . . . but of the rest of the world, you will find that the hand of pitiless power has been upon the shoulders of the great mass of mankind since time began, and that only with that glimmer of light which came at Calvary that first dawn which came with the Christian era, did men begin to wake to the dignity and light of the human soul." Although tyrants often declared their faith in Christ, Wilson professed, "the great body of our fellow beings have been kept under the will of men who exploited them and did not give them the full right to live and realize the purposes that God had meant them to realize."[60] The spreading of democracy, therefore, moved the world closer to fulfilling God's true plan for mankind.

A large number of Anglo-Saxon Protestant Americans had viewed the conflict similarly, as a significant step, perhaps the final one, to universal peace, enduring freedom, and the Kingdom of God. Yet a lasting peace had been there for the taking in Paris, and the world's leaders had failed to grasp it. In the United States, Wilson's speaking tour and health failed (he suffered a debilitating stroke in October) as the Senate refused to ratify the Treaty of Versailles; the country never joined the League of Nations.[61] For those who in 1917 viewed the war optimistically, as a millennial crusade to forge a more perfect brotherhood of man, such failures rubbed salt in the still-fresh physical and psychological wounds resulting from the war. While those who commemorated the war dead in the years immediately following the conflict regularly cited their loved ones' courage and sacrifice as justification for their deaths, very few evoked Wilson's progressive internationalism, which suggests that some Americans' confidence in a looming brotherhood of man (or nations) had receded or disappeared entirely.[62]

The seeds of such disillusionment with earthly progress had been sown during the war. For one, progress—industrial capitalism and technological innovations in particular—had made the bloodbath in the trenches and in "no man's land" possible. At the same time, the war allowed the victorious and most powerful earthly kingdoms to expand their imperial domains and oppress their subjects as brutally as ever. Democracy also did not appear to be any safer because of the war, even in the United States. While most Americans were aware that the advance of civilization was not necessarily linear, the massive casualties, draconian wartime policies, and intolerance toward others during World War I signified to many that progress itself was sham. As a result, millions abandoned their conviction that the world was improving steadily toward the millennium and joined premillennialist churches in increasing numbers in the decade following the war.[63] In short, while postmillennialists had dominated the wartime argument, the war proved to many that their faith in mankind's inherent goodness was misplaced. War could bring out the worst in many people, even those in God's New Israel.[64]

Despite the cynicism of some over the war's failed promises, those who had defined the war effort as a righteous campaign undertaken by a virtuous race had honorable objectives—to free the world of tyranny and overcome citizens' hesitancy to fight, die, save, spend, and work to bring the conflict to a successful conclusion. The Christian modernist vision of spiritual progress and moral uplift were motive forces for Americans of all stripes and greatly affected their perceptions of their role in the conflict. At the same time, premillennialists and the secular press also depicted the war as a showdown between pure light and pure darkness, absolute good and absolute evil. An apocalyptic understanding of the conflict, evident in arguments for military preparedness and anxiety over the alleged German conspiracy against the United States, was as much a part of American life and culture in the early twentieth century as was citizens' reverence for democracy.

Despite the purity of their objectives, ministers and propagandists often mixed apocalyptic or millennial definitions of the American war effort with racialized conceptions of the enemy and themselves. This mixture only deepened the Othering of the German enemy, adding an explicitly religious component to explanations of their Otherness. According to much postmillennialist propaganda, Germans' religion and understanding of God were backward, more fitting for the barbarians on the ancient Roman frontier than for a well-cultivated people. It was not just that the kaiser and the German people had lost their way spiritually. While some generous ministers and propagandists argued Germans had been duped into following a false god, the simple fact that they had been fooled or brainwashed in the first place implied that the overwhelming influence of Prussianism had morally or racially degenerated the Teuton. It was the Prussian kaiser, after all, who freely or inadvertently partnered with Satan and was willing to sacrifice the lives of his people while doing the Devil's bidding. Conversely, Nietzsche's writings epitomized the self-idolizing and Darwinistic German monarchy and the poor souls it commanded. In other words, the Satanism, paganism, or Nietzscheanism believed to be endemic to Prussian militarism was further proof of Germans' primitive and degenerated state and established them as the enemies of Christ.

Yet the United States' role as global messiah—a central feature of Anglo-Saxon American identity for generations—also was grounded in racial nationalism and a sense of Manifest Destiny. Their belief in an inherent connection between Christianity, democracy, and Anglo-Saxonism conditioned many ministers and propagandists to define the nation's war effort as a holy mission to smite the enemies of God and regression. The United States was the closest manifestation on earth of Christ's teaching, many white Americans believed, and for this reason it was the nation's responsibility to lead the fight against backwardness and toward the millennium.

After the war, however, many militantly muscular Christians came to lament postmillennial wartime propaganda because of the hatred it brought out in others and the doubt it elicited in themselves. Although not an enthusiastic disciple of liberal Christianity, the theologian and second-generation German American Reinhold Niebuhr described the feelings of many postwar American Christians in 1928 when he wrote, "When the war started I was a young man trying to be an optimist without falling into sentimentality. When it ended and the full tragedy of its fratricides had been revealed, I had become a realist trying to save myself from cynicism." The war had taught Niebuhr that he could no longer equate the progress of "civilization with the kingdom of God." "Civilization was not a victory of the human spirit over nature," he learned. "It was only partly that. It was also the arming of the brute in man."[65] Although the war did not completely dampen the myth that the United States was God's instrument and white Americans His chosen people, it had shown that progress was not intrinsically positive and that war could have a regressive impact on all who fought or supported it.

Fear, Othering, and Identity in the Postwar United States

> There is a simplicity about hate that makes it peculiarly attractive to a certain type of mind. It makes no demand of the mental processes, it does not require reading or thinking, estimate or analysis, and by reason of its instant removal of every doubt it gives an effect of decision, a sense of well-being.
>
> GEORGE CREEL, 1920

> Voice or no voice, the people can always be brought to the bidding of the leaders. That is easy. All you have to do is tell them they are being attacked, and denounce the peacemakers for lack of patriotism and exposing the country to danger. It works the same way in any country.
>
> HERMANN GOERING, April 18, 1946

The Great War's end "came swiftly, suddenly, and completely," according to *Current Opinion*.[1] New York on November 12, 1918, was a city on holiday as schools, banks, and offices closed in celebration of the previous day's signing of the armistice that abruptly ended Europe's Armageddon. The streets flooded with jubilant Americans waving flags, kissing strangers, and celebrating their country's triumph over the regressive forces of autocratic militarism.[2] Yet the sudden and surprising conclusion of the war deprived the American people of a catharsis or true sense of finality. Was the world now safe for democracy? Could foreign enemies still be plotting? Were wartime excesses justifiable? What lessons can be learned from the experience? Americans began debating these questions in the years immediately following the war and continued to do so over the next century. Fear of the foreign boogeyman, and the use and abuse of that fear, has been and continues to be an ever-present aspect of American life since the First World War.

The Othering of the German people, however, proved to be unsustainable. In regards to the enemy overseas, the kaiser's abdication and the creation of a democratic republic invalidated arguments that the Teuton had regressed so far as to be incapable of civilized government. The Treaty of Versailles also left the new Germany toothless through war reparations and by greatly limiting the size and scope of its military. On the wartime home front, anti-German sentiment actually played a significant role in the American Teuton's rehabilitation. Amidst the fear-inspired hyperpatriotism and crusade for a homogenous "100 percent American" society, most German Americans could not celebrate their ethnic identity—their culture, traditions, or language—without threat of reprisal or ostracism. Consequently, four years of suspicion and coercion accelerated American Teutons' assimilation into Anglo-Saxon American culture. At the same time, throughout the entire decade of the 1910s, American Teutons, especially those born in the United States, already had been finding multiple avenues of self-identification outside of their ethnic background, such as religion and popular culture. In reality, the un-Americanized German Other that Anglo-Saxons so feared had been slowly becoming an endangered species by the time the war started. With the passing of the wartime frenzy and gradually diminishing credibility of pseudoscientific views of whiteness, it became clear to most Anglo-Saxons by the 1920s that what had made Teutons a race of Others no longer applied.[3] One interesting example of this from fiction is the mystery surrounding the fabulously wealthy Jay Gatsby in F. Scott Fitzgerald's 1925 classic *The Great Gatsby*. Rumors that Gatsby enjoyed such infinite wealth because "he's a nephew or cousin of Kaiser Wilhelm's" or was "a German spy during the war" do not deter partygoers from his estate but attract them there instead.[4] That Germans could lose their Otherness at all, let alone relatively quickly, speaks both to how exceptional their Othering during the Great War had been and the degree to which international trauma can alter a nation's conception of another people's motives and capabilities.

In the short term, however, many white Americans had difficulty coming down from their wartime fever. As the pertinence of the Teuton's imperialist conspiracy and Otherness diminished, the primary target of American fear quickly and smoothly transitioned from Prussianism to Bolshevism, a danger deemed equally hostile, conspiratorial, degenerate, and undemocratic. Late in the war and for a short period after the armistice, commentators defined the world perils of Prussianism and Bolshevism as two sides of the same coin. In this paradigm, Russian Bolsheviks were the kaiser's pawns, while anti-war socialists and members of radical labor groups in the United States, many of whom were foreign-born, were the willing tools of both, thus lumping them all into the global German conspiracy. It did not matter, or perhaps too few cared to notice, that the Socialist Party of America (SPA) and the Industrial

Workers of the World (IWW) were fundamentally opposed to autocracy and militarism. Hundreds of moderate and radical socialists became political prisoners under the Espionage Act, their sedition and plotting against the draft supposedly providing aid and comfort to the German enemy.[5]

The nearly seamless conversion of American fear from German militarism to Bolshevik radicalism during the first Red Scare suggests that the successful conclusion of the war did little to cool many Americans' concerns about the prospect of foreign subjugation and the precariousness of Anglo-Saxon identity. The shifting of the role of chief Other from the Teuton to the Bolshevik occurred rather smoothly in part because factors similar to those which brought on the wartime Othering of the German were also at work regarding the Russian radical. Russians were understood to be an uncivilized race, and the undemocratic and degenerate ideology of Bolshevism, like Prussian militarism and the tsarist autocracy that preceded the communist takeover, was a manifestation of their primitive nature. The longstanding anxiety among Anglo-Saxons of radical working-class revolution, which had brought the Bolsheviks to power in Russia, had been a primary catalyst of the turn-of-the-century nativism that had been directed toward Teutons during wartime. Finally, the potential success of Bolshevism in the United States was said to promise apocalyptic consequences for American democracy and capitalism, hallmarks of Anglo-Saxon identity.

While concerns that the tandem of Russian Bolshevism and German militarism were plotting to dominate the United States and the world were entirely imaginary, the two had formed a temporary working relationship in Europe. The German government facilitated the return of the exiled Vladimir Lenin to St. Petersburg in April 1917. In November, Lenin's Bolsheviks seized power from the republican Provisional Government before signing the Treaty of Brest-Litovsk four months later, which ended the war on the Eastern Front in March 1918 and allowed Germany to move fifty divisions to the West.[6] The treaty and its repercussions on the battlefield added fuel to suspicions that Lenin, his compatriot Leon Trotsky, and the new Bolshevik government were the kaiser's partners in crime. Three weeks after the treaty was signed, the *Chicago Tribune* maintained that Bolshevism and German imperialism were one and the same. "Side by side march Hindenburg and Lenine, Ludendorf [sic] and Trotsky, over the torn bodies of republicans. The kaiser intends to impose kultur upon the world by force. The Bolsheviki intend to impose communism upon the world by force. They are allies against republicanism. One attacks it from without. The other attacks it from within."[7]

Political cartoonists also depicted the Bolshevik and German threats as indistinguishable, both being uniquely skilled in undermining American unity and wreaking death and destruction on civilized society. In April 1918, the *Chicago Tribune* published a cartoon of a socialist supporter of "Immediate Peace" walking through a tilled garden labeled "US" while dropping the seeds of "Sedition," which he carries in a sack around his neck. To his left on a wooden fence hangs a picture of the same man committing the same dastardly act in a garden marked "Russia," the only differences being his hat, a banner identifying him as a Bolshevik, and that his bag reads "Immediate Peace" instead of "Sedition." Uncle Sam, however, is aware of the plot and ready to club the militarist-socialist agent in the United States with a twenty-year prison sentence. The misspelling in the cartoon's heading, "Sowing Seeds that 'Germanate,'" was no typographical error (fig. E.1).[8] Rollin Kirby's rendering in the *New York World* of the danger of Bolshevism mimicked the theme of regression found in depictions of the apish, Prussianized German that terrorized the occupied territories in Europe. In his September 1918 cartoon entitled "Cain," a large, ogre-ish "Bolsheviki" with disheveled hair, peasants' clothing, and an unsettling expression walks away from a burning village, leaving those he murdered with his large bloody dagger scattered behind him (fig. E.2). The figure and the destruction he wrought is an unmistakable charge of Bolshevik savagery, reveals the apocalyptic consequences of Bolshevism run amok, and implicitly identifies Bolshevism with the mad German brute of wartime cartoon and poster art.

After the armistice, the press and influential Americans continued to present the Bolshevik menace in the same manner in which wartime propagandists had shown the German Other, perhaps because they knew no better way in which to describe the danger. The *New York Globe*, for instance, defined Bolshevism as "antidemocratic and autocratic" and "aggressive," all words that propagandists had routinely used to describe the German people and the kaiser's now-defunct regime. Some trusted public voices, like Frank H. Simonds of the *New York Tribune*, even warned of the possibility of renewed conflict, with the wartime Allies facing an alliance of Red Russia and a Bolshevik Germany, thus giving the dictatorship of the masses control over the dreaded *Mitteleuropa*.[9]

Attorney General A. Mitchell Palmer described the Bolshevik plot in the United States in terms almost identical to what many had used to explain the alleged plot to Germanize the United States from within—as a threat to American institutions and thus to Anglo-Saxon identity. The year 1919, Palmer

Figure E.1. "Sowing Seeds that 'Germanate,'" cartoon, *Chicago Tribune*, April 3, 1918.

Figure E.2. "Cain," cartoon, *New York World*, September 11, 1918.

claimed in early 1920, had been a particularly harrowing time: "Like a prairie-fire, the blaze of revolution was sweeping over every American institution of law and order." It had infiltrated American homes, churches, and schools, while morally "burning up the foundations of society." This revolutionary, immoral, and criminal campaign, Palmer claimed, was the work of a subversive band of aliens loyal not to the Stars and Stripes but to the banner of a foreign, tyrannical, undemocratic, and degenerate ideology. This menace to Anglo-Saxon democracy, though, was not German militarism but Bolshevism, or as Palmer put it, "the creed of any criminal mind." Like the wartime German conspiracy within the United States, the Bolshevik "criminal aliens" intended to place "the horror and terrorism of bolsheviki tyranny" that had wrecked Russia "in the place of the United States Government." The arrests and deportations that the Department of Justice had carried out to that point, though effective, had not stemmed the red tide completely. Palmer hoped "that American citizens will, themselves, become voluntary agents" for the DOJ "in a vast organization for mutual defense against the sinister agitation of . . . aliens, who appear to be either in the pay or under the criminal spell of Trotsky and Lenine." The nation was in "great need of [a] united effort to stamp it [Bolshevism] out," Palmer concluded. As was the case with the scourge of German agents, this task was too great for the DOJ to handle alone.[10]

Much of the clamor over Germany's alleged ties to labor radicals in the United States and Russia was based in Anglo-Saxon Americans' assumptions about the backwardness of southern and eastern European races, lingering anxiety over the inauspicious consequences of Teutonic Otherness, and apocalyptic concerns over their own racial-cultural vulnerability. Although the record number of striking workers in 1919 and the occasional anarchist bombing showed that the radicalism of decades past was alive and well, investigators found little reliable evidence of an imminent revolution in the United States or of a German–Bolshevik compact.[11] For many an Anglo-Saxon, however, actual proof of the connection was unnecessary, because the Others' inherent traits betrayed their behavior and temperament. Un-American and undemocratic forces, many believed, continued to strive for control of the United States.

Although the Great War had ended the threat of Germanization and regressive militarism, the racial undertones of the Red Scare suggested that apocalyptic nativism was growing more severe as the Anglo-Saxon United States moved into the 1920s. One of the most impactful and extreme expositions on the "race problem" and its threat to Anglo-Saxon identity may have been

Madison Grant's *The Passing of the Great Race*, which was written in 1916 but did not reach its peak influence until the early 1920s. Although completely unqualified to offer such a pointed analysis (he considered himself an amateur zoologist), Grant believed the country's reliance on cheap foreign labor and a romantic attachment to the "melting pot" theory left the Anglo-Saxon race vulnerable to extinction. "There exists today a widespread and fatuous belief in the power of environment, as well as of education and opportunity to alter heredity," he charged. A good environment allowed a race "to achieve its maximum development but the limits of that development are fixed for it by heredity and not by environment." Humanitarian reform and Americanization, therefore, were a waste of time. To rescue the Anglo-Saxon race from its misguided tolerance of the biologically inadequate, Grant prescribed sterilization, euthanasia, and an end to "sentimentalism." If Anglo-Saxons did not wake up soon, their country and identity would be lost to them forever. "If the Melting Pot is allowed to boil without control and we continue to follow our national motto and deliberately blind ourselves to all 'distinctions of race, creed, or color,' the type of native American of Colonial descent will become" a thing of the past.[12] Even more apocalyptic than Grant was eugenicist and Harvard Ph.D. Lothrop Stoddard, who wrote in his 1920 treatise *The Rising Tide of Color against White World Supremacy* that war, immigration, and interracial breeding had deteriorated the great white races of the world, leaving them easy prey for the "colored races" in an imminent global race war.[13]

Although it is unlikely that a majority of white Americans shared Grant's and Stoddard's extreme racial views, the passage of the Johnson-Reed National Origins Act in 1924 embodied the durability of the fear that allegedly inferior races threatened to take over the country and bring about the forced degeneration of the Anglo-Saxon race. The law severely restricted the influx of aliens from the backward corners of Europe while completely cutting off Asian immigration. Its impact was immediate. In 1925, only one-seventh of the total number of southern and eastern European newcomers in 1924 were allowed into the United States. It was no coincidence that at this time membership in the Ku Klux Klan, whose aversion to ethnic and social diversity mirrored that of the wartime period, jumped to anywhere between two million to five million.[14] The Johnson-Reed Act, the slew of state eugenics and sterilization statutes passed in this period, and the dramatic resurgence of the Klan grew from many Anglo-Saxon Americans' persisting desire for cultural homogeneity. The war against German militarism and its Bolshevik allies impeded the progress of ethnic and cultural tolerance and convinced many Americans that limiting contact with the problems and depravities of the wider world was the best way to assure their long- and short-term security.[15]

While the continued acceptance of virulent scientific racism suggested that popular notions of hierarchical whiteness were more entrenched than ever, the latter half of the 1920s saw a drastic shift in American nativism and racism. For one, with far fewer "undesirables" arriving on American shores, thanks to the wartime drop off in immigration and the new restriction law, the fears of Grant, Stoddard, and the Ku Klux Klan appeared less valid, and critics could more easily lampoon them as ignorant and intolerant. Again, Fitzgerald's *The Great Gatsby* offers an instructive example. In this instance, Daisy and Miss Baker openly mock Tom Buchanan as he preaches to Nick Carraway about the superiority of the "Nordics," of which he had learned from reading "'The Rise of the Colored Empires' by this man Goddard" (perhaps a mix of Grant and Stoddard).[16] Furthermore, with the natural population increase of second-generation white non-Anglos and the "Great Migration" of hundreds of thousands of African Americans out of the South, commonalities among whites became more salient in the North and West, while black–white segregation became the most pressing racial issue in the United States. As whites focused less on their differences, the cultural relativist theories of academics like Franz Boas, Otto Klineberg, and Ruth Fulton Benedict—that biology did not determine cultural differences—surpassed the biological determinism of Grant and Stoddard in the public mind. Finally, the Great Depression not only had a leveling impact on American society, but it also forced the federal government to pursue policies sympathetic to the working class, in which white non-Anglos were heavily represented. Despite blonde-haired, blue-eyed whiteness remaining the physical ideal, by the 1940s white Americans were far less afraid of each other than they were of the "Negroid" and "Mongoloid" races at home and abroad.[17] In short, American identity was no longer limited to "Anglo-Saxons" and those who closely mimicked Anglo-Saxon lifestyle and culture.

Immediate postwar concerns for democracy, however, were not all based on notions of race and whiteness. As Americans began to move past the German-specific hysteria of the period, some looked back on wartime propaganda with regret and cynicism.[18] Walter Lippmann was inspired by his experience producing propaganda for the US Army to offer a very pessimistic postwar critique of the future of American society and democracy. In 1922, Lippmann wrote in his treatise *Public Opinion* that the impact of wartime propaganda on Americans' actions and attitudes exposed their inability or unwillingness to formulate a vision of the world based on reason or facts.

Instead, he argued, people understood the relationship between events solely from "the pictures in their heads." The problem was that "the real environment is altogether too big, too complex, and too fleeting for direct acquaintance. We are not equipped to deal with so much subtlety, so much variety, so many permutations and combinations. And although we have to act in that environment, we have to reconstruct it on a simpler model before we can manage it." That reconstruction, however, was based solely on the information that the individual could or wished to access. Wartime propaganda had shown that those who understood this aspect of human nature and controlled the public's access to information could easily manipulate their audience's inner "pseudo-environment." Because of advances in mass communication and the lessons learned from the war, Lippmann lamented, "the manufacture of consent" had "improved enormously in technic [sic]." Democracy, which the United States had gone to war to defend, would never be the same. "It is no longer possible . . . to believe in the original dogma of democracy; that the knowledge needed for the management of human affairs comes up spontaneously from the human heart."[19]

Few faced more criticism for their role in the manufacturing of consent than George Creel. Late in the war, Creel began what would be his typical postwar line of defense. In a letter to *New York Evening Post* editor Thomas Lamont in late October 1918, Creel argued that "the greatest danger now facing the country is the present campaign of hate," a movement in which he claimed to have played no part. "I have always stood for free speech, for free opinion, against chauvinism and against base passions," he declared.[20] After the war, the former Committee on Public Information chief continued blaming others for wartime excesses. In his 1920 memoir of the CPI's activities, Creel contended that government propaganda was not responsible for wartime hysteria and nativism. "People generally, and the press particularly," were in a frenzy that manifested as "an excited distrust of our foreign population." Echoing his letter to Lamont, the ex-CPI head maintained that the fault laid with "a percentage of editors and politicians [who] were eager for a campaign of 'hate' at home." As he had during the war, Creel defended the CPI's work as having been grounded in truth. "Our effort was educational and informative throughout," Creel explained, "for we had such confidence in our case as to feel that no other argument was needed than the simple, straightforward presentation of facts."[21] He did not deny that his job was to manufacture consent. But to him, the CPI's work of informing the country of the nation's predicament did not weaken democracy. It served and protected it.

By the time of the Second World War, few Americans looked back at Creel's CPI as a credible source of facts or fairness. By contrast, American propaganda during World War II was often more muted than it had been a generation prior. The Office of War Information (OWI), the Franklin Delano Roosevelt administration's version of the CPI, was careful not to rile up the kind of frenzy that Creel and others had enflamed. While both the OWI and CPI purported to be the purveyors of "truth," the eras in which they operated shaped their messages. Propagandists during World War II rarely singled out German or Italian Americans as a race of potential spies, subverts, and enemy Others. Instead, their loyalty was championed far more often than it was questioned, and their Old World relatives were seen as having been duped by the charlatans Adolf Hitler and Benito Mussolini instead of being inherently brutal or evil. That most Americans found Nazi racism toward Jews and other white nationalities so repugnant speaks to the degree to which the old theories of Edward Ross, Madison Grant, Lothrop Stoddard, and Henry Fairfield Osborn had lost favor with Anglo-Saxon Americans.[22] While Lippmann viewed propaganda from the First World War as a discouraging sign of what democracy had become, the Roosevelt administration saw it as a Pandora's box that, if reopened, must be carefully controlled for the sake of maintaining democracy.

Yet race and millennialism still significantly affected how Americans viewed their enemy in the Pacific. Racialized depictions of the Japanese were a chip off the old fearmongering block. Compared to the process of Othering the Teuton a generation earlier, characterizing the Japanese people as racial Others was much easier for white Americans because of the starker differences in physical appearance and culture. Unlike the German foe from 1917 to 1918, before the Pearl Harbor attack white Americans had consistently viewed the Japanese enemy as a non-white alien people whose biology and culture established them as a subordinate race and the antithesis of white, western, Christian civilization. That Americans continued to view the Japanese through a similar prism as late as the trade wars of the 1980s, despite Japan having become a close political ally, speaks to the durability of non-white and non-western Otherness.[23] Although Teutonic Otherness was short lived, that white Germans were Othered just as intensely during the First World War as the non-white Japanese would be during the Second indicates how portrayals of a wartime enemy as an apocalyptic, existential threat to one's nation and family can shape a people's conception of race and identity.

Although demagoguery against destructive foreign Others and influences was relatively restrained throughout the remainder of the twentieth century, anxiety over the fragility of American identity continued to arise episodically during the Cold War with the Soviet Union. In a manner similar to the spy craze during the Great War, from the late 1940s to the mid-1950s, members of the House and Senate, most notably Wisconsin Senator Joseph McCarthy, and like-minded Americans fingered thousands of individuals, often with scant evidence, as being secret agents of the Soviet Union sent to undermine the country's democratic institutions. While few Americans directly participated in this second Red Scare, they had little problem with the purging of suspected communists from the nation's institutions. American nervousness and red-baiting continued into the 1960s when some reactionaries claimed that the African American bid for legal and political equality was a communist plot to undermine American identity and destabilize the United States by flipping the racial hierarchy on its head.[24]

Cries that the sky was falling because of dangerous outsiders and ideologies were not uncommon in the political discourse of the post–World War II United States, but the level of nationwide paranoia of the early twenty-first century, like that of a century earlier, has been in many ways exceptional. In the years since the terrorist attacks on the World Trade Center and Pentagon on September 11, 2001, the presumed Otherness of the Islamic world has been at the center of American political discourse. Muslim Othering, like that of Japan during the Second World War, was not unique in that for centuries the West had viewed the Middle East as a mysterious land filled with an exotic people and culture.[25] Yet the actions of fanatics, who make up a very tiny portion of the world's Muslims, led many Americans to fear most, if not all, Muslims, as well as the Islamic faith, which some commentators often described as a backward, even barbaric religion. Suicide attacks, many Americans believed, were the manifestation of that barbarism and Muslims' Otherness.

The federal government and the news media did not help matters, often asserting that Islamic terrorists could be anywhere, preparing to pounce on unsuspecting targets just like the German saboteurs who came before them. Although incidents of anti-Muslim violence were rare and largely condemned, Americans took warnings of unseen and impending foreign attacks seriously, just as they had during World War I. In early 2003, for instance, the Department of Homeland Security advised Americans to stock up on duct tape and rolls of plastic sheeting to cover their doors and windows in the event of a biological, chemical, or radiological terror attack, because "in the first 48 to 72 hours of an emergency, many Americans will likely have to look after themselves." In less than a day, anxious Americans had bought out local hardware stores' supplies of duct tape and plastic, neither of which are radiation proof.[26] Local authorities also were on alert. In 2005 the police chief of a small Maryland town of 1,400 convinced the Department of Homeland Security to pay for and install surveillance cameras around the town hall. According to the chief, the cameras were necessary because "you can't ever tell" if terrorists may pass through his sleepy town on the way to their target. DHS also installed cameras in bingo parlors throughout Kentucky to protect patrons from Islamic fanatics.[27]

At times, concerns over foreign influence or attacks were particularly strange. Similar to laws banning the teaching of the German language due to fear of Germanization, sixteen states have passed laws banning Sharia law—the rules in the Koran by which God regulates the private and political lives of Muslims—because of fears that the religious code aims to make Islam the supreme religion of the world.[28] In 2012, a county judge in Lubbock, Texas, publicly warned that the reelection of President Barack Obama, who many of his more extreme political opponents had claimed was a closet Muslim, and his inevitable usurpation of the Constitution would spark a civil war, which would lead the president to call in foreign troops from the United Nations to crush the freedom-loving and patriotic opposition.[29] Two years later, in a story that mirrored many of the rumor-based tales from 1917 of a German invasion across the Mexico–Texas border, a Texas sheriff warned on Fox News that an unidentified source had given him "an intelligence report that said that there were ISIS [Islamic State of Iraq and Syria] cells that were active in Juarez [Mexico]." When the anchor asked whether an invasion was imminent, the sheriff replied, "We have found copies, or people along the border, have found Muslim clothing, they have found Quran books that are laying on the side of the trail. So we know that there are Muslims that have come across, have been smuggled in the United States." The Department of Homeland Security, like the federal investigators of a century earlier, could provide no evidence to corroborate this story.[30]

Although the breadth of American fear during the War on Terror has not been quite as extensive as it was during the Great War, the circumstances that created this anxiety and many Americans' conception of the Islamic enemy Other share much in common with the American experience a century prior. In both cases, the United States was either at war or confronting the threat of impending war. American fears, in part, were based in real events, be they sunken ships, sabotaged factories, or jetliners crashing into skyscrapers. Government officials and the press consistently depicted the enemy Other as lurking in the shadows or scheming abroad, prepared to pounce on Americans in their own backyards at any moment. Commentators presented the enemy's values as the binary opposite of those of Americans. Both Kaiser Wilhelm II and Osama bin Laden hated Americans because of their freedom. Only through war and by surrendering a portion of their civil liberties—such as through the Espionage Act and warrantless surveillance—could Americans remain safe from the enemy Other.

These types of anxieties were more widespread from 1914 to 1918 because the belief that the enemy Other posed an existential threat to the nation and to American (or Anglo-Saxon) identity was more deeply embedded in the culture of the period. The vast majority of Americans used race, religion, or both to explain why certain nationalities fell into a particular place in the social and economic hierarchy. These factors explained why evil existed in the world and must be conquered. They explained Protestant Anglo-Saxon cultural and political dominance in the United States. They explained the success of American democracy and capitalism. Most importantly, they explained the perceived upward but tenuous trajectory of American history. Few countries at the turn of the century embraced progress as tightly as the United States. Yet Anglo-Saxons did not feel that their continued supremacy was guaranteed. Apathy or subjugation by an inferior people, they feared, could undermine the stock of a great white race and reverse the progress of civilization and Christianity. Fearful Americans recognized this danger in depictions of German agents in the United States and decivilized Teutons on European battlefields.

Through every available means of communication, propagandists reinforced this message of vulnerability. The hundreds of editorials written and cartoons drawn, thousands of speeches uttered, millions of pamphlets and posters printed, and scores of films produced about the war and the enemy reflected Anglo-Saxon Americans' fears, while also ensuring that the message was as ubiquitous as the imagined German spy. Its repetition alone is partly responsible for Americans' willingness to register for the draft, conserve food, buy Liberty Bonds, punish those who refused to sacrifice enough or at all, and smoke out the alleged Teutonic agents and pro-German radicals working to undermine democracy. Patriotism, the desire for personal gain, moral outrage at German atrocities, and peer pressure clearly were important in motivating much American support for the war effort. Defining the war as one for the preservation of one's nation and identity, though, made the struggle against Prussianism intensely personal and was a crucial factor in generating the critical mass of support the Wilson administration needed to conduct and help win the Great War. To many white Americans, the war was not a means of saving democracy abroad. It was a way to preserve this aspect of Anglo-Saxon heritage for themselves and their children.

Yet World War I was an existential crisis for the United States beyond the cultural and physical threat many imagined Germany to be. It was also a defining moment when circumstances forced Americans to closely examine who they were as a nation. Was the United States an Anglo-Saxon republic, upholding the traditions and culture that originated in England? Or had the United States finally transitioned fully into something new—a country that had blended the best traits from the various races, nationalities, and cultures· into a body politic where one's abilities and character trumped his or her ethnic background? These questions remain with us today. Although definitions of "foreign" and "American" have changed over time relative to political, social, and economic circumstances, Americans' perception of the foreign Other as an agent of anti-democratic conspiracy and a threat to their way of life has not changed significantly since the Great War. And this, paradoxically, makes the often-overlooked period of the First World War important to twentieth- and twenty-first-century American history. The war offered the American people an opportunity to strip the foreign boogeyman of its power by embracing instead of scorning those aspects of their ever-evolving society that scared them the most. By failing to unite to exorcise those demons, Anglo-Saxon Americans helped ensure that future encounters with foreign phantoms would take on a similarly menacing shape.

Abbreviations

APL, FBI, NARA: Records of the American Protective League, Records of the Federal Bureau of Investigation, RG 65, National Archives, College Park, MD

CPI, NARA: Records of the Committee on Public Information, RG 63, National Archives, College Park, MD

DOJ, NARA: Records of the Department of Justice, RG 60, National Archives, College Park, MD

Gen. Corr., MID, NARA: General Correspondence and Reports, Records of the Military Intelligence Division, RG 165, National Archives, College Park, MD

MD, LOC: Manuscript Division at the Library of Congress

"Negro Subversion," MID, NARA: "Correspondence of the MID, Relating to 'Negro Subversion,' 1917–1941," Records of the Military Intelligence Division, RG 165, National Archives, College Park, MD

OGF, FBI, NARA: Old German Files, Records of the Federal Bureau of Investigation, RG 65, National Archives, College Park, MD

PAH: Pamphlets in American History, microfiche, Sanford, NC: Microfilming Corporation of America

PPS, MID, NARA: Plant Protection Section, Records of the Military Intelligence Division, RG 165, National Archives, College Park, MD

PRWB, CPI, NARA: Pamphlets in the Red, White, and Blue Series, Records of the Committee on Public Information, RG 63, National Archives, College Park, MD

PTE: *Patriotism through Education Series*, National Security League

PWW: *Papers of Woodrow Wilson*

Women's Defense Work, CND, NARA: Committee on Women's Defense Work, Educational Propaganda Department, Records of the Council of National Defense, RG 62, National Archives, College Park, MD

Introduction

1. "An Appeal to the American People," August 18, 1914, in *PWW*, vol. 30, 394.

2. Wilson quoted in Cecil Arthur Spring Rice to Edward Grey, September 3, 1914, in *PWW*, vol. 30, 472.

3. "Diary of Colonel House," August 30, 1914, in *PWW*, vol. 30, 462. Historian Ross Kennedy maintains that a combination of Wilson's assessment that European power politics were inherently unstable and his fear that its continuation would force the United States to militarize drove the president's desire for the collective security offered in the League of Nations charter. Kennedy, *Will to Believe*. Frank Ninkovich makes a similar case but discusses Wilson's concerns within the context of the future "domino theory." The president, Ninkovich argues, worried that a European power that controlled the resources of the Eurasian continent through invasion could eventually threaten the security of the United States. Ninkovich, *Modernity and Power*, 37–68.

While I do not dismiss the strategic reasons that Wilson may have had to fret over a possible future with Germany as European hegemon, I maintain that such concerns were based as much on his cultural assumptions as on a clear reading of European politics.

4. In his study of the impetus behind wartime conformity and the ways in which it affected local politics and social tensions, Christopher Capozzola argues that Americans compensated for the federal government's lack of administrative competence in 1917 by emphasizing volunteerism and patriotic obligation. As the pressures of wartime increased, leading local citizens turned to vigilantism and coercion to enforce patriotism, which inspired the federal government to take a more active role in disciplining dissenters. To Americans, Capozzola concludes, the war was an opportunity to reshape and reorder their communities. Capozzola, *Uncle Sam Wants You*. Gary Gerstle also focuses on the obligations of citizenship but examines the interplay between and the incompatibility of what he terms "racial nationalism" and "civic nationalism." In the first two decades of the twentieth century, he argues, Theodore Roosevelt's conception of race and civic responsibility shaped American conceptions of identity and citizenship. During World War I and into the early 1920s, this "Rooseveltian nation" became a disciplinary state that aimed to Americanize unassimilated immigrants and radicals while homogenizing American society through coercion, education, and strict immigration restriction laws. Gerstle, *American Crucible*. I suggest, however, that obligations of citizenship and community cannot be divorced from the overlying meaning of the war to a large portion of the populace—that the war was one of national, racial, and spiritual self-defense.

5. Higham, *Strangers in the Land*, 133–134. Scholars of white American identity formation rarely have discussed the Great War and, when they have, do so only in passing. John Higham's 1955 treatise remains the standard work on American nativism. Higham argues that "the Anglo-Saxon tradition," which "characterized the in-group directly, the alien forces only by implication," distinguished the period from 1860 to 1925. *Strangers in the Land*, 9. I have found, however, that at least during the First World War era, the identity of the out-group—in this case, Germans— was just as important to Anglo-Saxon Americans' wartime identity as their views about themselves. Propagandists' very specific descriptions of German Otherness show that Anglo-Saxon Americans' identification of these specific "alien forces" was not "by implication." They took a hard look at the Germans in Europe and the United States and drew conclusions that were contingent upon their self-defense and self-identification.

Matthew Frye Jacobson skillfully argues that conceptions of whiteness shifted in response to the needs of the labor market and perceptions of immigrants' biological unfitness for self-government. Jacobson, *Whiteness of a Different Color*. In a separate study, Jacobson focuses on the intersection of ideas on race, progress, and imperialism in the Gilded Age and Progressive Era. Jacobson, *Barbarian Virtues*. In neither book, however, does Jacobson address Anglo-Saxons' wartime views of Germans as racially regressed—or, in a sense, un-whitened—despite his argument that notions of "civilization" were central to white Anglo-Saxon identity and beliefs about democracy. In a similar vein, Nell Irvin Painter pays very little attention to how the whiteness dynamics of the war years may have affected the spike in racial nationalism in the early 1920s that she discusses in impressive detail and clarity. Painter, *History of White People*.

6. Higham, *Strangers in the Land*, 9–10; and Painter, *History of White People*, 201–206.

7. Strong quoted in Lears, *Rebirth of a Nation*, 108. It is important to point out that Strong, like most imperialists subscribing to the idea of the "white man's burden," did not view his race's dominance of its inferiors as a perpetually violent affair. Instead, racial hegemony came by way of imparting American "civilization" and institutions to the natives in the hopes that one day their race could progress to the same point (or at least close to it) as that of the dominant Anglo-Saxons.

8. Crook, *Darwinism, War and History*, 73–74; and Degler, *In Search of Human Nature*, 20–25. Proponents of Lamarckism also believed that static environmental conditions could produce

congenital behaviors in future generations that a modified setting could not alter out of existence. In other words, some races were stuck in their present position within the racial hierarchy.

Thomas Dyer explains how the connection between race and language guided Theodore Roosevelt's very influential understanding of an "American" race. Dyer, *Theodore Roosevelt and the Idea of Race*, 6, 37–44.

9. Weiss, "Racism in the Era of Industrialization," 135. By 1916, however, most academics viewed Lamarckism and other theories declaring that environment directly shaped racial traits as obsolete, and the general population was moving in that direction as well. Degler, *In Search of Human Nature*, 22, 92–93. Still, the vehemence of the wartime "100% Americanism" crusade suggests that Lamarckism remained a central component of Anglo-Saxon attitudes toward "un-American" immigrants into the war years and beyond.

10. Hatch, *Democratization of American Christianity*; and Stearns, *American Fear*, 66–74.

11. See Said, *Orientalism*; and Dower, *War without Mercy*, 311–317. In recent years, scholars have built off Said's work to not only expand on the idea of Other formation but also to show that the dichotomy between imperial masters and subjects was anything but absolute. Imperialism functioned to integrate cultures as much as to denote their differences. See, for example, Van der Veer, *Imperial Encounters*; Camayd-Freixas (ed.), *Orientalism and Identity in Latin America*; and Ballantyne, *Orientalism and Race*. I have found *Orientalism and War*, a collection of essays, to be very informative in its discussions of the interconnectedness of Orientalism and Othering in modern wars between West and East. Barkawi and Stanski (eds.), *Orientalism and War*.

12. Through the postwar Treaty of Versailles, however, the United States and the Allies did seek to keep Germany in a state of perpetual military and diplomatic weakness by imposing heavy war reparations, limiting the size of its armed forces, and not allowing it to join the League of Nations. Yet there is no indication, at least from what I have seen, that this was a consequence of continued German Othering after the war. These terms appear to have been strictly punitive and preventative.

13. Kristin Hoganson's approach to her sources—that she "takes rhetoric seriously, treating it as something that illuminates motivations, convictions, and calculations of what is politically efficacious"—in her work on the political rhetoric of masculinity in the late 1890s informed my understanding of wartime propaganda in the late 1910s. Hoganson, *Fighting for American Manhood*, 14.

14. Propaganda scholars have tended to fall into two categories—those who contend that propaganda is inherently dangerous and those who do not. One of the pioneers of propaganda studies, sociologist Harold Lasswell, firmly believed the former, arguing that wartime propaganda revealed the ease with which the populace could be manipulated "into one amalgamated mass of hate and will and hope." Lasswell, *Propaganda Technique in World War I*, 221. In the isolationist 1930s, Charles W. Smith echoed Lasswell's sentiments. Smith, *Public Opinion in a Democracy*. After the Second World War, psychologist Leonard Doob took an equally negative view of propaganda, maintaining that its purpose is to direct groups of people to act in ways that are not necessarily productive for the individual. Doob, *Public Opinion and Propaganda*. Randal Marlin stands out as an exception to the scholarship of the past thirty years, agreeing with Lasswell and Doob that propaganda produced to further political or commercial ends is a means of coercing people to believe or act in ways that could be detrimental to their personal interests. Marlin, *Propaganda and the Ethics of Persuasion*.

Over the past two decades most scholars of propaganda have challenged the contention that it is inherently harmful and manipulative. Garth S. Jowett and Victoria O'Donnell argue that propaganda falls along a continuum, from "white" (where the information "tends to be accurate") to "gray" (source may not be identified and the accuracy of information is uncertain) to "black" (the "big lie," in which the source and information are both false). Jowett and O'Donnell, *Propaganda and Persuasion*, 16–20, 154–170. Oliver Thomson also views propaganda as existing along a scale, but his measure is based on the emotionality of the material and not the degree of truthfulness. The most emotionally powerful propaganda, he explains, is grounded in fear but also offers ways in which individuals can overcome the emotion. Thomson, *Easily Led*, 2–3, 46–48. I have found this to be common in American propaganda during World War I.

My view of propaganda, at least in the case of the United States during the First World War, falls somewhere in between these lines of argument. I maintain that propaganda is manipulative in nature. Yet, those doing the manipulating do not necessarily seek personal gain or fulfillment. Most wartime propagandists believed they were working on behalf of, not against, the American people. Many of them believed that Germany posed a very real threat to the United States and that too many Americans were unaware of the urgency of the situation. Their manipulation of the American people, at least in the minds of wartime propagandists, was for the common good.

My interpretation is unique in that few historians of American propaganda during the Great War have adequately examined the American wartime mindset. Jörg Nagler argues that Americans' "search for identity" defined their experience with wartime propaganda. I contend, however, that their Othering of the German in propaganda was based on a firm understanding of what "Americanism" meant. Nagler, "Pandora's Box," 500. In his 1996 book, Stewart Halsey Ross appears to have been interested in improving on H. C. Peterson's earlier study of the same name. Both narrow their examinations mostly to the anti-German print propaganda that Anglophile publishers and patriotic organizations in the United States happily disseminated on behalf of Great Britain, and neither attempts to place propaganda within the context of contemporary culture. Ross, *Propaganda for War*, and Peterson, *Propaganda for War*. Celia Malone Kingsbury examines wartime propaganda's impact on the family, especially the ways in which it attempted to coerce women into supporting the war effort and idealized military service for boys. Kingsbury, *For Home and Country*. The two scholarly studies on the Wilson administration's Committee on Public Information (CPI) have focused mostly on the agency's origins and administrative structure. In 1939, James R. Mock and Cedric Larson argued that the CPI had a calming influence on American society, which the authors hoped would repeat itself in the event of another major war. Mock and Larson, *Words That Won the War*. Four decades later, Stephen L. Vaughn spoke to how the progressivism of CPI chairman George Creel and his department heads led the agency to rely on voluntary censorship and compliance with administration policies. Vaughn cites examples of CPI-produced propaganda that did not correspond to Creel's vision and blames the decentralized nature of the agency for the discrepancy. Vaughn, *Holding Fast the Inner Lines*.

15. For this book, I consulted the primary instruments of the mostly well-intentioned propaganda employed during the Great War: editorials, political cartoons, novels, posters, pamphlets, speeches, and, to a much lesser extent, films. The impact of the messages expressed through these mediums is extremely difficult to assess in an era before public-opinion polling. Although widely circulated opinion journals, such as *Literary Digest* and *Current Opinion*, regularly surveyed editorial views on the significant issues of the day, the dialectic between editorial and public opinion is often weighted too much on the side of the editor to be a genuine expression of public attitudes. With little reliable wartime survey data, a close observation of citizens' actions and whether they adopted the slogans of propaganda are the clearest, yet admittedly quite limited, means of reading public opinion and the influence a well-constructed propaganda campaign can have on it. To gauge behavior and attitudes, I have relied on the wartime investigative reports of the Military Intelligence Division, Department of Justice, and the Bureau of Investigation, along with letters from mostly middle-class Americans to George Creel, Wilson, and other high-level functionaries who had a hand in the creation of propaganda. These sources suggest that a significant number of Americans believed the messages in the propaganda were true, repeated and passed on those messages to others in their community, and acted on the fear and anxiety that such messages and ensuing rumors instilled. Although the letters and follow-up

investigations are but a small sampling of what the government received, the sheer volume of correspondence suggests that genuine fear of German dominance was not atypical or uncommon.

16. See Mitchell, *Danger of Dreams*, 33–35.

17. Herwig, *Politics of Frustration*, 13–39, 67–84; and Herwig and Trask, "Naval Operations Plans between Germany and the U.S.A., 1898–1913." Nancy Mitchell makes a very convincing case that bellicose German rhetoric directed toward the United States in the first fifteen years of the century did not match Germany's aims or actions. Mitchell's work effectively counters the argument, attributed chiefly to Herwig and Trask, that German imperialist bombast and contingency war planning against the United States were proof that Germany had imperial ambitions in the Western Hemisphere and was willing to invade the United States to realize them. The policy Germany actually implemented vis-à-vis the United States and the Americas, Mitchell contends, was decidedly passive and limited in its aims compared to some other European powers, most notably Great Britain. Mitchell also shows that Germany's war plans, which included invasion routes, were unfinished and not taken seriously by the German army brass. Mitchell, *Danger of Dreams*. For a balanced account of the kaiser's imbalance, see MacDonogh, *Last Kaiser*.

18. Mitchell, *Danger of Dreams*, 29–30, 35, 64–107.

19. See Joll, *Origins of the First World War*; and Clark, *Sleepwalkers*, for the most evenhanded treatments of the war's origins.

20. Stevenson, *Cataclysm*, 148–156; and Morrow, *Great War*, 135.

21. John Horne and Alan Kramer offer a well-documented accounting of German actions. They suggest that British and American propaganda, though exaggerated, did not misrepresent the truth as much as many scholars have assumed. Horne and Kramer, *German Atrocities, 1914*. Despite all the attention German actions against civilians on the Western Front received during and after the war, Russian atrocities and mass deportations in East Prussia and Galicia were just as significant (in regards to the number of deaths relative to the population), and the Austro-Hungarian army's (especially the Hungarian Honvéd's) slaughter of between 25,000 and 30,000 of its own Ukrainian subjects was by far the bloodiest massacre of civilians during the war outside of the Armenian genocide. Watson, *Ring of Steel*, 127, 148–157, 171, 177–179.

22. Quoted in Doenecke, *Nothing Less than War*, 225.

23. Doenecke, *Nothing Less than War*, 113–114, 130–133, 173–174.

24. See Preston, *Lusitania*.

25. See Gilderhus, *Diplomacy and Revolution*; and Finnegan, *Against the Specter of a Dragon*.

26. See Tuchman, *Zimmermann Telegram*; and Boghardt, *Zimmermann Telegram*.

27. For the best treatment of how voluntarism worked nationally, see Schaffer, *America in the Great War*. Capozzola shows how a more "coercive" form of voluntarism worked at the local level. Capozzola, *Uncle Sam Wants You*.

28. MacMillan, *Paris 1919*. John Milton Cooper's study is the definitive work on Wilson's failure to win ratification of the treaty and American membership into the League. Cooper, *Breaking the Heart of the World*.

29. "Deadly Statistics," LifeInsuranceQuotes.org, accessed August 28, 2016, www.lifeinsurance quotes.org/additional-resources/deadly-statistics. Reportedly, Americans face a one-in-twenty-million chance of being killed in a terrorist attack and a one-in-two-hundred-thousand chance of being crushed by an asteroid. The website LifeInsuranceQuotes.org compiled their fatality statistics from various federal agencies and non-profit organizations.

Chapter 1 · Identity, Decline, and Preparedness, 1914–1917

1. "Speech of Hon. W. L. Harding," in *Mid-West Conference on Preparedness* (Davenport, IA: 1915), 109, 110, PAH.

2. Bederman, *Manliness and Civilization*, 1–43. Aside from Bederman, my thinking on masculinity and its connection to ideas on race in this period have been greatly informed by the

works of John Pettigrew and E. Anthony Rotundo. Pettigrew contends that "de-evolutionary masculinity" grew from men's "will to power over women" and an abject fear of appearing effeminate in front of other men. This drive led proponents of enhanced masculinity at the turn of the twentieth century to employ "Darwinian biology to classify brutishness as an essential and natural male trait." Pettigrew, *Brutes in Suits*, 2, 3 8. Rotundo insists that popular conceptions of manhood at the dawn of the twentieth century corresponded with new notions of the "self" in which one's manly identity was directly related to his passions. In this atmosphere, white American men valued aggressiveness and strenuous exertion while scorning emotional and physical weakness. Rotundo, *American Manhood*. Also see Kulhman, *Petticoats and White Feathers*.

3. Leonard, "Red, White and Army Blue," 176–190. Respect for primitive characteristics and races had been evident within the US Army as far back as the 1860s. Despite orders to eradicate the Native American population on the frontier plains and whites' lopsided military victories, American soldiers' tenacity often did not measure up to that of their primitive adversaries as well as their officers would have liked.

4. Beard, *American Nervousness*, vi, 92; and Bederman, *Manliness and Civilization*, 14, 85–87. Most physicians at the time claimed that women also were susceptible to neurasthenia because the overtaxing nature of civilization left them with less energy to put toward being nurturing mothers. See Rotundo, *American Manhood*, 189–190.

5. Hall, "Corporal Punishment," *New York Education* 3 (November, 1899), 163, 164.

6. MacLeod, "Socializing American Youth to Be Citizen-Soldiers," 142. Michael C. C. Adams has argued that aggressive and violent team sports were meant as outlets for repressed sexual energy and to segregate the sexes both physically and culturally in both the United States and Great Britain. The ultimate goal of violent sports, Adams concluded, was to brutalize boys and crush their individuality in order to make them better future soldiers. Adams, *Great Adventure*, 36–45. Also see Putney, *Muscular Christianity*, 33–39.

7. William James, "The Moral Equivalent of War," *Popular Science Monthly*, October 1910, 408, 409.

8. MacLeod, "Socializing American Youth," 157–161; and Putney, *Muscular Christianity*, 113–116. Although "Rough Riders" and ardent preparedness supporters Theodore Roosevelt and Leonard Wood envisioned the BSA as a premilitary organization, few in the organization shared their fear of military impotency. The predominance of less militaristic scout leaders angered Roosevelt and led Wood to terminate his affiliation with the BSA. Despite his distaste for militarism, Jordan was a devout Anglo-Saxon supremacist. White, "War Preparations and Ethnic and Racial Relations in the United States," 118.

9. Bederman, *Manliness and Civilization*, 218–221, Burroughs quote at 220. Also see Nash, *Wilderness and the American Mind*, 156; Reesman, *Jack London's Racial Lives*, 75–86; and Jacobson, *Barbarian Virtues*, 130.

10. Adherents came at the issue of preparedness from a variety of angles. Many liberal progressives—such as John Dewey, Walter Lippmann, Hamilton Holt, and, eventually, Woodrow Wilson—supported increases in American military power in order to strengthen the United States' ability to define the eventual European and global peace on democratic and progressive terms. Some only desired a larger navy to protect American shores and commerce, while others rejected universal military training on practical grounds but supported moderate increases in the size of the regular army and National Guard. In fact, for most of the neutrality period, supporters of universal military training were a diverse minority among preparedness supporters, as some believed it could unite a socially fractured nation or bring order, discipline, and efficiency to immigrants and the working class. See Chambers, *To Raise an Army*, 73–124; Clifford, *Citizen Soldiers*, 36–37; and Finnegan, *Against the Specter of a Dragon*, 3–4. My argument here stands apart from these works in that I discuss some of the deeper cultural foundations that drove the preparedness debate into such a hyperbolic direction.

11. "Battle, Murder, and Sudden Death," *Forum*, September 1914, 468–472, quote from 468. Also see "How the War Affects America," *Literary Digest*, August 15, 1914, 253–257, which provides a snapshot of newspaper editorial opinion from around the country.

12. Quotes from Cooper, *Vanity of Power*, 23–24.

13. Theodore Roosevelt, "The World War: Its Tragedies and Lessons," *Outlook*, September 23, 1914, 170.

14. Cooper, *Warrior and the Priest*, 269, 289–290, Wilson quote from 269. Cooper lists Henry Cabot Lodge, Augustus P. Gardner, and Elihu Root as the key Republican opponents of Wilson's response to Germany. None of these men, nor Roosevelt, nor the pro-preparedness National Security League, however, seriously suggested publicly that the United States declare war on Germany over the *Lusitania*. Cooper also reports that only six of one thousand newspaper editors polled favored intervention after the sinking. Cooper, *Vanity of Power*, 33–34.

15. Theodore Roosevelt to Arthur Lee Hamilton, June 17, 1915, in *Letters of Theodore Roosevelt*, vol. 8, 938.

16. Theodore Roosevelt to Henry Cabot Lodge, June 15, 1915 in *Selections from the Correspondence of Theodore Roosevelt and Henry Cabot Lodge*, 459. In speeches and published writings, Roosevelt limited his charges of timidity mostly to Wilson and the so-called "peace at any price" crowd. See Roosevelt, *America and the World War*.

17. Leonard Wood, Diary, May 11, 1915, Papers of Leonard Wood, MD, LOC.

18. Leonard Wood, Diary, November 25, 1915, Papers of Leonard Wood, MD, LOC.

19. "Remember the Lusitania!," *New York Tribune*, November 13, 1915.

20. "Preparedness," *World's Work*, June 1915, 135. For more examples of newspaper opinion see "America's Response to Germany's Challenge," *Literary Digest*, May 22, 1915, 1197–1199. David Lawrence includes a poll of newspaper editors on the issue. Lawrence, *True Story of Woodrow Wilson*, 197–198.

21. Ward, "The Origins and Activities of the National Security League, 1914–1919," 52–56, 55n15. The ADS formed after separating from the NSL in August 1915 over the NSL's hesitancy to publicly criticize Wilson's foreign and military policies. Robert D. Ward described the ADS as "in essence the Republican branch of the League, avowedly anti-Wilson in its campaign for preparedness" (55). Because of his personal and political qualms with Wilson, Roosevelt identified more closely with the ADS than with the NSL, although he actively supported both. Also see Edwards, *Patriots in Pinstripe*.

22. S. Stanwood Menken, *Remarks of S. Stanwood Menken at the Dinner of the Engineer's Society of Western Pennsylvania, Pittsburgh, February 14, 1916* (New York: 1916), PAH.

23. Theodore Roosevelt, *National Duty and International Ideals: Speech of Theodore Roosevelt before the Illinois Bar Association at Chicago, April 29, 1916* (New York: 1916), PAH.

24. H. S. Howland, *Unpreparedness: An Address Recently Delivered before the Members of the Saint Nicholas Club of the City of New York* (New York: 1916), 10–13, 17–20, quotes from 17–18, 22, PAH.

25. Henry L. Stimson, *The Basis for National Military Training* (New York: 1917), PAH.

26. William Menkel, "The Plattsburg Response: A Citizens' Movement Toward Military Preparedness," *Review of Reviews*, September 1915, 303, 307. Apparently not understanding the economic strains such training would cause less affluent families, Theodore Roosevelt often bragged that he had sent his sons to train at Plattsburg while condemning those who did not as un-American and effeminate. Lane, *Armed Progressive*, 184–202. A few (of many) examples of articles and editorials supporting the camps or training in schools include "An Efficiency Expert on Defense," *Review of Reviews*, January 1915, 48; "The Plattsburg Idea," *New Republic*, Oct. 9, 1915, 247–249; "National Defense at Plattsburg," *Literary Digest*, August 21, 1915, 336–338 (on newspaper opinion across the United States); "Compulsory Military Training in Schools and

the National Need for Physical Preparedness," *Current Opinion*, August 1916, 115–117; and "Universal Military Training," *Outlook*, January 10, 1917, 60–61.

27. Finnegan, *Against the Specter of a Dragon*, 112–113.

28. Richard Wayne Parker, *The Common Defense: Speech of Hon. Richard Wayne Parker of New Jersey in the House of Representatives, February 17, 1916* (Washington: 1916), 12–13, PAH.

29. For a thorough treatment of the United States' ugly experience in the Philippine War as well as the anti-imperialist movement it helped spawn, see Miller, *Benevolent Assimilation*.

30. The secretary of war explained in 1884 that transporting a European invasion force powerful enough to defeat American forces and hold ground in the United States "would demand a large part of the shipping of all Europe." Military theorist John Bigelow would point out ten years later that even Great Britain, master of the seas, did not control enough shipping to move an army of half a million men across the Atlantic without going bankrupt. Most military theorists in the early twentieth century, though, chose to ignore such fact-based conclusions. Weigley, *American Way of War*, 168–169, 503n4, secretary's quote from 168. Also see Linn, *Echo of Battle*, 55–56.

31. Cleveland Moffett, "Conquest of America, 1921," *McClure's Magazine*, May 1915, 9–12, 85–86, 88. The novel was published as Cleveland Moffett, *The Conquest of America: A Romance of Disaster and Victory* (New York: 1916). Also see *The American Defense Society, Inc.* (New York: 1915), PAH, for a complete listing of the ADS's Board of Trustees. Moffett was a member of a select group of authors and poets known as "The Vigilantes" who came together to inspire the nation to support military preparedness and, later, the war effort. Edwards, "America's Vigilantes and the Great War, 1916–1918," 277–286.

32. Moffett, "Conquest of America, 1921," *McClure's Magazine*, June 1915, 35–38, 90.

33. Moffett, "Conquest of America, 1921," *McClure's Magazine*, Aug. 1915, 35–37, 54–55. Reviews of Moffett's story were mixed. A letter to *McClure's* editors from a man claiming firsthand knowledge of the military aircraft industries of the European belligerents declared that Moffett's tale "could not be more timely or more graphically correct." The writer asserted that Americans were apathetic to potential foreign military threats that could turn the country into "a subjugated people long before" it was capable of responding. C. M. Wanzer, letter to the editor, *McClure's*, July 1915, 11. Conversely, the progressive *New Republic* predicted such stories would point the national conversation in a potentially dangerous direction. While hyperbolic narratives of unpreparedness "may thus do something to make the United States a little less unprepared for war . . . they cannot do this much until they have familiarized thousands upon thousands of readers with concrete pictures of German and Japanese invasions, until they have spread fear and suspicion and dislike of these two countries, until they have helped to create that international ill-will without which there would never be war." "Editorial Notes," *New Republic*, April 24, 1915, 292.

34. Moffett, "Conquest of America, 1921," *McClure's Magazine*, May 1915, 9, 10, quote from 11; Moffett, June 1915, 35; Moffett, August 1915, 36. Similar to Moffett's novel in its subtle allusions to American timidity is J. Barnard Walker's apocalyptic tale. Walker, *America Fallen!* Walker, a writer for *Scientific American*, was also the chair of the National Security League's Navy Committee. Finnegan, *Against the Specter of a Dragon*, 32.

35. Campbell, *Reel America and World War I*, 41, 161; and Dumenil, *Second Line of Defense*, 230–231. On harsh depictions of female pacifists during the war, see Zieger, "She Didn't Raise Her Boy to Be a Slacker," 19–20. In the non-fictional world, some women chose to actively prepare for their and their nation's defense by joining rifle clubs, and a select few briefly trained in military camps. Jensen, *Mobilizing Minerva*.

36. "America Is Invaded Again in the Films," *New York Times*, June 7, 1916. In the novel, a congressman, the son of an Americanized Polish immigrant, harangues his fellow lawmakers for their indifference to military readiness before the armies of a very German-like European

emperor invade the East Coast. The congressman and his beautiful love interest lead an underground insurgency after the American surrender that repels the invader and restores democracy. The story ends with the congressman, now Speaker of the House, presiding over the passage of a long-awaited defense bill. Through humiliation and submission, the nation had learned its lesson the hard way. Dixon, *Fall of a Nation.*

37. See Williamson, *Crucible of Race*, 140, 175–176. While most Wilson biographers have minimized his relationship with Dixon, his interest in *The Birth of a Nation*, and his role in the film's nationwide success, Lloyd Ambrosius shows that the president contributed heavily to the film's themes of white supremacy and war as a vehicle for millennial peace (Dixon even closely paraphrased Wilson's scholarly history of the United States) and looked to apply those ideas while in the White House. Ambrosius, "Woodrow Wilson and *The Birth of a Nation*," in *Woodrow Wilson and American Internationalism*, 63–92.

38. Disinterest in *The Fall of a Nation* and similar films, however, may have been due in part to the constraints inherent to filmmaking. Movies took months to finance and produce, making it nearly impossible for a filmmaker to tap directly into the immediate ire many Americans felt over a particular issue, such as the *Lusitania* sinking. This remained the case after the United States entered the war. War-related movies did not make up a significant portion of wartime films until September 1918. DeBauche, *Reel Patriotism*, 36, 38.

39. Maxim, *Defenseless America*, vii, 28–29, 304. Later that year, Maxim's macabre message in *Defenseless America* was translated to the silver screen as the film *The Battle Cry of Peace*, produced by the British-born J. Stuart Blackton. The *New York Times* described the film as "an animated, arresting, and sometimes lurid argument for the immediate and radical improvement of our national defenses." In between the scenes of burning buildings and unspeakable atrocities against man, woman, and child, several authorities on the state of the American military—such as General Leonard Wood, Admiral George Dewey, War Secretary Lindley Garrison, and Maxim himself—expounded on the images and lectured on the ways in which Americans could avoid such a fate in the future. Similar to Moffett's "Conquest of America, 1921," one of the most significant aspects of *The Battle Cry of Peace* was the thinly veiled allusion to Germany as the nation's primary foe. "Avowedly the invading force is of no particular nationality," the *Times* reported. "But it is difficult to escape the impression that you are expected to recognize the nationality. They are certainly not Portuguese, for instance." The implied identity of the foe also was not lost on many German Americans, who protested the film's four-week run at the Majestic Theater in Boston. "New York Shelled on 'Movie' Screen," *New York Times*, August 7, 1915. Historian Lynn Dumenil finds that Blackton's primary message was that a lack of military preparedness left the nation's women "subject to rape." Dumenil, *Second Line of Defense*, 232.

40. Patrick J. Quinn has examined each of these invasion tales as well, arguing that their authors' intention was to suggest a Manichean distinction between American self-government and German militaristic autocracy in order to foster, in case the nation went to war, a sense that men should risk their lives to defend their nation from such pure evil. Quinn, *Conning of America*, 72–100.

41. Some advocates for military preparedness also looked to the United States' past to find instances in which the nation was unprepared to fend off attack, most commonly the War of 1812 and the Civil War (in which the Union's lack of preparedness led to greater loss of life and property than was necessary). See "Could Washington Be Burned Now, and American Freedmen Run for Freedom as in 1814?," *Everybody's Magazine*, May 1915, 655–656; and Howland, *Unpreparedness*, 6–7.

42. Asada, *From Mahan to Pearl Harbor*, 18–23, Mahan quote from 20; and Herring, *From Colony to Superpower*, 355–357, 362. Preparedness leader General Leonard Wood's thoughts on Asian immigration was not far off from Mahan's. Writing to Roosevelt in 1905, Wood claimed the nation had "enough national weakness and humiliation from the negro to avoid further

trouble by the introduction of races with which we [Anglo-Saxons] can never mingle. . . . The introduction of any race with which we cannot intermarry is in my opinion a most horrible mistake." Quoted in White, "War Preparations and Ethnic and Racial Relations in the United States,"104–105. Although not widely read when published in 1913, military theorist Homer Lea's Darwinian treatise on what he saw as an inevitable racial and imperial showdown between Japan and the United States also spoke to similar themes as Mahan. Lea viewed immigration from Japan and the less modern corners of Europe as existential threats to the republic because it could lead to the mongrelization of the Anglo-Saxon race. Lea, *Valor of Ignorance*.

43. Dickinson, *War and National Reinvention*, 84–116.

44. Roosevelt, *National Duty and International Ideals*. Roosevelt was far from the only preparedness advocate to compare China's situation with that of the United States. Some examples from the press should suffice: "The Present Prospect of China," *Review of Reviews*, April 1915, 473–474; "Is Japan Aggressor or Protector in China?," *Review of Reviews*, August 1915, 230–231; "What Must We Do to Provide Adequate Military and Naval Defenses?," *Current Opinion*, July 1915, 5–8; and "What Japan Wins from China," *Literary Digest*, May 22, 1915, 1204–1205. The *Literary Digest* article provides examples of newspaper editors citing China's unpreparedness as a lesson for the United States.

45. "The Disadvantage of Being Busy, Peaceful and Unprepared," cartoon, *Current Opinion*, June 1915, 386. From the *Columbus (OH) Evening Dispatch*. Editorial opinion on the threat Japan posed to the United States was mixed. *Everybody's Magazine* saw the American conviction (a reasonable one, the editors claimed) that "the Occident and the Orient should not try to live together and intermarry" as the likely source of friction between the United States and Japan. "Straight Talk with *Everybody's* Publishers," *Everybody's Magazine*, February 1915, 272. Also see "Menace to the United States in Japan's Triumph Over China," *Current Opinion*, June 1915, 386–387; and "The Deeper Preparedness," *New Republic*, July 24, 1915, 299–300. Some, like the *Forum*, warned against growing Japanese aggression in the Pacific, its allegedly close ties with Germany (its wartime enemy), and its plans to land forces on the California coast, invade from Mexico, or take the Panama Canal Zone through Nicaragua. Sigmund Henschen, "What Is Behind the Japanese Peril?," *Forum*, July 1916, 63–78. *Review of Reviews* ran articles countering the argument that Japan and the United States were on a collision course. Instead, the nations were the bulwarks of peace and stability in the Pacific. "Japan's Challenge to England," *Review of Reviews*, April 1916, 456; and "Japan and America," *Review of Reviews*, April 1917, 398–401.

46. Gilderhus, *Diplomacy and Revolution*, 33–40.

47. *New York World* quoted in "Villa's Raid Secures the Right of Way for National Defense Measures," *Current Opinion*, May 1916, 307. For more examples of the press and editorials describing the failure of the Punitive Expedition as indicative of the United States' unpreparedness, see "Our Unpreparedness Revealed by Villa," *Literary Digest*, April 1, 1916, 883–886, and "The Weakness of Our Second Line," *Literary Digest*, December 23, 1916, 1646–1647. *Review of Reviews* reported that pro-Allied voices in the press were claiming that Germany would likely use Mexico as a springboard for future invasion. The editors, to their credit, said there was little evidence to support this claim. "Carranza and the Germans," *Review of Reviews*, March 1917, 246.

48. Theodore Roosevelt, *National Preparedness, Military, Industrial, Social: Speech of Theodore Roosevelt at Kansas City, Missouri, Memorial Day, 1916* (New York: 1916), PAH.

49. Roosevelt, *National Duty and International Ideals*.

50. *Omaha World-Herald* quoted in "Villa's Raid Secures the Right of Way for National Defense Measures," 307–308.

51. Finnegan, *Against the Specter of a Dragon*, 141, 154–155. Preparedness advocates intensified their campaign for UMT in the latter half of 1916 and found some success. The National Association for Military Training polled a number of newspapers (very selectively, one would guess) and found that 93 percent of editors supported UMT generally. *Literary Digest* reported in early

January 1917 that editors from major newspapers in Chicago, New York, Washington, Philadelphia, Seattle, and even Sioux City, Iowa, threw their wholehearted support behind the cause. The attitudes of selected newspaper editors, however, is a weak measure of public opinion. "To Make Our Boys Soldiers," *Literary Digest*, January 6, 1917, 4.

52. *Omaha World-Herald* quoted in "How Zimmerman United the United States," *Literary Digest*, March 17, 1917, 689.

Chapter 2 · *The Emergence of the Internal Enemy Other, 1914–1917*

1. Melville Davisson Post, "The Invisible Army," *Saturday Evening Post*, April 10, 1915, 3–5.

2. According to Frederick C. Luebke, examples of actual espionage "were based on nothing more substantial than rumor and suspicion." Luebke fails to point out that although many of the stories in the press were exaggerated, some were not. Luebke, *Bonds of Loyalty*, 171. Don Heinrich Tolzmann's broad history of German Americans also underplays the importance of real-life intrigue in the rise of anti-German nativism during neutrality and wartime. Tolzmann, *German-American Experience*, 268–294. La Vern J. Rippley and Russell Kazal focus on how the war led most German Americans to turn their backs on their Old World culture (or maintain multiple identities in Kazal's case) and assimilate. Rippley, *German-Americans*, 180–195; and Kazal, *Becoming Old Stock*.

German historian Reinhard R. Doerries looks at how German propaganda and espionage affected relations between the two governments prior to April 1917, but he also attempts to correct what he sees as a misconception: that the US government exaggerated the extent and danger of German intrigue for propaganda purposes. The Wilson administration had known of German plots since the fall of 1914, Doerries argues, and also received incriminating evidence of spy activity from the British. Doerries's overreliance on German, British, and American government documents, however, appears to lead him to overlook the degree to which the spy menace in the United States was also a creation of the government–press–public opinion dialectic and Americans' collective imagination. Doerries, *Imperial Challenge*, 141–190.

3. This was not the case regarding European Germans, whom white Americans saw as possessing similar yet more barbaric traits due to the allegedly backwards society that Germany's autocratic militarism had established. See chapter 4.

4. Jacobson, *Whiteness of a Different Color*, 168.

5. Bodnar, *Transplanted*, 85–116. Despite the fears of many in the middle and upper classes, most labor radicals did not seek social or political revolution, nor were they uniformly foreign born. Also see Goldstein, *Political Repression in Modern America*, 34–44.

6. Higham, *Strangers in the Land*, 9–10; and Painter, *History of White People*, 201–206.

7. Luebke, *Bonds of Loyalty*, 29–31.

8. Ross, *Old World in the New*, 46–66, quotes from 51, 63, 65. *Century* magazine published Ross's chapter on Germans in May, roughly two months before the Great War began. Ross, "The Germans in America," *Century Magazine*, May 1914, 98–104.

9. Ross, *Old World in the New*, 65–66.

10. Luebke, *Bonds of Loyalty*, 45–48, 70–71.

11. Thayer, *Life and Letters of John Hay*, vol. 2, 291. Hay's Germanophobia was so important to his worldview that an early biographer dedicated an entire chapter, entitled "The German Menace Looms Up," to Hay's supposed prescience on German militarism's threat to world peace while secretary of state. Hay showed a tendency to overreact in traumatic domestic incidents, as evidenced by a letter he wrote to his father-in-law during the violent nationwide railroad strike of 1877 in which he said, "Any hour the mob chooses it can destroy any city in the country— that is the simple truth." Quote from Foner, *Great Labor Uprising of 1877*, 9.

12. Johnson, *Culture at Twilight*, 15; and Luebke, *Bonds of Loyalty*, 68, 70–72. For more on the Pan-German League, see Chickering, *We Men Who Feel Most German*.

13. The few German Americans who actively worked with German government representatives acted as financial agents, provided on-site support for some sabotage incidents, or printed German-friendly newspaper articles in the German-language press. Millman, *Detonators*, 6–7, 42–44; and Luebke, *Bonds of Loyalty*, 91–95.

14. "German Blows Up Canadian Bridge," *New York Times*, February 3, 1915. While holding Horn in the county jail in Machias, Maine, the local sheriff thought it wise to place extra guards in the building because he assumed other German agents in the vicinity may attempt to break the prisoner free. The extra manpower was a smart move; after the war, investigators learned that Horn's mission was part of a larger plot coordinated from the German Embassy to destroy several bridges to Canada. "Horn Lodged in Jail: Extra Precautions at Machias to Guard against a Rescue," *New York Times*, February 6, 1915; and Doerries, *Imperial Challenge*, 180.

15. Quoted in Gregory Morton, "If It Comes to War," *Outlook*, June 9, 1915, 307.

16. "Where the German-Americans Stand," *Literary Digest*, May 22, 1915, 1200–1201. The editors also cited two German American newspapers that professed their disgust with the sinking and two others that pledged loyalty to the United States in the event of war. Also see "German-Americans in the Event of War," *Current Opinion*, June 1915, 384–385.

17. Newspapers quoted in "German-American Loyalty," *Literary Digest*, May 29, 1915, 1262–1264.

18. Link, *Wilson*, vol. 3, 554–560. After the discovery, however, the Wilson administration did little to suppress suspected German propagandists or chastise the German Embassy. Few laws had been broken and, although the administration did not appreciate Germany's cloak and dagger methods, it did not see censuring the German representatives as worth damaging the country's neutrality. Consequently, the exposed plots had little immediate bearing on US–German diplomatic relations. The Wilson administration acted similarly in late 1914 and early 1915 when the Department of Justice found that employees of the Hamburg-American Company, with the help of the embassy, had been forging passports so German reservists in the United States could return to Germany. Although the forgers were tried and convicted, the administration did not view the plot as an infringement of the country's neutrality.

American authorities, however, did not discover until much later that in April 1915 German financial agents had acquired the *New York Evening Mail* to act as a propaganda rag for the kaiser's regime. Its run of pro-German articles and editorials, though, did not last long. To avoid detection, the editors had little choice but to avoid angering an increasingly pro-Allied readership. Germany's most ambitious propaganda operation in the United States turned out to be an utter failure. Doenecke, *Nothing Less than War*, 113.

19. "Move to Punish Teuton Plotters," *New York Times*, November 22, 1915.

20. Link, *Wilson*, vol. 4, 56–58; and Doerries, *Imperial Challenge*, 167–168, 176–177, 182–183.

21. *New York Herald* quoted in "German Bomb-Plots in the United States," *Literary Digest*, November 6, 1915, 993–994.

22. "Remember the Lusitania!," *New York Tribune*, November 13, 1915. Also see "Atrocities and Asininities," *World's Work*, December 1915, 128–129.

23. Millman, *Detonators*, 91–97, 270–272. The conclusion that the Black Tom and Kingsland blasts were industrial accidents remained the official verdict until the Mixed Claims Commission, which handled postwar lawsuits against Germany over wartime damages, decided on June 15, 1939, that agents of the Imperial German Government were in fact guilty of starting the infernos. Also see Landau, *Enemy Within*, which utilized the commission's case files but was published before the commission made its findings public, and Witcover, *Sabotage at Black Tom*. For a good yet very brief summary of the German sabotage campaign in the United States prior to the American declaration of war, see Richelson, *Century of Spies*. For a contemporary press source on these and other unsolved cases of alleged sabotage, see *A Partial Record of Alien Enemy*

Activities, 1915–1917 (New York: [1917?]), PAH, a pamphlet that was prepared from articles published in the ardently anti-German and pro-Ally *Providence Journal*.

24. Newspapers quoted in "What the German-Americans Are Organizing For," *Literary Digest*, February 13, 1915, 299.

25. Newspapers quoted in "German-Americans in Politics," *Literary Digest*, February 20, 1915, 361.

26. "Pan-Germanism in the United States," *World's Work*, June 1915, 135L.

27. James Middleton, "Are Americans More German than English?," *World's Work*, December 1915, 141–147, quotes from 144, 145, 146.

28. In terms of propaganda in the United States, the British had an edge from the start. The Royal Navy cut Germany's undersea cables between the New and Old Worlds in August 1914. Its relative dominance on the high seas guaranteed the free importation of the Allies' descriptions of the war and severely limited German propaganda efforts. Ross, *Propaganda for War*, 27–29.

29. The starting point for all studies of immigrant assimilation remains Higham, *Strangers in the Land*. John F. McClymer concludes that the racial and cultural exclusivity of the period from 1915 to the passing of the National Origins Act in 1924 was "a coherent era in American politics and society." McClymer, *War and Welfare*, 74. Also see McClymer's essay, "The Federal Government and the Americanization Movement, 1914–24," 23–41. Gary Gerstle concludes that a disciplinary state arose during this period to Americanize the immigrant and homogenize American society. Gerstle, *American Crucible*. Christina Ziegler-McPherson attempts to counter Gerstle's coercion argument by pointing out the limited funds appropriated to state Americanization agencies and the lack of immigrant participation in such programs. Ziegler-McPherson, *Americanization in the States*.

30. Quoted in Higham, *Strangers in the Land*, 242.

31. Theodore Roosevelt, *National Duty and International Ideals: Speech of Theodore Roosevelt Before the Illinois Bar Association at Chicago, April 29th, 1916* (New York: 1916), PAH.

32. Ray Stannard Baker to Theodore Roosevelt, January 14, 1916, reel 28, Ray Stannard Baker Papers, General Correspondence, MD, LOC. Interestingly, Baker is one of the few Americans who ever called out Roosevelt for his often-dangerous speech. It does not appear that Baker ever sent a similar letter to Wilson, whom he admired greatly.

33. Winston Churchill, "A Plea for the American Tradition," *Harper's Monthly Magazine*, January 1916, 249–256, quotes from 249, 250.

34. Margaret Sherwood, "Our Immigrant Young and the Anglo-Saxon Ideal," *Forum*, September 1916, 317–322, quotes from 320, 321. On calls for assimilation through education in the press, also see "Americanization and the Lack of a National Epic Consciousness," *Current Opinion*, September 1916, 182–183. A large number of Americanizers hoped to tie the need for immigrant assimilation to the desire for a more prepared military, the most prominent being Kellor, *Straight America*; Henry Breckinridge, "The Solving of the Hyphen," *Forum*, November 1916, 583–588; and John Dewey, "Universal Service as Education," *New Republic*, April 22, 1916, 309–310.

35. For most of the article, the editors were citing the thoughts of the American missionary Sidney L. Gulick. "The Immigration Question Again," *World's Work*, August 1916, 374–375. The editors of this mainstream publication appear to have opposed the literacy test on the same grounds—that it was not effective in keeping immigrants of poor "quality and character" out of the country—earlier in the neutrality period. See "The Limit of the Melting Pot," *World's Work*, March 1915, 491–492.

36. Quoted in Link, *Wilson*, vol. 4, 59.

37. Woodrow Wilson to Edward M. House, August 4, 1915, in *PWW*, vol. 34, 79; Edward M. House to Woodrow Wilson, August 23, 1915, in *PWW*, vol. 34, 309; and Edward M. House to Woodrow Wilson, Aug. 26, 1915, *Intimate Papers of Colonel House*, vol. 2, 34–35. House's title of

"colonel" was merely honorary, having been bestowed upon him by the governor of Texas, Jim Hogg, for helping him win his election. Hodgson, *Woodrow Wilson's Right Hand*, 2. Wilson reportedly said at one time of his relationship with House, "Mr. House is my second personality. . . . His thoughts and mine are one." Quoted in Knock, *To End All Wars*, 20.

38. For a couple excellent examples of Wilson's "anti-hyphen" commentary before the 1916 election year, see "An Appeal to the American People," August 18, 1914, in *PWW*, vol. 30, 393–394; and "Annual Address on the State of the Union," December 7, 1915, in *PWW*, vol. 35, 307.

39. Wiebe, *Search for Order*, 160–161, 189. Congress's diminished ability to handle the wide range of problems stemming from the country's rapid modernization was a primary reason for the rise of the "public man."

40. With the federal government offering few services, citizens compensated in the late nineteenth and early twentieth centuries with local volunteer organizations. Volunteer groups, not the national government, were responsible for defining and maintaining common notions of patriotism and nationalism before the federal government tried to take on these tasks in 1917. See O'Leary, *To Die For*; and Capozzola, *Uncle Sam Wants You*.

41. "A Flag Day Address," June 14, 1916, in *PWW*, vol. 37, 223. New York *Sun* reporter John Price Jones contended that in early 1915 a German agent attempted to bribe "*seven or eight different Congressmen*" to lobby and vote for an embargo on munitions sales to the Allies. Jones, *America Entangled*, 215. Emphasis in the original.

42. Quoted in Tumulty, *Woodrow Wilson As I Knew Him*, 191.

43. Samuel G. Blythe, "Harpooning the Hyphenates," *Saturday Evening Post*, July 29, 1916, 24.

44. Joseph P. Tumulty to Wilson, June 13, 1916, in *PWW*, vol. 37, 219. Tumulty could have merely been playing off his boss's known anxieties about the threat Germany could pose to the country in order to gain approval for this political tactic. After citing this change to the party platform in his memoirs, Tumulty then discussed how formidable Hughes was as an opponent and how much Wilson admired the judge's work as governor of New York. Tumulty, *Woodrow Wilson As I Knew Him*, 191–192.

45. Link, *Woodrow Wilson and the Progressive Era*, 232. For editorial opinion on Hughes's courting of immigrant voters and on how immigrants voted, see "Mr. Hughes and the Hyphen," *Literary Digest*, September 16, 1916, 658; "How the Hyphen Voted," *Literary Digest*, November 25, 1916, 1394–1395; and "The Candidates and the Hyphenates," *Current Opinion*, July 1916, 5–6.

46. Cooper, *Woodrow Wilson*, 357–358. The election was so close that Wilson won New Hampshire by 52 votes, Hughes took Minnesota by 392, and three others—California, New Mexico, and North Dakota—were too close to call for two days after the election. Hughes waited two weeks to concede.

47. Newspapers quoted in "To Make Us Spy-Proof and Bomb-Proof," *Literary Digest*, March 10, 1917, 610–612.

48. Louis F. Post to Thomas W. Gregory, February 21, 1917, file 184973-1, box 2077, Straight Numerical File, DOJ, NARA.

49. Elmira Advertiser Association to War Department, March 10, 1917, and F. H. Duehay to Elmira Advertiser Association, March 19, 1917, file 185379, box 2098, Straight Numerical File, DOJ, NARA.

50. L. H. Baekeland to H. E. Coffin, March 9, 1917, and J. Daniels to T. W. Gregory, March 19, 1917, file 185382-1, box 2098, Straight Numerical File, DOJ, NARA.

51. Jones, *America Entangled*, 212, 214. The claims in Jones's book were broadcast to a very wide audience in "Lusitania Decoyed into Trap, Book Says," *New York Times*, March 5, 1917.

52. *Minneapolis Tribune* quoted in "To Make Us Spy-Proof and Bomb-Proof," 610. That Allied secret agents and propagandists roamed American streets appears to have not caused the president to lose any sleep. At the same time, as much as the British Royal Navy's illegal seizures of American ships, goods, and American mail increased tensions between the two countries

during neutrality, the Wilson administration and the American press, while angered, most often described these affronts as unfortunate misunderstandings, rarely mentioning publicly the possibility of war between the United States and Great Britain over neutral rights. Germany's transgressions, albeit in most cases more serious than Britain's, rarely were given the benefit of the doubt. Finally, only in rare cases (such as in German American or Irish American neighborhoods or some sections of the populist-minded South) was "pro-British" a pejorative term, unlike the near-universally panned moniker "pro-German." Historian Robert W. Tucker blames Wilson's pro-Allied neutrality for the deterioration of US–German relations that ultimately ended in war. Tucker, *Woodrow Wilson and the Great War*. For a brief discussion of British violations of US sovereignty and the Wilson administration's response early in the war, see Doenecke, *Nothing Less Than War*, 47–50.

53. "An Address to a Joint Session of Congress," April 2, 1917, in *PWW*, vol. 41, 524.

Chapter 3 · The War on the Internal Enemy Other, 1917–1918

1. The Military Intelligence Division was known at the time of this investigation as the Military Intelligence Section (MIS), which was originally formed in May 1917. In August 1918, the MIS became the MID, a new division within the Army General Staff. For the sake of clarity and to stay consistent with the title of the records collection at the National Archives, I will refer to the agency as the MID throughout the text and notes. Bidwell, *History of the Military Intelligence Division*, 110, 116–117.

2. "In Re: Bolge, Osprey, Fla. German Neutrality," September 16, 1917, file 10218–20, reel 1, "Negro Subversion," MID, NARA.

3. Koenig, *Fourth Horseman*.

4. A great example of propagandists' reliance on the 1915 incidents of intrigue is a widely circulated Committee on Public Information (CPI) pamphlet that reviewed every incident of German sabotage, intrigue, and propagandizing prior to 1917—real and imagined. Not surprisingly, the pamphlet's authors, Earl E. Sperry and Willis M. West, do not include incidents of post-1917 German intrigue. In fact, they admit at the end of the pamphlet that "all the criminal plots and conspiracies" discussed in the work took place "prior to the summer of 1915." Earl E. Sperry and Willis M. West, *German Plots and Intrigues in the United States during the Period of Our Neutrality* (Washington, DC: 1918), 61, entry 41, PRWB, CPI, NARA.

5. The common stance among historians of the Progressive Era has been that native-born Americans' desire for cultural homogeneity drove wartime fear of immigrant disloyalty and of all things German, leading directly to wartime repression and Americanization campaigns. John Higham describes Anglo-Saxons' wartime suspicion of German Americans as part of the same "crusading spirit" and "yearning idealism" that had driven domestic reform but had transformed into "the most strenuous nationalism and the most pervasive nativism that the United States had ever known." Higham, *Strangers in the Land*, 194–197, quotes from 194, 195. Frederick Luebke portrays the spy frenzy as the creation of political and social elites who were frustrated with the seeming dearth of pro-war sentiment among the public. Luebke, *Bonds of Loyalty*. More recently, Richard Slotkin has maintained that the popular conception of nationalism, "that national politics and culture were expressions of racial character," led Anglo-Saxon Americans to describe German brutality and treachery in the same manner they did the nation's traditional non-white enemies, as unassimilable barbarians and savages. Those who supported the nation's "racial enemy," then, were liable to the same punishments historically meted out to Native Americans and African Americans. Slotkin, *Lost Battalions*, 215–218, quote form 215. According to Christopher Capozzola, Americans' acceptance of or engagement in the repression of German Americans and their alleged partners had its origins in the perception that some Americans, both native and foreign born, were not living up to the unwritten obligations of citizenship. Capozzola, *Uncle Sam Wants You*. Also see Gary Gerstle's take on the connection between racial and civic nationalism

in *American Crucible*. Although I do not believe that the momentum of progressive reform, the urgency of fashioning a pro-war consensus, and the pressure to conform were insignificant, I argue in this chapter that wartime anti-German nativism was the result of several intersecting factors, race being the most significant in my judgment.

6. Samuel Hopkins Adams, "Invaded America," *Everybody's Magazine*, December 1917, 9–16, 86, quotes from 9, 10, 86; and "Invaded America: The Winning Battle in the Middle West," *Everybody's Magazine*, February 1918, 74–83, quotes from 74. In the later installments Adams levels further charges and criticism on the presumably disloyal German Americans and touts enemy alien confinement and Americanization as key elements of US national security. "Invaded America: Making Over the Alien," *Everybody's Magazine*, March 1918, 55–64. John R. Rathom of the *Providence Journal* began an identical series in the *World's Work* in February 1918. Rathom's participation in the series, though, lasted for only one edition as the *Providence Journal* sought to reap the subscription benefits of their employee's fearmongering. French Strother, the *World's Work*'s managing editor, took over the series for the rest of its run. John R. Rathom, "Germany's Plots Exposed," *World's Work*, February 1918, 394–415; French Strother, "Fighting Germany's Spies," March 1918, *World's Work*, 513–528; *World's Work*, April 1918, 652–669; *World's Work*, May 1918, 78–102; *World's Work*, June 1918, 134–153; *World's Work*, July 1918, 303–317; *World's Work*, August 1918, 393–401; and *World's Work*, September 1918, 542–552.

7. Shailer Mathews, *Why the United States Is at War* (New York: 1917), 3–4, 7, PAH.

8. Wallace Notestein and Elmer E. Stoll (eds.) *Conquest and Kultur: Aims of the Germans in Their Own Words* (Washington, DC: 1917), 87, 96–97, entry 41, box 5, PRWB, CPI, NARA. The CPI circulated 1,225,000 copies of *Conquest and Kultur* in 1918. Vaughn, *Holding Fast the Inner Lines*, 70.

9. Private organizations also got involved in the bashing of the NGAA, sometimes to advance their own agendas. The Anti-Saloon League went so far as to connect the NGAA and Germany's conspiracy to the United States Brewers' Association. "The most patriotic act that Congress . . . can do this year," they concluded, was "to abolish the un-American, pro-German, crime-producing, food-wasting, youth-corrupting, home-wrecking, treasonable liquor traffic." *A Disloyal Combination* (Westlake, OH: 1918), 18, PAH. Opponents of Prohibition were also quick to use the war emergency to push their agenda. The *Buffalo Enquirer* argued that the kaiser would be delighted if "this country [were] torn asunder" by the division between the moralistic, tee-totalling middle class and laborers on the issue of alcohol. Interestingly, the *Enquirer*'s editors relied upon readers' understanding of Germans' conspiratorial nature. "If the Kaiser thought he could foment discontent by keeping prohibition stirred up during the war," they argued, "does anyone doubt that he would do it?" The concluding line of the editorial was equally ridiculous: "Germany might be behind the prohibition movement. You can never tell." "Is Prohibition German Propaganda?," *Buffalo Enquirer*, July 13, 1918, PAH.

10. David Lawrence, "Americans for America," *Saturday Evening Post*, June 15, 1918, 44. Some other representative examples in the press include "The 'German-American Alliance,'" *Literary Digest*, March 9, 1918, 16; "Pan-Germanism in America," *Review of Reviews*, August 1918, 208; and "America Votes for Americans!," *Everybody's Magazine*, August 1918, 4.

11. Kazal, *Becoming Old Stock*, 181–182.

12. David Lawrence, "Swat the Spy!," *Saturday Evening Post*, January 12, 1918, 14, 15. The ambivalence of the neutrality period, however, did not completely disappear, as an examination of the *Saturday Evening Post* shows. Journalists such as Irvin Cobb and David Lawrence were responsible for some of the most exaggerated anti-German stories in the wartime press. The newspaper's editors, though, occasionally printed front-page stories portraying German Americans as victims of wartime excesses and describing how the United States could benefit from their contribution to American society. Some writers even refuted their fellow *Post* contributors' claims of an active conspiracy, such as Carl W. Ackerman, who in November 1917 claimed that

the US Secret Service's campaign against German intrigue had been so effective that "for the first time during the war" Americans could "speak of the checkmating of the enemy's intelligence service." Carl W. Ackerman, "The Last Spy Offensive," *Saturday Evening Post*, November 10, 1917, 18–19, 50, quote from 18; and Edward G. Lowry, "Germans and Germans," *Saturday Evening Post*, June 30, 1917, 3–4, 85.

13. Lewis Allen Browne, "Our Danger—Tomorrow's German-Americans," *Forum*, May 1918, 570–571, 577.

14. Flagg produced this cartoon on behalf of the patriotic troop of writers and artists known as the Vigilantes. See Edwards, "America's Vigilantes and the Great War."

15. Luebke, *Bonds of Loyalty*, 76. The relevant section of the Delbrück Law, Section 25, is quoted in Schieber, *Transformation of American Sentiment toward Germany*, 208.

16. *Disloyal Combination*, 10.

17. Mathews, *Why the United States Is at War*, 3.

18. Elihu Root to Richard D. Harlan, July 17, 1918, box 136, General Correspondence, Elihu Root Papers, MD, LOC.

19. Quotes from Kennedy, *Over Here*, 54. See also Peterson and Fite, *Opponents of War*, 195–196; and Luebke, *Bonds of Loyalty*, 250–254.

20. "Why Teach German," *Leipsic (OH) Free Press*, February 7, 1918, in George Smith to G. Creel, February 7, 1918, box 18, folder 34, Creel Correspondence, CPI, NARA.

21. National Committee of One Hundred, "Germany's 'Peaceful Penetration' of the United States in Population, Language, Education," no date, box 631, Women's Defense Work, CND, NARA. For wartime opinions on Americanization, see Frances Kellor, *Neighborhood Americanization: A Discussion of the Alien in a New Country and of the Native American in His Home Country* (New York: 1918), PAH; Lois Kimball Matthews Rosenberry, *The Making of Americans* (US: [1918?]), PAH; and Winthrop Talbot, "The Faith that Is in Us: A Rallying Cry to Americans," *Forum*, November 1917, 613–618.

22. W. H. Hobbs to S. Stanwood Menken, August 22, 1917, box 1, Robert M. McElroy Papers, MD, LOC. Hobbs was able to reach a national audience in April 1918 when the *Outlook* published an article he wrote on the danger of German parochial schools, which he claimed were bastions of German *kultur* and a massive roadblock to the Americanization of German children. W. H. Hobbs, "A Pioneer Movement for Americanization," *Outlook*, April 24, 1918, 666.

23. Document containing Duluth Board of Education resolution, n.d., box 18, folder 34, Creel Correspondence, CPI, NARA.

24. Superintendent to E. J. Orear, January 4, 1918, box 14, folder 411, Creel Correspondence, CPI, NARA.

25. Luebke, *Bonds of Loyalty*, 247–250, quote from 249; and Herries and Herries, *Last Days of Innocence*, 295. Also see "Fighting the German Propaganda in the United States," *Current Opinion*, May 1918, 305–306.

26. For more on progressives and propaganda, see Thompson, *Reformers and War*; and Vaughn, *Holding Fast the Inner Lines*.

27. Harvey O'Higgins, *The German Whisper* (Washington, DC: 1918), 3, 29, entry 41, box 6, PRWB, CPI, NARA. O'Higgins also was likely the author of another CPI pamphlet with a similar theme that offered the same prescription: inform the federal government of any suspicious talk. *The Kaiserite in America: One Hundred and One German Lies* (Washington, DC: 1918).

28. "Spies and Lies," poster, 1917, entry 1, box 13, Creel Correspondence, CPI, NARA. It was also published as an ad in popular magazines and newspapers. See *Everybody's Magazine*, August 1918, 73; and *Saturday Evening Post*, August 3, 1918, 23.

29. Thomas Watt Gregory to Woodrow Wilson, June 14, 1917, in *PWW*, vol. 42, 510–511.

30. Daniels, *Cabinet Diaries of Josephus Daniels*, 173.

31. Smith, *War & Press Freedom*, 40.

32. Rosnow and Fine, *Rumor and Gossip*; and Shibutani, *Improvised News*. Seeking to understand wartime hysteria through literary works, Celia Malone Kingsbury argues that rumor and gossip can be used to whip the emotions of even the most even-tempered into a frenzy. Kingsbury, *Peculiar Sanity of War*, xx, 4.

33. Conference Report of the Department of Educational Propaganda, transcript, [1918?], box 629, Women's Defense Work, CND, NARA. Catt proved a good fit for her post as she appears to have fully subscribed to the CPI's line that German propaganda had been a menace to the country for quite some time and that guilty citizens must be informed of their unwitting treachery. See Breen, *Uncle Sam at Home*, 129, on the formation of the DEP in October 1917 and its renaming as the Americanization Section.

34. Woman's Committee, Council of National Defense, New Hampshire Division, Circular, January 12, 1918, box 628, Women's Defense Work, CND, NARA.

35. Stories of German-inspired black insurrection, in the South especially, found their way into the mainstream press, thus completing the rumor cycle. Two widely circulated examples are "German Plots among Negroes," *Literary Digest*, April 21, 1917, 1153; and Adams, "Invaded America," *Everybody's Magazine*, December 1917, 13.

36. Ellis, *Race, War, and Surveillance*, 8–9.

37. Kornweibel, *"Investigate Everything,"* 45.

38. "In Re: German Propaganda Among Negroes, at Old Point, Virginia," January 22, 1918, file 10218-85, reel 1, "Negro Subversion," MID, NARA.

39. "In Re: Otto Marle, Alien Enemy, Seditious Remarks," April 6, 1918, file 10218-134, reel 2, "Negro Subversion," MID, NARA. In a similar vein, rumors also swirled through southern black communities that if the United States won the war whites would return African Americans to slavery. Bill Harris, report, January 11, 1918, file 10218-82, reel 1; and Office of Naval Intelligence to MID, March 11, 1918, file 10218-112, reel 2. Both from "Negro Subversion," MID, NARA.

40. "In Re: Glass Found in Food Stuffs," April 6, 1918, file 10218-123, reel 2, "Negro Subversion," MID, NARA.

41. D. J. Kirton to J. W. Ragsdale, April 6, 1917, file 3057, reel 304, OGF, FBI, NARA. For similar cases from the BI and the MID, see Unsigned to A. J. Devlin, April 2, 1917; and A. Bruce Bielaski to the Blockton, AL Postmaster, April 2, 1917. Both from file 3057, reel 304, OGF, FBI, NARA. L. O. Thompson, report, July 1, 1917, file 10218-2, reel 1; Ralph H. Daughton, report, January 22, 1918, file 10218-85, reel 1; and Major M. D. Wheeler to Branch Babcock, May 8, 1918, file 10218-113, reel 2. All from "Negro Subversion," MID, NARA.

42. Branch Bocock, report, May 11, 1917, file 3057, reel 304, OGF, FBI, NARA.

43. It is possible that some of these and similar reports coming out of the South also were inspired by the much less well-known Plan of San Diego that Mexican and African American conspirators had concocted in 1915. Their aim was to conquer the lands the United States had taken from Mexico in the late 1840s, reestablish Mexican sovereignty, form an all-black nation between the newly expanded Mexico and the United States, and invite Native Americans and the Japanese to take part in the conquest. The plot was never a realistic threat to the United States and had been abandoned by early 1917. Germany was not involved. Sandos, "Pancho Villa and American Security," 295–297. For a thorough discussion of the Plan of San Diego and its long-term consequences for future Mexican immigration, see Johnson, *Revolution in Texas*.

44. "In re AGITATION AMONG NEGROES: Unknown Parties," September 11, 1917, file 10218-23, reel 1, "Negro Subversion," MID, NARA. The BI also investigated the case. R. L. Barnes, report, "In re: Unknown Party at Yoakum, Texas Trying to Cause Agitation Among the Negroes," September 4, 1917, file 3057, reel 304, OGF, FBI, NARA. Also see Ruth E. Crevering to Josephus Daniels, August 2, 1917; and B.C. Baldwin, report, September 1917. Both from file 3057, reel 304, OGF, FBI, NARA.

45. Kornweibel, *"Investigate Everything,"* 41–43. For a similar case, see J. P. Cooper to Chief Post Office Inspector, April 20, 1917, file 3057, reel 304, OGF, FBI, NARA. The MID's leadership also was concerned about a black exodus to Mexico. Van Deman to Spencer Roberts, May 17, 1918, file 10218-147, reel 2, "Negro Subversion," MID, NARA.

46. "Memorandum on the Loyalty of the American Negro in the Present War," August 27, 1917, file 10218-7, reel 1, "Negro Subversion," MID, NARA.

47. *Boston Guardian* quoted from "German Plots Among Negroes," 1153.

48. "Propaganda," *Baltimore Afro-American*, July 19, 1918.

49. "Loyalty," *Crisis*, May 1917, 8.

50. Special Employee Beasley, report, "In Re: Chef at 'Puss 'n Boots' Confectionary Co.," July 13, 1917, file 10218-4, reel 1, "Negro Subversion," MID, NARA.

51. P. T. Rellihan, report, "Re: Kuhn, Loeb & Co.," July 28, 1917, file 10218-113, reel 2, "Negro Subversion," MID, NARA.

52. Office of Naval Intelligence to MID, March 11, 1918, file 10218-112, reel 2 (from Washington, DC, on rumors among blacks that white Americans would re-enslave them if Germany lost the war); Spencer Roberts to Chief of MID, May 22, 1918, file 10218-147, reel 2 (from Philadelphia, on a Mr. McElrone who works for a "certain Government" and calls himself the "negro liberator"); and William Frew to Chief of MID, August 6, 1918, file 10218-200, reel 3 (from Grosse Pointe, MI—near Detroit—on Michigan and Georgia state Councils of National Defense teaming up to end German propaganda among African Americans in the Detroit and Atlanta areas). All from "Negro Subversion," MID, NARA.

53. J. F. Trazzare to Military Intelligence—Plant Protection, June 1, 1918, Reports on Fires, box 3, PPS, MID, NARA.

54. Leon Bone, report, "In re Destruction of Dam at Fairview, Utah (German Activities)," July, 23, 1917, file 10095-35, box 2477, Gen. Corr., MID, NARA.

55. Division Superintendent to George H. Murdock, May 26, 1917, file 5910, reel 319, OGF, FBI, NARA.

56. The APL's mere existence, historian David Kennedy explains, "testifies to the unusual state of American society in World War I, when fear corrupted usually sober minds." Kennedy, *Over Here*, 81–83, quote from 82. Also see Hyman, *To Try Men's Souls*, 267–315; Jensen, *Price of Vigilance*; and Hough, *The Web*. The APL's membership came exclusively from the educated, white-collar class, with only "the highest type of business and professional men" being recruited "for the highest type of intelligent, aggressive and patriotic work." Detroit Superintendent to prospective applicant, April 10, 1917, file 5910, reel 320, OGF, FBI, NARA. Wilson was not a fan of the APL, telling Gregory, "It seems to me that it would be very dangerous to have such an organization operating in the United States, and I wonder if there is any way in which we could stop it." Woodrow Wilson to Thomas Watt Gregory, June 4, 1917, in *PWW*, vol. 42, 446. The APL was far from the only organization of volunteer sleuths operating during the war. A postwar list of similar "Volunteer Secret Service Organizations" shows fifteen in the southwestern United States alone. Pierson W. Banning, *Hun Hunting at Home* (Los Angeles, CA: 1919), PAH.

57. The founding of the local High Point, North Carolina, branch provides a good example of the bias typical of the APL. While informing the APL's chairman A. M. Briggs that High Point was not in need of any out-of-town assistance from the APL, local man A. J. Parker betrayed his distrust of all things foreign. "The cases of disloyalty and evasion of the draft would be very few here," he explained, "owing to the fact that we have comparatively few people who are of foreign birth." Apparently, native-born Americans were incapable of disloyalty. The apparent dearth of alien threats in High Point, however, did not stop Parker from offering up his services to Briggs as "chief" of a newly-formed APL branch in the town, which would "be glad to co-operate with you." A. J. Parker to A. M. Briggs, April 16, 1918, box 10, Correspondence with Field Offices, APL, FBI, NARA.

58. James H. Daly, report, "In Re: Herman Shauer (M[a]rquette, Mich.)," August 2, 1918, Reports on Fires, box 1, PPS, MID, NARA.

59. Roland Ford, report, April 18, 1917, file 5910, reel 320, OGF, FBI, NARA.

60. J. L. O'Brian to T. W. Gregory, April 18, 1918, in *PWW*, vol. 47, 364–365. In most of the reports in the records of the MID's Plant Protection Section, the agents merely surmised that insurance fraud was behind the fires. I only came across one reported incident where investigators found a clear desire to commit insurance fraud to be the cause of a fire. George Black to Edmund Leigh, May 28, 1918, Reports on Fires, box 1, PPS, MID, NARA.

61. "Port Newark Fire Seen as Part of Wide German Plot," *New York Times*, January 27, 1918.

62. Thomas F. J. Cavanagh and William J. McCahill to Commanding Officer, Neutrality Squad, January 28, 1918, Reports on Fires, box 1, PPS, MID, NARA.

63. Military Intelligence Branch, *Propaganda in Its Military and Legal Aspects*, 7, 73–109, 112–124, 128–132, quotes from 14, 101. In its discussion of the NGAA, the MID quoted extensively from the same David Lawrence article in the June 15, 1918, *Saturday Evening Post* cited in note 10 of this chapter. Also see the collection of wartime MID documents in Challener (ed.), *United States Military Intelligence Weekly Summaries.*

64. Murphy, *World War I and the Origins of Civil Liberties*, 79–81. Wilson initially ordered Attorney General Gregory to draft the bill that would become the Espionage Act in 1916, but Congress chose not to act on the proposed legislation until after the United States declared war. Stone, "Mr. Wilson's First Amendment," 191–192.

65. A. S. Burleson to M. Bronner, October 22, 1917, Albert Sidney Burleson Papers, vol. 19, MD, LOC. For the mainstream press's opinion on Burleson's wartime powers, see "Mr. Burleson to Rule Press," *Literary Digest*, October 6, 1917, 12.

66. The Wilson administration also took direct measures against German nationals, including requiring them to register with the federal government. Roughly 6,000 German Americans spent time in internment camps at one point or another during the war, but most received parole. All enemy aliens—that is, not German American citizens—were compelled to stay at least one-half mile from military bases and industrial and transportation facilities deemed crucial to the war effort unless their employer was able to acquire passes for essential workers. Worse was the work of the Office of the Alien Property Custodian, run by the future Attorney General A. Mitchell Palmer. His office confiscated enemy aliens' American bank accounts, stocks, bonds, and property in order to keep them out of the hands of German agents. Yet instead of holding the property in trust as ordered, Palmer sold much of it off to the benefit of American banks and certain industries. Capozzola, *Uncle Sam Wants You*, 187–189, 204. None of these measures, though, affected more than a few thousand Teutons and, regarding their draconian nature, paled in comparison to both the Espionage Act and the Japanese internment order during World War II.

67. Victor Berger to A. S. Burleson, July 12, 1917, Burleson Papers, vol. 19, MD, LOC. In February 1918, Berger was indicted under the Espionage Act only to post bail and run, unsuccessfully but with the support of a significant minority of voters, as the Socialist candidate for Senate from Wisconsin in April. Murphy, *Origins of Civil Liberties*, 218–219. For more on Berger's tortuous experience with wartime sedition laws, see Thomas, *Unsafe for Democracy*, 113–118, 137–140.

68. Smith, *War & Press Freedom*, 40, 57, 59; and Polenberg, *Fighting Faiths*, 212–213. For a fine legal explanation of the Espionage Act, see Rabban, *Free Speech in Its Forgotten Years*, 248–298.

69. The mainstream press and many in the legal profession praised Clayton for his diatribe. The *New York Times* said Clayton "deserve[d] the thanks of the city and of the country for the way he conducted the trial," while a New York lawyer claimed Clayton's speech made his "blood tingle—with pride, with approbation." Quotes from Polenberg, *Fighting Faiths*, 142.

70. Another famous example of a judge's prejudices getting the better of him in an Espionage Act case is the trial of Kate Richards O'Hare, whom the judge sentenced to ten years in prison,

not because of the words she uttered against the draft, but because her words showed "what was in her heart." Kennedy, *Disloyal Mothers and Scurrilous Citizens*, 18–38. Also see Murphy, *Origins of Civil Liberties*, 210–218; and Rabban, *Free Speech in Its Forgotten Years*, 255–279.

71. *The Duties of the Home Defense Leagues* (New York: 1917), PAH. The editors of the *Forum* gave the ADS's call to arms and volunteerism a wider audience when it printed, mostly word for word, sections of the pamphlet in a story on combating spies and disloyalty. "What Constitutes Treason?," *Forum*, October 1917, 433–446. The National Security League, the ADS's parent organization, also called for Americans to organize local defense leagues, but differed in that their appeal was less urgent, stating that the work of federal and local authorities as well as the great distance between the United States and Europe had "almost entirely destroyed the possibility of an uprising." The point of home defense leagues to the NSL was to encourage Americans to spy on suspicious neighbors. *Home Defense Leagues: Suggestions for their Organization* (New York: 1917), 4, PAH.

72. "Too Easy with the Enemy," *Washington Post*, August 30, 1917.

73. Roosevelt quoted in Slotkin, *Lost Battalions*, 219.

74. Daniels quoted in Luebke, *Bonds of Loyalty*, 278.

75. Peterson and Fite, *Opponents of War*, 196–207, Tulsa Council of Defense quote from 200.

76. "Re: H.F. Bittner, German Lutheran Minister, American Security Matter," October 29, 1917, file 10332-9, box 3070, Gen. Corr., MID, NARA. For similar investigations in Iowa and Wisconsin, see "In Re: Rev. Schumann. Pomeroy, Iowa. Neutrality Matter," February 13, 1918, file 10332-11; and "IN RE REV. JOHN WILLIAM REU," November 5, 1917, file 10332-7. Both from box 3070, Gen. Corr., MID, NARA.

77. Peterson and Fite, *Opponents of War*, 202–203. Also see "The First War-Lynching," *Literary Digest*, April 20, 1918, 16–17; and "Is Lynching a Good Way to Fight Germany?," *Outlook*, April 17, 1918, 609. The fact Prager's lynch mob was made up mostly of laborers suggests his murder may not have been merely a manifestation of fears of a German conspiracy. At the same time, one of the ring leaders was a German American who himself faced charges of disloyalty. DeWitt, *Degrees of Allegiance*, 59–60. Also see Weinberg, *Loyalty, Labor & Rebellion*.

78. Peterson and Fite, *Opponents of War*, 204. Perhaps few Americans should have been shocked by the lynching of Prager and other supposed disloyalists because, as Richard M. Brown argues in his classic study of American vigilantism, extralegal violence had been part of an informal, dual system of law and order that Americans throughout the United States had sanctioned throughout most of the country's history. Brown, *Strain of Violence*.

79. "High Time," *Everybody's Magazine*, June 1918, 4.

80. T. U. Taylor to Thomas Watt Gregory, April 10, 1918; and Gregory to Taylor, April 15, 1918, Thomas Watt Gregory Papers, box 1, MD, LOC. Also of note is Gregory's correspondence with Josephus Daniels on press coverage of the Walter Spoorman case from Norfolk, Virginia. After seeing that the press claimed Spoorman kept a German uniform and letters from the former German ambassador Count Bernsdorff in his trunk, Gregory lamented that the DOJ would be criticized yet again for not shooting the accused, although there was no evidence supporting the press's outlandish claims. Thomas Watt Gregory to Josephus Daniels, January 16, 1918, reel 51, Special Correspondence, Josephus Daniels Papers, MD, LOC. John Lord O'Brian offered a seven-step solution to reducing mob violence and improving the DOJ's public image. John Lord O'Brian to Thomas Watt Gregory, April 18, 1918, in *PWW*, vol. 47, 363–365. Also, while Gregory seemed to have been joking about shooting spies, the editors of the *Outlook* did not think this was such a bad idea. "George Washington and German Spies," *Outlook*, November 28, 1917, 490.

81. A. Bruce Bielaski, "Memorandum for the Attorney General," January 10, 1918, file 83627, reel 455, OGF, FBI, NARA.

82. Gregory quoted in Thomas, *Unsafe for Democracy*, 155–156. For newspaper calls for a tougher Espionage Act after the Prager lynching, see "Stronger Curb on Enemies at Home," *Literary Digest*, May 4, 1918, 19; and "'Enemy Aliens' and the Spy Problem," *Literary Digest*, May 25, 1918, 25, 95. As one would expect, the African American press was unhappy that Gregory's and Wilson's regret over Prager's lynching was accompanied by silence on the issue of the lynching of blacks in the South. See "Mr. Gregory on Judge Lynch," *Baltimore Afro-American*, May 10, 1918.

83. Thomas Watt Gregory, "How the Rear of Our Armies Was Guarded during the World War," 1919, box 26, Gregory Papers, MD, LOC.

Chapter 4 · Resisting Regressive Militarism, 1917–1918

1. Samuel Harden Church, "Fighting the Dragon," No. 34 (New York: 1918), PTE.

2. John A. Thompson shows that from the 1880s through the Cold War, American policy-makers often have employed concerns over a foreign attack on the United States as justification for foreign or military policies. He argues, however, that warnings of an imminent attack, be it from Imperial Germany or an atomic strike by the Soviet Union, were meant to further cynical political goals, not because policymakers believed that conquest was possible. Thompson, "Exaggeration of American Vulnerability," 23–43. Although I do not discount the manipulative nature of wartime invasion propaganda, I argue that the stated fears of most politicians, commentators, and propagandists during World War I were, for the most part, genuine expressions of their personal anxieties and beliefs.

3. Chase, *Legacy of Malthus*, 48, 185.

4. Sadler, *Long Heads and Round Heads*, 60–63, quote from 63.

5. William S. Sadler to George Creel, March 18, 1918; and George Creel to William S. Sadler, March 21, 1918. Both from entry 1, box 21, Creel Correspondence, CPI, NARA.

6. E. A. Hooton, "Review of *Long Heads and Round Heads*," 364. As historian Allan Chase sardonically put it, "by 1916, no serious scientific worker" saw craniology as "a measurement of anything other than the size of a person's hat." Chase, *Legacy of Malthus*, 185.

7. Newton Diehl Baker, "Address of the Secretary of War, Annual Dinner of the Grand Army of the Republic," February 7, 1918, box 244, Speeches and Writings, Newton Diehl Baker Papers, MD, LOC.

8. Franklin K. Lane, *Why Do We Fight Germany? A Cabinet Officer States the Truth about the War* (New York: 1917), PAH.

9. Elihu Root to Joseph Buffington, September 7, 1918, box 136, General Correspondence, Elihu Root Papers, MD, LOC.

10. Robert McNutt McElroy, untitled draft of a speech, June 27, 1917, box 20, Robert McNutt McElroy Papers, MD, LOC. McElroy, however, was no racial nationalist. In a July 1917 speech, he argued that demands for Anglo-Saxon unity were counterproductive and mischaracterized what it meant to be American. "The only call which can command the support of the American nation," he maintained, "is the call to defend a law that is higher than race loyalty, that transcends mere ethnic prejudices." Robert McNutt McElroy, "The Ideals of Our War," July 3, 1917, No. 5 (New York: 1917), 4–5, PTE.

11. Robert Herrick, *Jungle Law* (New York: [1917?]), PAH.

12. Notestein and Stoll (eds.), *Conquest and Kultur*, 7.

13. Elmer Ellsworth Rittenhouse, *Know Your Enemy* (New York: 1918), 2, 5, 6, and 7, PAH.

14. Irvin S. Cobb, "Thrice Is He Armed," *Saturday Evening Post*, April 21, 1917, 137.

15. James, "Introduction: Reading World War I Posters," 20–21. While Pearl James and the contributors to the volume analyze poster art exclusively, I find that their analyses are applicable to political cartoons as well, which were only slightly more nuanced and no less sensational.

16. Herford also appears to have given the kaiser a large, hooked nose, which appears to link the corrupt German mind with that of the allegedly double-dealing, morally suspect, and

acquisitive Jewish Other, whom some Anglo-Saxon patricians and agrarian populists had viewed as a prime threat to the American economy and Anglo-Saxon identity in the late nineteenth century. Anti-Semitic references in anti-German propaganda, however, were far from the norm. Most scholars of anti-Semitism maintain that such bigotry, although not uncommon, was not particularly widespread in the United States, which may explain why propagandists rarely employed stereotypical Jewish traits as an "Other" template. See Higham, "Anti-Semitism in the Gilded Age," 573–574; Dinnerstein, *Anti-Semitism in America*; and Gerber, "Anti-Semitism and Jewish-Gentile Relations in American Historiography and the American Past," 30–31.

17. "Can the World Make Peace with This Thing?," cartoon. *New York Times Current History*, June 1918, 558. From the *Columbus (OH) Dispatch*. Historian Nicoletta F. Gullace has examined the racialized nature of many of the posters that I discuss in this chapter (plus some from Great Britain and Australia), and we share some similarities in our analysis. Gullace, however, focuses solely on poster art, while I place the posters in the broader context of print, oral, and cartoon propaganda. By looking at the posters as part of a wider campaign, the representations look less specifically "Asiatic," as Gullace claims, than they do generic illustrations of Germany's alleged regression. Gullace, "Barbaric Anti-Modernism," 61–78. Descriptions of Prussian militarism as being of a bygone era of European history or renderings of Germany as a caveman suggest most Americans at the time continued to view degenerated Teutons as fundamentally European.

18. See Rawls, *Wake Up, America!*, 28, 210. From February 1918 to January 1919, *Everybody's Magazine* ran a series on the history of Germany's occupation of Belgium based largely on British accounts of atrocities, most of which were rooted in rumor. The fact that the series ran into the postwar months is indicative of the series' popularity and, perhaps, the editors' desire for a harsh peace. *Everybody's Magazine*, February 1918–January 1919, vols. 38–40. Nicoletta F. Gullace examined German atrocity propaganda in Britain, arguing that stories and images of German soldiers defiling women and towns supported "an image of international law and a definition of the liberal state that located the safety of women and the family as the primary issue of the public realm." Raleigh's "Hun or Home?" and Young's "Remember Belgium" show that Americans often viewed this type of propaganda in such way. Gullace, "Sexual Violence and Family Honor," 725–728.

19. Other, presumably later, editions of this poster included a caption along the shoreline to the right of the gorilla's foot reading "If this war is not fought to a finish in Europe, it will be on the soil of the United States." See Rawls, *Wake Up, America!*, 66. Art historian David M. Lubin appears to find a dual meaning in the poster. On the one hand, he maintains, it was a projection of white fears of black (and possibly Jewish) rape. On the other, the ape was a figure many Americans, even women, "might have admired [for] his unconstrained physicality, emotionality, and freedom from middle class strictures of behavior, sexual or otherwise." Lubin, *Grand Illusions*, 27–41, quote from 39. While my research supports Lubin's first assertion to a large degree, to me, his second interpretation does not appear to hold up when examined in the context of wartime attitudes about racial progress. As chapter 1 shows, a large number of Americans during neutrality accepted the notion that a touch of savagery was necessary for individual, racial, and national growth. Hopps's rapacious "mad brute," however, has devolved far more than what was deemed admirable or desirable.

20. See Ayers, *Vengeance and Justice*, 239–245; and Hall, *Revolt Against Chivalry*, 145–149. Ideas of racial progress, identity, and apocalyptic destruction, however, were no less significant in African Americans' understanding of the war, the threat posed by Germany, and their identity as Americans. Such thoughts were perhaps more salient to their daily lives. Throughout the war and before, the African American press regularly applied the adjectives "barbaric" and "uncivilized" to the white South, doing so much more frequently than they did to the German enemy. How could one so quickly condemn German atrocities and autocracy, many black editors asked, when Jim Crow oppression and lynching showed the white South was just as atrocious? Yet, with

their country at war, many of the most prominent African American newspapers and organizations felt compelled to support the national cause and join in the chorus of voices warning about the consequences to the American people if Germany won the war. When they did, however, they often described the difference between Germany and the South as being one of degree but not substance. One illustrative example is W.E.B. DuBois's editorial in the May 1917 edition of the *Crisis* in which he wrote that the Great War itself "is an appeal to barbarism," which racial discrimination and lynching had shown was not alien to the United States. While in no way pardoning whites for their cruelty toward blacks, DuBois claimed that German barbarism was, in fact, uniquely savage and dangerous, even compared to what southern blacks faced on a regular basis. "Bad as [American racism and lynching] is, slavery is worse; German dominion is worse; the rape of Belgium and France is worse." "The World Last Month," *Crisis*, May 1917, 8. DuBois, who described the conflict as both a war of white imperialism and an opportunity for dark-skinned peoples to free themselves from colonization, considered the Allies the lesser of many evils, with Germany being the most brutal of Europe's imperial overlords. "World War and the Color Line," *Crisis*, November 1914, 28–30; "Germany," *Crisis*, February 1916, 186–187; and "A Philosophy in Time of War," *Crisis*, August 1918, 164–165. For examples of black newspapers placing lynching and German atrocities on near-equal footing, see "Uncle Sam Speaks: Barbarous Unchristian Europe!," cartoon. *Crisis*, March 1916, 236; "Civilization," *Crisis*, August 1916, 165; "Civilization in the South," *Crisis*, March 1917, 215–216; "Tennessee Lynching Outrivals Worst German Atrocities," *Baltimore Afro-American*, December 8, 1917; "Me and God," *Baltimore Afro-American*, January 19, 1918; and "Autocracies, Germany and Elsewhere," *Baltimore Afro-American*, February 2, 1918. The best scholarly works on African Americans' wartime challenges, setbacks, and victories are Lentz-Smith, *Freedom Struggles*; and Williams, *Torchbearers of Democracy*.

21. As Lynn Dumenil points out, women in wartime visual propaganda (primarily posters and films) were portrayed as either modern, independent heroines doing their bit for their country or vulnerable "objects in need of masculine protection." In posters depicting a woman as a victim (or potential victim) of rape or violence, she effectively argues, the female character often symbolizes the nation, suggesting the Teutonic perpetrator could endanger "both patriarchal and national power" in the United States. Dumenil, *Second Line of Defense*, 204–211, quotes from 205, 211. Pearl James views the victimization themes of such propaganda as a feminization of victimhood meant to strike fear in the hearts of American women while shielding men from the more likely prospect that they would be the victim of the bloodthirsty Hun. James, "Images of Femininity in American World War I Posters," 284–285. In my mind, my argument on the centrality of racial and millennial interpretations of such scenes does not detract from Dumenil's and James's interpretations but considers additional cultural forces that inspired many Americans' actions and feelings toward the war.

22. Richard Slotkin perhaps takes the metaphor too far, claiming that the link many whites made between the alleged black rapist and the subhuman German defiler incited American vigilantism against German Americans and pro-German whites. Slotkin, *Lost Battalions*, 218–219. The pictorial metaphor of the subhuman beast—be it an ape, gorilla, wolf, or other hairy creature—also had been applied to Irish, Germans, Italians, and other non-Anglo immigrants during the nineteenth and early twentieth centuries and often denoted presumed racial inferiority in general, not necessarily a metaphorical reference to African Americans or rape.

23. Charles Wadsworth, Jr., *Perils of the United States: Address of Rev. Charles Wadsworth, Jr., D.D., before the Colonial Society of Pennsylvania, April 13, 1918* (Philadelphia, PA: 1918), 3–4, PAH. Similarly, representations of the subhuman enemy as ape-like would not suffice to explain early Japanese victories over the United States during World War II. American propaganda depicted the Japanese as bestial in terms of their aggressiveness yet also capable of effectively wielding the tools of modern warfare to their advantage. Such propaganda suggested to Ameri-

cans that overcoming such "supermen" would take a herculean effort. Dower, *War without Mercy*, 94–117.

24. Rawls, *Wake Up, America!*, 208–214.

25. Rawls, *Wake Up, America!*, 195–233. While most invasion posters were attached to the Liberty Loan and War Savings Stamp campaigns, not all posters in these drives employed fear to persuade Americans to monetarily support the war. Many attempted to shame Americans into doing their part or depicted patriotic scenes of Uncle Sam, Columbia, marching soldiers, or Americans (both native- and foreign-born) giving because of their love for liberty.

26. British Prime Minister David Lloyd George stressed the urgency of the situation to Wilson in his "Crisis Telegram," sent on March 28, 1918, a week after the first shots of the German offensive. Lloyd George claimed it was "impossible to exaggerate the importance of getting American reinforcements across the Atlantic in the shortest possible space of time." The formal British appeal to the United States for 120,000 men per month came two days later. Beaver, *Newton D. Baker and the American War Effort*, 134.

27. "America, Wake Up! Cease Living in a Fool's Paradise," *New York Tribune*, May 2, 1917.

28. Quoted in "What the United States Is Fighting For," *Current Opinion*, July 1917, 6. Also see "Germany's Larger Aims and America," *Review of Reviews*, February 1918, 116–117; Sartell Prentice, *What Doest Thou Here, America?* (Nyack, NY: 1917), 4, 6, PAH; André Chéradame, "The United States and Pan-Germanism" (New York: 1917), PAH; *Why We Are at War, Why You Must Help, What You Can Do* (New York: 1917), PAH; and "America in the Battle Line of Democracy," *World's Work*, April 1917, 581–586.

29. Lane, *Why Do We Fight Germany?* Lane repeated the scenario of a German invasion force launching from Canada in a letter to a soldier-in-training in March 1918. Franklin K. Lane to John Lyon, March 15, 1918, in *The Letters of Franklin K. Lane*, eds. Lane and Wall, 280.

30. David F. Houston, *Why We Went to War* (Washington, D.C.: 1918), 12, PAH. Also see Newton D. Baker to Woodrow Wilson, August 14, 1918, box 244, Speeches and Writings, Newton Diehl Baker Papers, MD, LOC; and Louis F. Post, *Why We Are at War* (New York: [1917?]), PAH.

31. Robert Lansing, "A War of Self-Defense," *Literary Digest*, December 29, 1917, 33, 100.

32. "The Liberty Loan," May 22, 1917, entry 62, box 2, CPI, NARA. Also see "The Liberty Loan," *Four Minute Men Bulletin*, June 9, 1917, no. 3, entry 62, box 2, CPI, NARA, 1, 3. The definitive work on the CPI's band of over 10,000 speakers is Cornebise, *War as Advertised*.

33. Shailer Mathews, "Democracy and World Politics," July 4, 1917, No. 10 (New York: 1917), 14–15, PTE. Other speeches relevant to this point from the Chautauqua training camp include William H. Hobbs, "The Outlook for Democracy," July 7, 1917, No. 8; McElroy, "The Ideals of Our War," July 3, 1917; Pomeroy Burton, "Hurry Up, America!," July 2, 1917, No. 11; and Franklin D. Roosevelt, "The Navy and the War," July 7, 1917, No. 12, all from PTE.

34. George Creel, "An American War and an American Victory," box 1, George Creel Papers, MD, LOC.

35. Woodrow Wilson to George Creel, July 29, 1918, box 1, George Creel Papers, MD, LOC.

36. "A Flag Day Address," June 14, 1917, in *PWW*, vol. 42, 501. Wilson remained consistent on the *Mitteleuropa* and German imperialism points throughout the war. See "An Address in Buffalo to the American Federation of Labor," November 12, 1917, in *PWW*, vol. 45, 13; and "An Address," April 6, 1918, in *PWW*, vol. 47, 267–270. An author in the *World's Work* crafted a similar scenario late in the war to justify American military involvement in Siberia. J.B.W. Gardiner, "Save Russia—Or Face Defeat," *World's Work*, October 1918, 599–603. Wilson's concern over German dominance of Eurasia mirrored that of future presidents, Harry Truman in particular, who feared an unstoppable and aggressive Soviet Union supported by the same resource base. Leffler, *Preponderance of Power*.

37. John S. P. Tatlock, *Why America Fights Germany*, War Information Series, No. 15 (Washington, DC: 1918), 8–9. For Gerard's account of his meeting with the kaiser, see Gerard, *My Four*

Years in Germany, 251–253. The author of another widely distributed CPI pamphlet made the same case. *How the War Came to America*, June 15, 1917, entry 41, box 5, PRWB, CPI, NARA, 1, 10, 11.

38. Not surprisingly, newspaper and magazine articles about the likelihood of a German attack on the metropolis were quite common. In April 1917, for instance, *Review of Reviews* ran an article that mimicked the oft-repeated preparedness argument that New York's fall to an invading force would leave the rest of the nation open to conquest because the vast majority of the American arms industry was within two-hundred miles of the city. Waldemar Kaempffert and Carl Dienstbach, "The Defense of New York," *Review of Reviews*, April 1917, 418–419. Looking to go back to this well again a year later, the magazine's editor Albert Shaw asked George Creel about the propriety of printing a speculative article about what would happen if New York came under attack by German bombers. Shaw claimed that such a story would "stimulate Americans to greater effort." Albert Shaw to George Creel, entry 1, box 21, Creel Correspondence, CPI, NARA. Creel was either indifferent or gave his blessing because the next month Shaw published the article, which concluded that "if we cherish the illusion that New York and other coast cities are safe from aerial bombardment, we live in a fool's paradise." "Can the Germans Bomb New York from the Air?," *Review of Reviews*, May 1918, 492–496, quote from 496.

39. Pennell, *Joseph Pennell's Liberty Loan Poster*, 7.

40. Emily Palmer Cape, "What Will America Lose if She Loses the War," n.d., box 629, Women's Defense Work, CND, NARA. Several of the speeches found in these records, such as the one cited here, clearly were delivered at some time during the war. The author's edits are visible in the margins and the length of the speeches—one typed page—meant they were short in duration. The inclusion of *Four Minute Men Bulletins* within these same files suggests that the CPI guided the speech-making of the Committee on Women's Defense Work.

41. "4-Minute Talk: 'Your Country Appeals to You!'" n.d., box 628, Women's Defense Work, CND, NARA.

42. S. Stanwood Menken to Elihu Root, September 13, 1917, box 136, General Correspondence, Elihu Root Papers, MD, LOC.

43. Albert Payson Terhune, *What the Victory or Defeat of Germany Means to Every American* (New York: [1917?]), PAH.

44. Agnes Repplier, *What Does the Victory or Defeat of Germany Mean to the United States?* (New York: [1917?]), PAH. The slight difference in title with the other pamphlets is of negligible importance in that Repplier was asked to speak to the same point and, presumably, their dates of production were close.

The YMCA, of all organizations, made a similarly hyperbolic point on the spread of German cruelty to the United States and its impact on the American family in a poster that claims American homes "will be brought low" like those already labeled "German-enemy territory." "The Security and Happiness of Your Home Are Threatened," n.d., entry 1, box 22, Creel Correspondence, CPI, NARA.

45. Walter Camp, *What the Victory or Defeat of Germany Means to Every American* (New York: [1917?]), PAH. Also see the contributions of Owen Johnson, James H. Collins, Granville Fortescue, Booth Tarkington, Cosmo Hamilton, and Prince and Princess Pierre Troubetzkoy, which shared the same title as Camp's pamphlet and cited similar or identical concerns.

46. The future conditions propagandists described were similar to the national security state that would arise after World War II. See Friedberg, *In the Shadow of the Garrison State*; and Hogan, *Cross of Iron*. For the militarizing effects the Cold War garrison state had on American culture and politics, see Sherry, *In the Shadow of War*; and Craig and Logevall, *America's Cold War*.

47. "A Flag Day Address," June 14, 1917, in *PWW*, vol. 42, 502. Wilson's "peace without victory" speech of January 1917 called for a return to the *status quo ante bellum* as the quickest means of ending the bloodshed, which in some ways contradicted his argument that civilization was not safe as long as autocracy reigned in Germany. But over time he became increasingly

more frustrated with German intransigence. After receiving an unsatisfactory response from Germany in October 1918 on accepting his Fourteen Points and his call for them to disarm and evacuate all occupied territories, the president concluded that the autocratic regime must go. Cooper, *Woodrow Wilson*, 442–445. Before then, some of the most ardent opponents of the League of Nations used Wilson's own argument, that militaristic Germany would likely strike the United States in the future, against him. See Henry Cabot Lodge, "The War Work of Congress," *Forum*, June 1918, 686; William Howard Taft, "The Things Against Which We Are Fighting: The Attempt to Conquer and Prussianize the World," in *A Reference Book for Speakers* (New York: 1918), 18, box 630, Women's Defense Work, CND, NARA; and William Howard Taft, *The Menace of a Premature Peace: An Address Delivered at Montreal, Canada, September 26, 1917* (New York: 1917), PAH.

48. Roosevelt, "The Navy and the War," 11.

49. *The President's Flag Day Address* (Washington, DC: 1917), 5, 28. The Flag Day pamphlet was one of the most widely circulated CPI pamphlets, with a distribution of 6,813,340 copies. Mock and Larson, *Words That Won the War*, 171.

50. Josephus Daniels, "War Against Junkerism," February 22, 1918, in Daniels, *The Navy and the Nation*, 97. That long-term militarization threatened the advances made by labor during the Progressive Era was a fairly common theme. Some fitting examples include Daniels, "Patriotism Before Business," March 29, 1917, in *The Navy and the Nation*, 35; John R. Commons, *Why Workingmen Support the War* (New York: [1918?]), PAH; and Woodrow Wilson, "A Labor Day Address," September 2, 1918, in *PWW*, vol. 49, 414–415.

51. "Statement of Hon. Newton D. Baker," May 1, 1918, box 244, Speeches and Writings, Newton Diehl Baker Papers, MD, LOC.

52. Franklin K. Lane to J. O'H. Cosgrove, December 21, 1917, in *Letters of Franklin K. Lane*, 263. Secretary of Agriculture David F. Houston stayed on message as well. Houston, *Steps to Victory: Address Delivered before the Economic Club, New York City, December 6, 1917* (New York: 1917), PAH.

53. *News and Courier* quoted in "What the United States Is Fighting For," *Current Opinion*, July 1917, 6.

54. Elihu Root to B. Lorenzo Hill, March 5, 1918, box 136, General Correspondence, Elihu Root Papers, MD, LOC.

55. Bielaski to R. H. Van Deman, May 7, 1917; Van Deman to Intelligence Officer, May 8, 1917 (two letters); C. B. Treadway, report, May 5, 1917; and Van Deman to Bielaski, June 13, 1917 and June 20, 1917; all from file 9140-470, box 2028, Gen. Corr., MID, NARA. In August 1917, two informants gave the MID detailed accounts of a German spy and propaganda campaign head-quartered in New York City but apparently conspiring to sabotage the Canal Zone. Anonymous, report, August 1917, file 9140-859, box 2037, Gen. Corr., MID, NARA.

56. John L. Zurbrick to Howard P. Wright, April 14, 1917 (two letters), file 9140-438, box 2028, Gen. Corr., MID, NARA.

57. Robert Bridges, *Patriotism and War: An Address Delivered at Renton and Issaquah, Washington on July Fourth, 1917* (Seattle, WA: 1917), PAH. Emphasis in the original.

58. "New York Given Air Raid Scare," *Chicago Tribune*, July 2, 1918.

59. *Everybody's Magazine*, November 1917, 79.

60. "The Liberty Loan," *Four Minute Men Bulletin*, June 9, 1917, no. 3, entry 62, box 2, CPI, NARA, 1.

61. See Preston, *Aliens and Dissenters*; Polenberg, *Fighting Faiths*; and Keith, *Rich Man's War, Poor Man's Fight*. The year 1917 saw more strikes than any other year in US history—4,450 to be exact—as those who felt left behind by the war boom, particularly those in mining and lumber industries in the West, lashed out at those they felt exploited them for large war profits. Kennedy, *Over Here*, 262–263.

62. "Explanatory Note for the Benefit of War Lecturers," enclosure to "Report of Speaker's Bureau, Council of Defense and Food Administration for Kansas," February 2, 1918, entry 82, box 6, General Correspondence Regarding Speakers, CPI, NARA. Emphasis in the original.

63. "Community Action in a Government at War," enclosure to "Report of Speaker's Bureau, Council of Defense and Food Administration for Kansas," February 2, 1918, entry 82, box 6, General Correspondence Regarding Speakers, CPI, NARA. Emphasis in the original.

64. By the same token, Dixon believed that the "tendency to servility in the Slav nation" of Russia allowed the autocratic Romanov dynasty to thrive for centuries. Frederick Dixon to Grosvenor Clarkson, September 4, 1917, entry 1, box 5, Creel Correspondence, CPI, NARA.

65. Alice Upton Pearmain, Circular No. 2, November 22, 1917, box 628, Women's Defense Work, CND, NARA. Emphasis in the original. Also see Melvyn Ryder to George Creel, November 5, 1917, entry 1, box 21, Creel Correspondence, CPI, NARA.

66. Conference Report, Department of Educational Propaganda, [1918?], box 629, Women's Defense Work, CND, NARA. Also, see Edmund Leigh Pell to Josephus Daniels, October 4, 1917, reel 47, Special Correspondence, Josephus Daniels Papers, MD, LOC.

67. Francis H. Weston to Thomas W. Gregory, August 6, 1917, box 1, Thomas W. Gregory Papers, MD, LOC.

68. Summary of letter from G. H. Mathis to CPI, September 28, 1917, entry 82, box 4, General Correspondence Regarding Speakers, CPI, NARA.

69. Allen Bartlit Pond to Woodrow Wilson, July 13, 1917, in *PWW*, vol. 43, 168, 169.

70. Richard Hathaway Edmonds to Woodrow Wilson, October 4, 1917, in *PWW*, vol. 44, 305, 306. Wilson replied to Edmonds the next day and perhaps revealed the degree to which he was closed off from the public or blind to its sentiments: "I get widely variant accounts of the matter [apathy and opposition toward the war] from different parts of the country, or rather it would be more correct to say that from most parts of the country I get the report that the people do very distinctly comprehend what the war is about and are thoughtfully back of the administration." Woodrow Wilson to Richard Hathaway Edmonds, October 5, 1917, in *PWW*, vol. 44, 308.

71. Frank Irving Cobb to Woodrow Wilson, August 27, 1917, in *PWW*, vol. 44, 74; and Woodrow Wilson to Frank Irving Cobb, September 1, 1917, in *PWW*, vol. 44, 118.

72. Leon B. Bacon to George Creel, March 5, 1918, entry 1, box 1, Creel Correspondence, CPI, NARA.

73. B. Gamble to George Creel, November 26, 1917, entry 1, box 9, Creel Correspondence, CPI, NARA. Emphasis in the original.

74. Charles F. Oursler to Newton D. Baker, March 4, 1918, entry 1, box 9, Creel Correspondence, CPI, NARA. The War Department forwarded the letter to Creel.

75. B. Hart Wright to George Creel, April 4, 1918, entry 1, box 26, Creel Correspondence, CPI, NARA.

76. Orr Buffington to Newton D. Baker, October 31, 1917; and George Creel to Orr Buffington, November 7, 1917. Both from entry 1, box 3, Creel Correspondence, CPI, NARA.

Chapter 5 · *Toward the Democratic Millennium, 1914–1918*

1. "Germans Seek Help of Devil, Not God, Says Dr. Bricker," *Atlanta Constitution*, May 7, 1917.

2. Weber, *Living in the Shadow of the Second Coming*, 9–13, 115. Admittedly, my description of premillennialism in the text glosses over the diversity of belief within the various premillennial sects. What I describe in the text refers to the dispensationalist view because, as scholar Timothy Weber points out, it was the most popular form of premillennialism in the period before the war. Additionally, wartime premillennialists believed that Kaiser Wilhelm, though a bad seed, could not be the Antichrist because he did not possess the qualities found in prophecy.

The qualifications for the Antichrist, according to premillennialists, were that he be born in former Roman territory, rule a coalition of ten nations, and falsely proclaim he was God, none of which fit Wilhelm II, although Germany's allies Austria-Hungary and Ottoman Turkey had been part of the Roman Empire.

3. Much of my understanding of postmillennialism has come from Marsden, *Fundamentalism and American Culture*, 48–54; and Hutchinson, *Modernist Impulse in American Protestantism*.

4. Marsden, *Fundamentalism and American Culture*, 146. Although not directly responsible for wartime millennialist propaganda, Catholic "modernists" at the turn of the century were models from which many liberal Protestant ministers formed their interpretation of millennialism. Hutchinson, *Modernist Impulse in American Protestantism*, 179–182.

5. See Cherry (ed.), *God's New Israel*.

6. Walters, *American Reformers*, 25–26.

7. See Smith, *Revivalism and Social Reform in Mid-Nineteenth Century America*, 235; and Moorhead, *American Apocalypse*, 81.

8. Griffen, "The Progressive Ethos," 120–149. Ronald G. Walters claims that early American secular reformers also employed the language of millennialism. Walters, *American Reformers*, 37.

9. Henry W. Wright, "The Religion of Democracy," *Forum*, March 1915, 332, 334. Also see Putney, *Muscular Christianity*, 11–44.

10. "The Meaning of the War," *Collier's*, August 22, 1914, 14.

11. "Why Not Try Christianity?," *Outlook*, December 9, 1914, 810. For an example of the mainstream press defining World War I as a literal Armageddon, see "The War as a Presage of the World's End," *Current Opinion*, February 1917, 117.

12. Garet Garrett, "When Christians Fight, Are They Christians?," *Everybody's Magazine*, December 1914, 844–846.

13. Agnes Repplier, "Christianity and War," *Atlantic Monthly*, January 1915, 12.

14. Many Americans understood the New Testament as advocating non-violence and love for one's enemy when confronted with physical violence. Several Protestant churches, such as the Society of Friends, the Mennonites, and the Church of the Brethren, renounced war completely, maintaining that any act that led directly or indirectly to the death of another human being violated God's commandment that "thou shall not kill." Preparedness advocates and, later, pro-war ministers and propagandists saw peace churches, which represented a small minority of Christian voices, as enough of a threat that they consistently attacked pacifist beliefs as naïve, effeminate, and un-Christian. Wartime legislation against disloyal rhetoric also quieted pacifist Christians through intimidation and incarceration. Much of the propaganda calling for Christian courage was meant as a direct counter to the religious underpinnings of isolationism and pacifism. Piper, *American Churches in World War I*, 11–12. For representative examples of vigilantism against and the legal persecution of pacifist ministers, see Peterson and Fite, *Opponents of War*, 113–120.

15. "Christianity and War," *Outlook*, January 13, 1915, 61–62.

16. "The Crime of Cowardice," *Outlook*, October 13, 1915, 355–356. Calls for Christian courage continued after April 1917 but were not as prevalent as during the preparedness debate, the peak year of 1915 especially. See *What Ye Fight For? Answer of a Catholic Priest* (New York: 1917), PAH; and "Why Not?," *Outlook*, March 6, 1918, 360.

17. Dudley Field Malone, "National Defense," *McClure's Magazine*, March 1916, 19.

18. Quoted in "Not a Failure, but a Denial of Christianity," *Literary Digest*, January 9, 1915, 59. McKim's comments about the un-Christian nature of German bellicosity and a man's responsibility to protect one's homeland "from unprovoked attack" was likely a reflection of his devotion to the prevailing Lost Cause myth that Union aggression was among the chief reasons for southern secession and the start of the Civil War. See Wilson, *Baptized in Blood*, 49 and 164–165.

19. *Christian World* quoted in "Germany's 'New Spirituality,'" *Literary Digest*, May 15, 1915, 1154–1155.

20. William Jewett Tucker, "The Ethical Challenge of the Times," *Atlantic Monthly*, June 1915, 800–801.

21. "Lutheran Protests of Loyalty," *Literary Digest*, August 4, 1917, 40.

22. It is important to point out that I found no evidence that propagandists or angry citizens targeted German Catholics specifically. Perhaps this was because the presumed source of Germans' spiritual deterioration was militarist Prussia, which was predominantly Protestant.

23. Abrams, *Preachers Present Arms*, 29, 31, 211–213. Some German American Lutheran ministers even acted as informants for the federal government, ratting out pro-German pastors or members of their congregations.

24. Luebke, *Bonds of Loyalty*, 280–281.

25. Irvin S. Cobb, "The Prussian Paranoia," *Saturday Evening Post*, May 5, 1917, 3–4, 49, 51, quote from 4.

26. "Germany in Need of a New God," *Current Opinion*, November 1917, 329–330. The *Providence Journal* quote is from 330.

27. Cyrus Townsend Brady, *What the Victory or Defeat of Germany Means to Every American* (New York: [1917?]), PAH.

28. Joseph C. Lincoln, *What the Victory or Defeat of Germany Would Mean* (New York: [1917?]), PAH.

29. In reality, the mass casualties were the result of tactics employed by both sides throughout 1918. The highest casualty rates of the conflict occurred during Germany's spring offensives and the Allied counteroffensives through the summer and fall. In this decisive period of the war, soldiers spent far less time in the safety of their trenches and more time advancing against machine guns and rapid-firing artillery across open ground. The results were horrific. For example, during the German army's spring offensives, when German soldiers were ordered to cross "no man's land" in droves, it lost roughly 900,000 men in four months. By contrast, in ten months of fighting at Verdun in 1916—the longest battle of the war—Germany lost around 450,000 soldiers killed, wounded, and missing. Morrow, *Great War*, 129, 246.

30. "His God," cartoon. *New York Times Current History*, March 1918, 569. From the *Providence Journal*.

31. William E. Barton, *The Moral Meanings of the World War: A Sermon in the First Congregational Church of Oak Park, Illinois, Sunday, June 16, 1918* (Oak Park, IL: 1918), 17, PAH.

32. Francis J. Oppenheimer, *No "Made in Germany" Peace* (New York: [1917?]), PAH.

33. Lyman Abbott, "The Spiritual Meaning of Democracy," *Outlook*, April 17, 1918, 616.

34. Carl Krusada, "There Is No Christ in Germany," *Forum*, February 1918, 227–228, 230.

35. Marsden, *Fundamentalism and American Culture*, 146, 148–149.

36. Rittenhouse, *Know Your Enemy*, 614, PAH.

37. "Nietzsche's Religion," *Outlook*, January 23, 1918, 131.

38. Henry A. Wise Wood, *Christ, or the Sword?* (New York: 1918), PAH.

39. McLoughlin, *Billy Sunday Was His Name*, 125–126.

40. Sunday quoted in Bruns, *Preacher*, 130.

41. Martin, *Hero of the Heartland*, 121.

42. Peter Clark MacFarlane, "Sunday Salvation," *Everybody's Magazine*, May 1915, 363. MacFarlane, while acknowledging the massive audiences who came to see Sunday, believed the preacher's theology was "absurd" and outdated. For a short yet informative summary of Sunday's theology, see Dorsett, *Billy Sunday and the Redemption of Urban America*, 70–74.

43. Sunday's closest competitor in terms of his hyperbolic sermons was Congregationalist minister Newell Dwight Hillis. Hillis explained, "For three years the Kaiser has had the Devil all

mixed up with God,—being unable to distinguish between them." The German military, he reported, distributed tokens to German soldiers that promised "that your Kaiser and your War Staff" would protect them from God's ultimate judgment for atrocities committed against civilians. Hillis thought a more accurate description of the arrangement was that Satan would not judge soldiers for their monstrous actions. "Hell and damnation are fully satisfied with all you Germans have done," he concluded. Hillis, *German Atrocities*, 34; and Abrams, *Preachers Present Arms*, 98–99.

44. Bruns, *Preacher*, 249–250. Quotes from McLoughlin, *Billy Sunday*, 258, 259–260; and Marsden, *Fundamentalism and American Culture*, 142. Tagging Germany as the source of the global pandemic does not seem to have been common. See Barry, *Great Influenza*, 343–344; and Koenig, *Fourth Horseman*, 263–264.

45. Gamble, *War for Righteousness*, 149–154, quotes from the Senate pastor, McAdoo, and Hulbert on 149, 150, 153. Lane quoted in Leuchtenberg, *Perils of Prosperity*, 45–46. Wilson quote from "An Address to a Joint Session of Congress," April 2, 1917, in *PWW*, vol. 41, 523.

46. Harold Bell Wright, "The Sword of Jesus," *American Magazine*, February 1918, 7, 8, 57.

47. John H. Boyd, *The Unmasking of Germany* (Portland, OR: [1918?]), 5–7, 11, PAH.

48. George Frederick Pentecost, *The Presbyterian Church in the War: A Sermon Preached at Bethany Presbyterian Church, Philadelphia, Pa., July 1st, 1917* (Philadelphia: 1917), 4, 8, PAH. Emphasis in the original.

49. Abbott, "Spiritual Meaning of Democracy," 615–616.

50. Lyman Abbott, "Which?," *Outlook*, January 2, 1918, 10. The National Americanization Committee produced an interesting pamphlet making a similar comparison between Lincoln and the kaiser, including a letter the kaiser sent to the bereaved mother of nine dead German soldiers in which Wilhelm thanked her for her and her sons' sacrifices and included a photograph of himself. Lincoln's letter to the mother of five Union soldiers killed during the Civil War, however, expressed only empathy, regret, and his condolences. *Why America Is at War: Where Will You Make Your Home?* (New York: [1917?]), PAH.

51. Tatlock, *Why America Fights Germany*, 7.

52. Notestein and Stoll (eds.) *Conquest and Kultur*, 7, 15, 17.

53. "This Is Kultur," *Everybody's Magazine*, October 1918, 104. The following publications also printed the ad, giving it a tremendously wide circulation: *The Independent*, October 12, 1918, 60; *Collier's*, September 28, 1918, 31; and, strangely, among advertisements for purchasing gold as well as dental and medical devices in *The Journal of the National Dental Association*, October 1918, 1114.

54. Charles Elbert Whelan, *The Liberty Loan: A Stand for God and Humanity, A Test of Patriotism* (Madison, WI: [1918?]), 1–3, PAH.

55. David James Burrell, "Onward, Christian Soldiers, to the Golden Age!" in "Is God in the War?," *Forum*, December 1917, 675.

56. Edgar Saltus, *What the Victory or Defeat of Germany Means to Every American* (New York: [1917?]), PAH.

57. Charles S. Medbury, *Mobilizing the Mind of America* (New York: 1918), 12–13, PAH. Also see "Jesus No 'Peace-At-Any-Price' Man," *Current Opinion*, April 1918, 271–272.

58. Knock, *To End All Wars*, 4, 8, 33.

59. Quoted in Tuveson, *Redeemer Nation*, 211. While Wilson's religious faith was a key factor in his desire and fight for a League of Nations, he also sought universal peace for political and strategic reasons. As the recent and the next world war would indicate, imperialism and militarism, not just in Germany but in all of Europe, was a problem that needed fixing.

60. "An Address in the Oakland Municipal Auditorium," September 18, 1919, in *PWW*, vol. 63, 354–355.

61. Knock, *To End All Wars*, 252–254; and Cooper, *Breaking the Heart of the World*.

62. On the seeming irrelevance of Wilsonian internationalism on immediate postwar memory, see Trout, *On the Battlefield of Memory*, 35–37.

63. Marsden, *Fundamentalism and American Culture*.

64. To maintain that the war led to universal "disillusionment," religious or otherwise, would be an oversimplification. Although the nation failed to live up to its lofty millennial goals, many still looked back at the war as a time of national unity and strength. Memory of the United States' experience during the First World War would be contested throughout the interwar years. Trout, *On the Battlefield of Memory*.

65. Reinhold Niebuhr, "What the War Did to My Mind," *Christian Century*, September 27, 1928, 1161–1162.

Epilogue · *Fear, Othering, and Identity in the Postwar United States*

1. "The Collapse of Autocracy and the Peril of Bolshevism," *Current Opinion*, December 1918, 345.

2. "Nation Rejoices at War's End," *New York Times*, November 12, 1918.

3. See Luebke, *Bonds of Loyalty*, 311–320, 328–331; and Kazal, *Becoming Old Stock*.

4. Fitzgerald, *Great Gatsby*, 32, 44.

5. Charges of SPA and IWW collaboration with Germany became quite common in the press during the first summer of American belligerency. A few examples include "Our Socialists," *Chicago Tribune*, June 5, 1917; and "He Charges I.W.W. Conspire with Foe," *New York World*, June 29, 1917.

6. Morrow, *Great War*, 237.

7. "Wake Up, America!," *Chicago Tribune*, March 24, 1918.

8. The Wilson administration also put its reputation behind charges that radicals in the United States were in cahoots with Germany by releasing the pamphlet *The German-Bolshevik Conspiracy* in the fall of 1918 through the Committee on Public Information. Edgar Sisson, an associate head of the CPI and chief of the agency's Foreign Section, smuggled several seemingly incriminating documents out of Russia that he believed verified that the Bolshevik leadership "are German agents" who worked with German officials to smuggle "agents-agitators, and agents-destructors" into the United States. Despite two American scholars testifying to their authenticity, British intelligence concluded that the documents were forgeries. This did not deter the Wilson administration and CPI. The documents had a significant impact on Woodrow Wilson, who, after seeing them in May, found sending American soldiers to assist anti-Bolshevik forces in the Russian Civil War more appealing. Foglesong, *America's Secret War against Bolshevism*, 171, 196. Quotes from *The German-Bolshevik Conspiracy* (Washington, DC: 1918), entry 41, box 5, PRWB, CPI, NARA.

9. The *New York Globe* quoted from "Bolshevism Threatening the World," *Literary Digest*, November 23, 1918, 9.

10. A. Mitchell Palmer, "The Case against the 'Reds,'" *Forum*, February 1920, 174, 180, 182.

11. Murray, *Red Scare*, 112.

12. Grant, *Passing of the Great Race*, 16, 18–19, 49, 263. Also see Guterl, "'Absolute Whiteness,'" 149–166.

13. Quoted in Jacobson, *Whiteness of a Different Color*, 96–97.

14. Hawley, *Great War and the Search for a Modern Order*, 58; and Pegram, *One Hundred Percent American*, 26.

15. Despite such sentiments, the United States did not remove itself from global affairs completely. The Dawes and Young plans as well as the Washington Naval Conference are the three most well-known examples of American diplomatic and economic intervention abroad. Herring, *From Colony to Superpower*, 436–483.

16. Fitzgerald, *Great Gatsby*, 12–13.

17. Painter, *History of White People*, 327–348; and Jacobson, *Whiteness of a Different Color*, 91–96. Also see Barkan, *Retreat of Scientific Racism*; Hale, *Making Whiteness*; Roediger, *Wages of Whiteness*; and Roediger, *Working toward Whiteness*.

18. Postwar disillusionment was particularly stark in the 1930s, the decade of the Great Depression, as scholars such as Walter Millis and politicians like Gerald Nye provided populist critiques of the war effort that claimed American intervention was a means of securing banks' investments by ensuring Allied victory and, thus, greater profits for the arms industry. Millis, *Road to War*; and Kennedy, *Freedom from Fear*, 386–388. European writers of the 1920s fit the label "disillusioned" far better than those in the United States. See Fussell, *Great War and Modern Memory*; and Eksteins, *Rites of Spring*, 275–299.

19. Lippmann, *Public Opinion*, 4, 16, 248–249. Lippmann's new appraisal of democracy differed from his contention in 1914 that a rational progressive state could save the masses from their ignorance. Lippmann, *Drift and Mastery*. Just a few short years after the publication of *Public Opinion*, Adolf Hitler took a similarly pessimistic view of democracy and the masses when examining anti-German propaganda produced in Great Britain and the United States during World War I. He wrote in *Mein Kampf*, his autobiography and political testimony, that a propagandist can overcome the "slow-moving" masses' poor memory "only after the simplest ideas are repeated thousands of times." The message, though, should not only be simple. "The art of propaganda lies in understanding the emotional ideas of the great masses and finding, through a psychologically correct form, the way to the attention and thence to the heart of the broad masses." To Hitler, American and British depictions of Germans as inherently brutal were "as ruthless as [they were] brilliant." "The rabid, impudent bias and persistence with which this lie was expressed" was masterful because it "took into account the emotional, always extreme, attitude of the great masses and for this reason was believed." Hitler, *Mein Kampf*, 180, 183–184, 185.

20. George Creel to Thomas W. Lamont, October 23, 1918, entry 1, box 14, folder 383, Creel Correspondence, CPI, NARA.

21. Creel, *How We Advertised America*, 4–5, 169. Creel had made these thoughts public the year before, saying in an article in *Everybody's Magazine*, "The average newspaper . . . made for confusion rather than clarity; its appeals were to the emotions not to the mind; it cluttered public discussion with rumors, distortions, false report and hysteria." The CPI, on the other hand, tried to forge "a public opinion bed-rocked in *truth* and built high and strong with *facts*." George Creel, "The American Newspaper: What It Is and What It Isn't," *Everybody's Magazine*, April 1919, 41. Emphasis in the original.

22. See Polenberg, *War and Society*, 51–54; Winkler, *Politics of Propaganda*; Jeffries, *Wartime America*, 178; and Takaki, *Double Victory*, 131–136.

23. Dower, *War without Mercy*, 301–314.

24. See Patterson, *Grand Expectations*, 165–205; Griffith, *Politics of Fear*; and Dudziak, *Cold War Civil Rights*. The perceived precariousness of American identity, though, was not a factor in Americans' fear of dying in a fiery, thermonuclear Armageddon with the Soviet Union. Americans were able to live with that fear by trivializing it. See May, *Homeward Bound*; and Winkler, *Life under a Cloud*.

25. See Said, *Orientalism*.

26. Jeanne Meserve, "Duct Tape Sales Rise amid Terror Fears," *CNN*, February 11, 2003, www.cnn.com/2003/US/02/11/emergency.supplies/.

27. Stearns, *American Fear*, ix.

28. Andrea Elliot, "The Man behind the Anti-Shariah Movement," *New York Times*, July 31, 2011, www.nytimes.com/2011/07/31/us/31shariah.html.

29. Josh Levs, "Texas Democrats: Judge Who Said Obama Could Trigger Civil War Should Quit," *CNN*, August 24, 2012, www.cnn.com/2012/08/23/us/texas-judge-warning.

30. Esther Yu-Hsi Lee, "Texas Sheriff Claims 'Quran Books' Found at Mexican Border May Mean ISIS Infiltration," ThinkProgress.com, September 15, 2014, thinkprogress.org/immigration /2014/09/15/3567351/texas-sheriff-claims-isis-penetrate-united-states.

Federal Records—National Archives, College Park, Maryland
Records of the Department of Justice, Record Group 60

Straight Numerical File, 1904–1974

Records of the Council of National Defense, Record Group 62

Women's Defense Work Division, Educational Propaganda Department

Records of the Committee on Public Information, Record Group 63

Bulletins for Cartoonists
Correspondence of the Chairman, George Creel
Four-Minute Men Bulletins
General Correspondence of the Speaking Division
Pamphlets—"Red, White, and Blue" Series
Pamphlets—War Information Series

Records of the Federal Bureau of Investigation, Record Group 65

American Protective League, Correspondence with Field Offices, 1917–1919
Old German Files (microfilm)

Records of the War Department, Military Intelligence Division, Record Group 165

Correspondence Relating to Negro Subversion
General Correspondence and Reports
Plant Protection Section

Archived Personal Papers—Library of Congress, Washington, DC

Newton D. Baker Papers
Ray Stannard Baker Papers
Albert Sidney Burleson Papers
George Creel Papers
Josephus Daniels Papers

Thomas Watt Gregory Papers
Robert McNutt McElroy Papers
Louis F. Post Papers
Elihu Root Papers
Leonard Wood Papers

Published Papers, Document Collections, and Memoirs

Challener, Richard D., ed. *United States Military Intelligence Weekly Summaries.* Vol. 5, New York: Garland Publishing, 1978.

Creel, George. *How We Advertised America: The First Telling of the Amazing Story of the Committee on Public Information that Carried the Gospel of Americanism to Every Corner of the Globe.* New York: Harper & Bros., 1920.

Daniels, Josephus. *The Cabinet Diaries of Josephus Daniels, 1913–1921.* Edited by E. David Cronon. Lincoln: University of Nebraska Press, 1963.

——. *The Navy and the Nation: War-time Addresses by Josephus Daniels.* New York: George H. Doran Company, 1919.

Hitler, Adolf. *Mein Kampf.* Translated by Ralph Manheim. 1925. Reprint, New York: Houghton Mifflin, 1999.

Lane, Anne Wintermute, and Louise Herrick Wall, eds. *The Letters of Franklin K. Lane, Personal and Political.* New York: Houghton Mifflin, 1922.

Link, Arthur S., et al., eds. *The Papers of Woodrow Wilson.* 69 vols. Princeton, NJ: Princeton University Press, 1966–1994.

Lodge, Henry Cabot and Charles F. Redmond, eds. *Selections from the Correspondence of Theodore Roosevelt and Henry Cabot Lodge, 1884–1918.* 2 vols. 1925. Reprint, New York: De Capo Press, 1971.

Morison, Elting E., John M. Blum, and Alfred D. Chandler, eds. *The Letters of Theodore Roosevelt.* Vol. 8, *The Days of Armageddon, 1914–1919.* Cambridge, MA: Harvard University Press, 1954.

Propaganda in Its Military and Legal Aspects. Washington, DC: Military Intelligence Branch, Executive Division, General Staff, 1918.

Seymour, Charles, ed. *The Intimate Papers of Colonel House.* 4 vols. Boston: Houghton Mifflin, 1926–1928.

Tumulty, Joseph P. *Woodrow Wilson As I Knew Him.* Garden City, NY: Doubleday, Page & Company, 1924.

Contemporary Periodicals

American Journal of Physical
    Anthropology
American Magazine
Atlanta Constitution
Atlantic Monthly
Baltimore Afro-American
Century Magazine
Chicago Tribune
Christian Century
Collier's Weekly
Crisis
Current Opinion
Everybody's Magazine
Forum
Harper's Monthly Magazine

Life
Literary Digest
McClure's Magazine
Nation
New Republic
New York Times
New York Times Current History
New York Tribune
New York World
Outlook
Review of Reviews
Saturday Evening Post
Washington Post
World's Work

Contemporary Novels and Non-Fiction Works

Beard, George M. *American Nervousness: Its Causes and Consequences, A Supplement to Nervous Exhaustion (Neurasthenia).* New York: G. P. Putnam, 1881.

Dixon, Thomas. *The Fall of a Nation.* New York: D. Appleton and Company, 1916.

Fitzgerald, F. Scott. *The Great Gatsby.* 1925. Reprint, New York: Scribner, 2004.

Gerard, James W. *My Four Years in Germany.* New York: George H. Doran Company, 1917.

Grant, Madison. *The Passing of the Great Race.* 1916. Reprint, New York: Scribner's, 1922.

Hall, G. Stanley. "Corporal Punishment." *New York Education* 3 (November 1899), 163–165.

Hillis, Newell Dwight. *German Atrocities: Their Nature and Philosophy.* New York: Fleming H. Revell Company, 1918.

Hooton, E. A. Review of *Long Heads and Round Heads; or, What's the Matter with Germany,* by William Samuel Sadler. *American Journal of Physical Anthropology* 1, no. 3 (1918), 363–366.

Hough, Emerson. *The Web.* Chicago: Reilly & Lee, 1919.

Jones, John Price. *America Entangled: The Secret Plotting of German Spies in the United States and the Inside Story of the Sinking of the Lusitania*. New York: A. C. Laut, 1917.

Kellor, Frances. *Straight America: A Call to National Service*. New York: Macmillan, 1916.

Lawrence, David. *The True Story of Woodrow Wilson*. New York: George H. Doran Company, 1924.

Lea, Homer. *The Valor of Ignorance*. 1909. Reprint, New York: Harper and Bros., 1942.

Lippmann, Walter. *Drift and Mastery: An Attempt to Diagnose the Current Unrest*. New York: M. Kennerley, 1914.

———. *Public Opinion*. New York: Harcourt, Brace and Company, 1922.

Maxim, Hudson. *Defenseless America*. New York: Hearst International Library, 1915.

Moffett, Cleveland. *The Conquest of America: A Romance of Disaster and Victory*. New York: George H. Doran Company, 1916.

Pennell, Joseph. *Joseph Pennell's Liberty Loan Poster: A Text-Book for Artists and Amateurs, Governments and Teachers and Printers, with Notes, an Introduction and Essay on the Poster by the Artist, Associate Chairman of the Committee on Public Information, Division of Pictorial Publicity*. Philadelphia and London: J. B. Lippincott Company, 1918.

Roosevelt, Theodore. *America and the World War*. New York: Scribner's, 1915.

Ross, Edward A. *The Old World in the New: The Significance of Past and Present Immigration to the American People*. New York: The Century Company, 1914.

Sadler, William Samuel. *Long Heads and Round Heads; or, What's the Matter with Germany*. Chicago: A. C. McClurg & Co., 1918.

Thayer, William Roscoe. *The Life and Letters of John Hay*. 2 vols. Boston and New York: Houghton Mifflin Company, 1915.

Walker, J. Barnard. *America Fallen!: The Sequel to the European War*. New York: Dodd, Mead, and Company, 1915.

Scholarly Sources

Abrams, Ray H. *Preachers Present Arms*. New York: Round Table Press, 1933.

Adams, Michael C. C. *The Great Adventure: Male Desire and the Coming of World War I*. Bloomington: Indiana University Press, 1990.

Ambrosius, Lloyd. "Woodrow Wilson and *The Birth of a Nation*." In *Woodrow Wilson and American Internationalism*, 36–93. New York: Cambridge University Press, 2017.

Asada, Sadao. *From Mahan to Pearl Harbor: The Imperial Japanese Navy and the United States*. Annapolis, MD: Naval Institute Press, 2006.

Ayers, Edward L. *Vengeance and Justice: Crime and Punishment in the 19th-Century American South*. New York: Oxford University Press, 1984.

Ballantyne, Tony. *Orientalism and Race: Aryanism and the British Empire*. New York: Palgrave, 2002.

Barkan, Elazar. *The Retreat of Scientific Racism: Changing Concepts of Race in Britain and the United States between the World Wars*. New York: Cambridge University Press, 1992.

Barkawi, Tarak, and Keith Stanski, eds. *Orientalism and War*. New York: Columbia University Press, 2012.

Barry, John M. *The Great Influenza: The Epic Story of the Deadliest Plague in History*. New York: Viking, 2004.

Beaver, Daniel R. *Newton D. Baker and the American War Effort, 1917–1919*. Lincoln: University of Nebraska Press, 1966.

Bederman, Gail. *Manliness and Civilization: A Cultural History of Gender and Race in the United States, 1880–1917*. Chicago: University of Chicago Press, 1995.

Bidwell, Bruce W. *History of the Military Intelligence Division, Department of the Army General Staff, 1775–1941*. Frederick, MD: University Publications of America, 1986.

Bodnar, John. *The Transplanted: A History of Immigrants in Urban America*. Bloomington: Indiana University Press, 1985.

Boghardt, Thomas. *The Zimmermann Telegram: Intelligence, Diplomacy, and America's Entry into World War I*. Annapolis, MD: Naval Institute Press, 2012.

Bourke, Joanna. *Fear: A Cultural History*. London: Virago, 2005.

Breen, William J. *Uncle Sam at Home: Civilian Mobilization, Wartime Federalism, and the Council of National Defense, 1917–1919*. Westport, CT: Greenwood Press, 1984.

Brewer, Susan A. *Why America Fights: Patriotism and War Propaganda from the Philippines to Iraq*. New York: Oxford University Press, 2009.

Bristow, Nancy K. *Making Men Moral: Social Engineering during the Great War*. New York: New York University Press, 1996.

Brown, Richard M. *Strain of Violence: Historical Studies of American Violence and Vigilantism*. New York: Oxford University Press, 1975.

Bruns, Roger A. *Preacher: Billy Sunday and Big-Time American Evangelism*. New York: W. W. Norton, 1992.

Camayd-Freixas, Erik, ed. *Orientalism and Identity in Latin America: Fashioning Self and Other from the (Post) Colonial Margin*. Tucson: University of Arizona Press, 2013.

Campbell, Craig W. *Reel America and World War I: Film in the U.S., 1914–1920*. Jefferson, NC: McFarland, 1985.

Capozzola, Christopher. *Uncle Sam Wants You: World War I and the Making of the Modern American Citizen*. New York: Oxford University Press, 2008.

Chambers, John Whiteclay, II. *To Raise an Army: The Draft Comes to Modern America*. New York: Free Press, 1987.

Chase, Allan. *The Legacy of Malthus: The Social Cost of the New Scientific Racism*. New York: Knopf, 1977.

Cherry, Conrad, ed. *God's New Israel: Religious Interpretations of American Destiny*. Chapel Hill: University of North Carolina Press, 1998.

Chickering, Roger. *We Men Who Feel Most German: A Cultural Study of the Pan-German League, 1886–1914*. Boston: Allen & Unwin, 1984.

Clark, Christopher. *The Sleepwalkers: How Europe Went to War in 1914*. New York: Harper, 2013.

Clifford, John Garry. *The Citizen Soldiers: The Plattsburg Training Camp Movement, 1913–1920*. Lexington: University of Kentucky Press, 1972.

Cooper, John Milton, Jr. *Breaking the Heart of the World: Woodrow Wilson and the Fight for the League of Nations*. New York: Cambridge University Press, 2001.

———. *The Vanity of Power: American Isolationism and the First World War, 1914–1917*. Westport, CT: Greenwood Press, 1970.

———. *The Warrior and the Priest: Woodrow Wilson and Theodore Roosevelt*. Cambridge, MA: Harvard University Press, 1983.

———. *Woodrow Wilson: A Biography*. New York: Knopf, 2009.

Cornebise, Alfred E. *War as Advertised: The Four-Minute Men and America's Crusade, 1917–1918*. Philadelphia: American Philosophical Society, 1984.

Craig, Campbell, and Frederik Logevall. *America's Cold War: The Politics of Insecurity*. Cambridge, MA: The Belknap Press of Harvard University Press, 2012.

Crook, Paul. *Darwinism, War and History: The Debate over the Biology of War from the "Origin of Species" to the First World War*. New York: Cambridge University Press, 1994.

DeBauche, Leslie Midkiff. *Reel Patriotism: The Movies and World War I*. Madison: University of Wisconsin Press, 1997.

Degler, Carl N. *In Search of Human Nature: The Decline and Revival of Darwinism in American Social Thought*. New York: Oxford University Press, 1991.

DeWitt, Petra. *Degrees of Allegiance: Harassment and Loyalty in Missouri's German-American Community during World War I*. Athens: Ohio University Press, 2012.

Dickinson, Frederick R. *War and National Reinvention: Japan in the Great War, 1914–1919*. Cambridge, MA: Harvard University Press, 1999.

Dinnerstein, Leonard. *Anti-Semitism in America*. New York: Oxford University Press, 1995.

Doenecke, Justus D. *Nothing Less Than War: A New History of America's Entry into World War I*. Lexington: University of Kentucky Press, 2011.

Doerries, Reinhard R. *Imperial Challenge: Ambassador Count Bernsdorff and German-American Relations, 1908–1917*. Translated by Christa D. Shannon. Chapel Hill: University of North Carolina Press, 1989.

Doob, Leonard. *Public Opinion and Propaganda*. New York: H. Holt, 1948.

Dorsett, Lyle W. *Billy Sunday and the Redemption of Urban America*. Grand Rapids, MI: William B. Eerdmans, 1991.

Dower, John. *War without Mercy: Race and Power in the Pacific War*. New York: Pantheon Books, 1986.

Dudziak, Mary L. *Cold War Civil Rights: Race and the Image of American Democracy*. Princeton, NJ: Princeton University Press, 2000.

Dumenil, Lynn. *The Second Line of Defense: American Women and World War I*. Chapel Hill: University of North Carolina Press, 2017.

Dyer, Thomas. *Theodore Roosevelt and the Idea of Race*. Baton Rouge: Louisiana State University Press, 1980.

Edwards, John Carver. "America's Vigilantes and the Great War, 1916–1918." *Army Quarterly and Defense Journal* 106, no. 3 (July 1976), 277–286.

———. *Patriots in Pinstripe: Men of the National Security League*. Washington, DC: University Press of America, 1982.

Eksteins, Modris. *Rites of Spring: The Great War and the Birth of the Modern Age*. Boston: Houghton Mifflin, 1999.

Ellis, Mark. *Race, War, and Surveillance: African Americans and the United States Government during World War I*. Bloomington: Indiana University Press, 2001.

Finnegan, John Patrick. *Against the Specter of a Dragon: The Campaign for American Military Preparedness, 1914–1917*. Westport, CT: Greenwood Press, 1974.

Foglesong, David S. *America's Secret War against Bolshevism: U.S. Intervention in the Russian Civil War, 1917–1920*. Chapel Hill: University of North Carolina Press, 1995.

Foner, Philip S. *The Great Labor Uprising of 1877*. New York: Monad, 1977.

Friedberg, Aaron L. *In the Shadow of the Garrison State: America's Anti-Statism and Its Cold War Grand Strategy*. Princeton, NJ: Princeton University Press, 2000.

Fussell, Paul. *The Great War and Modern Memory*. New York: Oxford University Press, 1977.

Gamble, Richard M. *The War for Righteousness: Progressive Christianity, the Great War, and the Rise of the Messianic Nation*. Wilmington, DE: ISI Books, 2003.

Gerber, David A. "Anti-Semitism and Jewish-Gentile Relations in American Historiography and the American Past." In *Anti-Semitism in American History*, edited by David A. Gerber, 3–56. Urbana: University of Illinois Press, 1986.

Gerstle, Gary. *American Crucible: Race and Nation in the Twentieth Century*. Princeton, NJ: Princeton University Press, 2001.

———. "Race and Nation in the Thought and Politics of Woodrow Wilson." In *Reconsidering Woodrow Wilson: Progressivism, Internationalism, War, and Peace*, edited by John Milton Cooper, Jr., 93–124. Baltimore: Johns Hopkins University Press, 2008.

Gilbert, G. M. *Nuremberg Diary*. New York: Farrar, Straus and Company, 1947.

Gilderhus, Mark T. *Diplomacy and Revolution: U.S.-Mexican Relations under Wilson and Carranza*. Tucson: University of Arizona Press, 1977.

Glassner, Barry. *The Culture of Fear: Why Americans Are Afraid of the Wrong Things.* New York: Basic Books, 1999.

Goldstein, Robert, J. *Political Repression in Modern America: 1870–1976.* Urbana: University of Illinois Press, 2001.

Gossett, Thomas F. *Race: The History of an Idea in America.* New York: Schocken, 1965.

Griffen, Clyde. "The Progressive Ethos." In *The Development of an American Culture*, edited by Stanley Coben and Lorman Ratner, 120–149. Eaglewood Cliffs, NJ: Prentice-Hall, 1970.

Griffith, Robert. *The Politics of Fear: Joe McCarthy and the Senate.* Lexington: University of Kentucky Press, 1970.

Gullace, Nicoletta F. "Barbaric Anti-Modernism: Representations of the 'Hun' in Britain, North America, Australia, and Beyond." In *Picture This: World War I Posters and Visual Culture*, edited by Pearl James, 61–78. Lincoln: University of Nebraska Press, 2009.

———. "Sexual Violence and Family Honor: British Propaganda and International Law during the First World War." *American Historical Review* 102, no. 3 (June 1997), 714–747.

Guterl, Matthew. "'Absolute Whiteness': Mudsills and Menaces in the World of Madison Grant." In *Fear Itself: Enemies Real & Imagined in American Culture*, edited by Nancy Lusignan Schultz, 149–166. West Lafayette, IN: Purdue University Press, 1999.

Hale, Grace Elizabeth. *Making Whiteness: The Culture of Segregation in the South, 1890–1940.* New York: Pantheon, 1998.

Hall, Jacquelyn Dowd. *Revolt Against Chivalry: Jessie Daniel Ames and the Women's Campaign against Lynching.* New York: Columbia University Press, 1979.

Hatch, Nathan O. *The Democratization of American Christianity.* New Haven, CT: Yale University Press, 1989.

Hawley, Ellis W. *The Great War and the Search for a Modern Order: A History of the American People and Their Institutions, 1917–1933.* Prospect Heights, IL: Waveland, 1992.

Herries, Meirion, and Susie Herries. *The Last Days of Innocence: America at War, 1917–1918.* New York: Random House, 1997.

Herring, George C. *From Colony to Superpower: U.S. Foreign Relations since 1776.* New York: Oxford University Press, 2008.

Herwig, Holger H. *Politics of Frustration: The United States in German Naval Planning, 1889–1941.* Boston: Little, Brown, 1976.

Herwig, Holger H., and David Trask. "Naval Operations Plans between Germany and the U.S.A., 1898–1913: A Study of Strategic Planning in the Age of Imperialism." *Militärgeschichtliche Zeitschrift* 8, no. 2 (December 1970), 5–32.

Higham, John. "Anti-Semitism in the Gilded Age: A Reinterpretation." *Mississippi Valley Historical Review* 43, no. 4 (March 1957), 559–578.

———. *Strangers in the Land: Patterns of American Nativism, 1860–1925.* New Brunswick, NJ: Rutgers University Press, 1955.

Hodgson, Godfrey. *Woodrow Wilson's Right Hand: The Life of Colonel Edward M. House.* New Haven, CT: Yale University Press, 2006.

Hofstadter, Richard. *The Paranoid Style in American Politics.* New York: Knopf, 1965.

———. *Social Darwinism in American Thought.* 1944. Reprint, New York: George Bariller, 1959.

Hogan, Michael J. *Cross of Iron: Harry S. Truman and the Origins of the National Security State, 1945–1954.* New York: Cambridge University Press, 1998.

Hoganson, Kristin. *Fighting for American Manhood: How Gender Politics Provoked the Spanish-American and Philippine-American Wars.* New Haven, CT: Yale University Press, 1998.

Horne, John, and Alan Kramer. *German Atrocities, 1914: A History of Denial.* New Haven, CT: Yale University Press, 2001.

Hutchinson, William R. *The Modernist Impulse in American Protestantism.* Cambridge, MA: Harvard University Press, 1976.

Hyman, Harold. *To Try Men's Souls: Loyalty Tests in American History.* Berkley: University of California Press, 1959.

Jacobson, Matthew Frye. *Barbarian Virtues: The United States Encounters Foreign Peoples at Home and Abroad, 1876–1917.* New York: Hill and Wang, 2000.

———. *Whiteness of a Different Color: European Immigrants and the Alchemy of Race.* Cambridge, MA: Harvard University Press, 1998.

James, Pearl. "Images of Femininity in American World War I Posters." In *Picture This: World War I Posters and Visual Culture*, edited by Pearl James, 273–311. Lincoln: University of Nebraska Press, 2009.

———. "Introduction: Reading World War I Posters." In *Picture This: World War I Posters and Visual Culture*, edited by Pearl James, 1–36. Lincoln: University of Nebraska Press, 2009.

Jeffries, John W. *Wartime America: The World War II Home Front.* Chicago: Ivan R. Dee, 1996.

Jensen, Joan M. *Price of Vigilance.* Chicago: Rand McNally, 1969.

Jensen, Kimberly. *Mobilizing Minerva: American Women in the First World War.* Urbana: University of Illinois Press, 2008.

Johnson, Benjamin Heber. *Revolution in Texas: How a Forgotten Rebellion and Its Bloody Suppression Turned Mexicans into Americans.* New Haven, CT: Yale University Press, 2003.

Johnson, Charles T. *Culture at Twilight: The National German-American Alliance, 1901–1918.* New York: Peter Lang, 1999.

Joll, James. *The Origins of the First World War.* New York: Longman, 1984.

Jowett, Garth S., and Victoria O'Donnell. *Propaganda and Persuasion.* New York: Sage, 1986.

Kazal, Russell. *Becoming Old Stock: The Paradox of German-American Identity.* Princeton, NJ: Princeton University Press, 2004.

Keith, Jeanette. *Rich Man's War, Poor Man's Fight: Race, Class, and Power in the Rural South during the First World War.* Chapel Hill: University North Carolina Press, 2004.

Kennedy, David M. *Freedom from Fear: The American People in Depression and War, 1929–1945.* New York: Oxford University Press, 1999.

———. *Over Here: The First World War and American Society.* New York: Oxford University Press, 1980.

Kennedy, Kathleen. *Disloyal Mothers and Scurrilous Citizens: Women and Subversion during World War I.* Bloomington: Indiana University Press, 1999.

Kennedy, Ross A. *The Will to Believe: Woodrow Wilson, World War I, and America's Strategy for Peace and Security.* Kent, OH: Kent State University Press, 2009.

Kingsbury, Celia Malone. *For Home and Country: World War I Propaganda and the Home Front.* Lincoln: University of Nebraska Press, 2011.

———. *The Peculiar Sanity of War: Hysteria in the Literature of World War I.* Lubbock: Texas Tech University Press, 2002.

Knock, Thomas J. *To End All Wars: Woodrow Wilson and the Quest for a New World Order.* New York: Oxford University Press, 1992.

Koenig, Robert. *The Fourth Horseman: One Man's Mission to Wage the Great War in America.* New York: PublicAffairs, 2006.

Kornweibel, Theodore, Jr. *"Investigate Everything": Federal Efforts to Compel Black Loyalty during World War I.* Bloomington: Indiana University Press, 2002.

Kuhlman, Erika A. *Petticoats and White Feathers: Gender Conformity, Race, the Progressive Peace Movement, and the Debate over War, 1895–1919.* Westport, CT: Greenwood Press, 1997.

Landau, Henry. *The Enemy Within: The Inside Story of German Espionage in America.* New York: Putnam, 1937.

Lane, Jack C. *Armed Progressive: General Leonard Wood.* San Rafael, CA: Presidio Press, 1978.

Lasswell, Harold D. *Propaganda Technique in World War I.* Rev. ed. Cambridge: Massachusetts Institute of Technology Press, 1971.

Lears, T. J. Jackson. *No Place of Grace: Antimodernism and the Transformation of American Culture, 1880–1920.* New York: Pantheon, 1981.

——. *Rebirth of a Nation: The Making of Modern America, 1877–1920.* New York: Harper-Collins, 2009.

Leffler, Melvyn. *A Preponderance of Power: National Security, the Truman Administration, and the Cold War.* Stanford, CA: Stanford University Press, 1992.

Lentz-Smith, Adriane. *Freedom Struggles: African Americans and World War I.* Cambridge, MA: Harvard University Press, 2009.

Leonard, Thomas C. "Red, White and Army Blue: Empathy and Anger in the American West." *American Quarterly* 26, no. 2 (May 1974), 176–190.

Leuchtenberg, William E. *The Perils of Prosperity, 1914–32.* Chicago: University of Chicago Press, 1958.

Link, Arthur S. *Wilson.* 5 vols. Princeton, NJ: Princeton University Press, 1947–1964.

——. *Woodrow Wilson and the Progressive Era, 1910–1917.* New York: Harper, 1954.

Linn, Brian McAllister. *The Echo of Battle: The Army's Way of War.* Cambridge, MA: Harvard University Press, 2007.

Lubin, David M. *Grand Illusions: American Art & the First World War.* New York: Oxford University Press, 2016.

Luebke, Frederick C. *Bonds of Loyalty: German-Americans and World War I.* DeKalb: Northern Illinois University Press, 1974.

MacDonogh, Giles. *The Last Kaiser: The Life of Wilhelm II.* New York: St. Martin's Press, 2001.

MacLeod, David L. "Socializing American Youth to Be Citizen-Soldiers." In *Anticipating Total War: The German and American Experiences, 1871–1914,* edited by Manfred F. Boemke, Roger Chickering, and Stig Förster, 137–166. Washington, DC: Cambridge University Press, 1999.

MacMillan, Margaret. *Paris 1919: Six Months that Changed the World.* New York: Random House, 2002.

Marlin, Randal. *Propaganda and the Ethics of Persuasion.* Orchard Park, NY: Broadview Press, 2002.

Marsden, George M. *Fundamentalism and American Culture: The Shaping of Twentieth Century Evangelicalism, 1870–1925.* New York: Oxford University Press, 1980.

Martin, Robert F. *Hero of the Heartland: Billy Sunday and the Transformation of American Society, 1862–1935.* Bloomington: Indiana University Press, 2002.

May, Elaine Tyler. *Homeward Bound: American Families in the Cold War.* New York: Basic Books, 1988.

McClymer, John. F. "The Federal Government and the Americanization Movement, 1915–24." *Prologue* 10, no. 1 (Spring 1978), 23–41.

——. *War and Welfare: Social Engineering in America, 1890–1925.* Westport, CT: Greenwood Press, 1980.

McLoughlin, William G., Jr. *Billy Sunday Was His Name.* Chicago: University of Chicago Press, 1955.

Miller, Creighton. *"Benevolent Assimilation": The American Conquest of the Philippines, 1898–1903.* New Haven, CT: Yale University Press, 1982.

Millis, Walter. *Road to War: America, 1914–1917.* Boston: Houghton Mifflin, 1935.

Millman, Chad. *The Detonators: The Secret Plot to Destroy America and an Epic Hunt for Justice.* New York: Little, Brown, 2006.

Mitchell, Nancy. *The Danger of Dreams: German and American Imperialism in Latin America.* Chapel Hill: University of North Carolina Press, 1999.

Mock, James R., and Cedric Larson. *Words That Won the War: The Story of the Committee on Public Information, 1917–1919.* Princeton, NJ: Princeton University Press, 1939.

Moorhead, James M. *American Apocalypse: Yankee Protestants and the Civil War, 1860–1869.* New Haven, CT: Yale University Press, 1978.

Morrow, John H., Jr. *The Great War: An Imperial History.* New York: Routledge, 2004.

Murphy, Paul L. *World War I and the Origins of Civil Liberties in the United States.* New York: W. W. Norton, 1979.

Murray, Robert K. *The Red Scare: A Study in National Hysteria, 1919–1920.* Minneapolis: University of Minnesota, 1955.

Nagler, Jörg. "Pandora's Box: Propaganda and War Hysteria in the United States during World War I." In *Great War, Total War: Combat and Mobilization on the Western Front, 1914–1918,* edited by Roger Chickering and Stig Förster, 485–500. New York: Cambridge University Press, 2000.

Nash, Roderick. *The Nervous Generation: American Thought, 1917–1930.* 1970. Reprint, Chicago: Elephant, 1990.

———. *Wilderness and the American Mind.* New Haven, CT: Yale University Press, 1967.

Neal, Arthur G. *National Trauma and Collective Memory: Extraordinary Events in the American Experience,* 2nd ed. Armonk, NY: M. E. Sharpe, 2005.

Ninkovich, Frank. *Modernity and Power: A History of the Domino Theory in the Twentieth Century.* Chicago: University of Chicago Press, 1994.

O'Leary, Cecilia Elizabeth. *To Die For: The Paradox of American Patriotism.* Princeton, NJ: Princeton University Press, 1999.

Olmstead, Kathryn S. *Real Enemies: Conspiracy Theories and Democracy, World War I to 9/11.* New York: Oxford University Press, 2009.

Painter, Nell Irvin. *The History of White People.* New York: W. W. Norton, 2010.

Patterson, James T. *Grand Expectations: The United States, 1945–1974.* New York: Oxford University Press, 1996.

Pegram, Thomas R. *One Hundred Percent American: The Rebirth and Decline of the Ku Klux Klan in the 1920s.* Chicago: Ivan Dee, 2011.

Peterson, H. C. *Propaganda for War: The Campaign against American Neutrality, 1914–1917.* 1939. Reprint, Port Washington, NY: Kennikat, 1968.

Peterson, H. C., and Gilbert C. Fite. *Opponents of War, 1917–1918.* Madison: University of Wisconsin Press, 1957.

Pettigrew, John. *Brutes in Suits: Male Sensibility in America, 1890–1920.* Baltimore: Johns Hopkins University Press, 2007.

Piper, John F., Jr. *The American Churches in World War I.* Athens: University of Ohio Press, 1985.

Polenberg, Richard. *Fighting Faiths: The Abrams Case, the Supreme Court, and Free Speech.* New York: Viking, 1987.

———. *War and Society: The United States, 1941–1945.* Philadelphia: Lippincott, 1972.

Preston, Diana. *Lusitania: An Epic Tragedy.* New York: Walter & Company, 2002.

Preston, William. *Aliens and Dissenters: Federal Suppression of Radicals, 1903–1933.* Urbana: University of Illinois Press, 1963.

Putney, Clifford. *Muscular Christianity: Manhood and Sports in Protestant America, 1880–1920.* Cambridge, MA: Harvard University Press, 2001.

Quinn, Patrick J. *The Conning of America: The Great War and American Popular Literature.* Atlanta, GA: Rodopi, 2001.

Rabban, David M. *Free Speech in Its Forgotten Years.* New York: Cambridge University Press, 1997.

Rawls, Walton. *Wake Up, America!: World War I and the American Poster.* New York: Abbeville Press, 1988.

Reesman, Jeanne Campbell. *Jack London's Racial Lives: A Critical Biography.* Athens: University of Georgia Press, 2009.

Richelson, Jeffrey T. *A Century of Spies: Intelligence in the Twentieth Century.* New York: Oxford University Press, 1995.

Rippley, La Vern J. *The German-Americans*. Boston: Twayne, 1976.

Robin, Corey. *Fear: The History of a Political Idea*. New York: Oxford University Press, 2004.

Roediger, David. *The Wages of Whiteness: Race and the Making of the American Working Class*. London: Verso, 1991.

———. *Working toward Whiteness: How America's Immigrants Became White*. New York: Basic Books, 2005.

Rosnow, Ralph L. and Gary Alan Fine. *Rumor and Gossip: The Social Psychology of Hearsay*. New York: Elsevier, 1976.

Ross, Stewart Halsey. *Propaganda for War: How the United States Was Conditioned to Fight the Great War of 1914–1918*. Jefferson, NC: McFarland, 1996.

Rotundo, E. Anthony. *American Manhood: Transformations in Masculinity from the Revolution to the Modern Era*. New York: Basic Books, 1993.

Said, Edward W. *Orientalism*. New York: Pantheon Books, 1978.

Sandos, James A. "Pancho Villa and American Security: Woodrow Wilson's Mexican Diplomacy Revisited." *Journal of Latin American Studies* 13, no. 2 (November 1981), 293–311.

Schaffer, Ronald. *America in the Great War: The Rise of the War Welfare State*. New York: Oxford University Press, 1991.

Schieber, Clara Eve. *The Transformation of American Sentiment toward Germany, 1870–1914*. 1923. Reprint, New York: Russell & Russell, 1973.

Sherry, Michael S. *In the Shadow of War: The United States since the 1930s*. New Haven, CT: Yale University Press, 1995.

Shibutani, Tamotsu. *Improvised News: A Sociological Study of Rumor*. Indianapolis, IN: Bobbs-Merrill, 1966.

Slotkin, Richard. *Lost Battalions: The Great War and the Crisis of American Nationality*. New York: H. H. Holt, 2005.

Smith, Charles W. *Public Opinion in a Democracy*. New York: Prentice-Hall, 1939.

Smith, Jeffrey Alan. *War & Press Freedom: The Problem of Prerogative Power*. New York: Oxford University Press, 1999.

Smith, Timothy L. *Revivalism and Social Reform in Mid-Nineteenth Century America*. New York: Abingdon Press, 1957.

Stearns, Peter N. *American Fear: The Causes and Consequences of High Anxiety*. New York: Routledge, 2006.

Sterba, Christopher M. *Good Americans: Italian and Jewish Immigrants during the First World War*. New York: Oxford University Press, 2003.

Stevenson, David. *Cataclysm: The First World War as Political Tragedy*. New York: Basic Books, 2004.

Stone, Geoffrey R. "Mr. Wilson's First Amendment." In *Reconsidering Woodrow Wilson: Progressivism, Internationalism, War, and Peace*, edited by John Milton Cooper, Jr., 189–224. Baltimore: Johns Hopkins University Press, 2008.

Takaki, Ronald T. *Double Victory: A Multicultural History of America in World War II*. Boston: Little, Brown, 2000.

Thomas, William H., Jr. *Unsafe for Democracy: World War I and the Justice Department's Covert Campaign to Suppress Dissent*. Madison: University of Wisconsin Press, 2008.

Thompson, John A. "The Exaggeration of American Vulnerability: The Anatomy of a Tradition." *Diplomatic History* 16, no. 1 (1992), 23–43.

———. *Reformers and War: American Progressive Publicists and the First World War*. New York: Cambridge University Press, 1987.

Thomson, Oliver. *Easily Led: A History of Propaganda*. Thrupp, Stroud, Gloucestershire, Great Britain: Sutton Publishing, 1999.

Tolzmann, Don Heinrich. *The German-American Experience*. Amherst, NY: Humanity Books, 2000.

Trout, Steven. *On the Battlefield of Memory: The First World War and American Remembrance, 1919–1941*. Tuscaloosa: University of Alabama Press, 2010.

Tuchman, Barbara W. *The Zimmermann Telegram*. New York: Macmillan, 1966.

Tucker, Robert W. *Woodrow Wilson and the Great War: Reconsidering American Neutrality, 1914–1917*. Charlottesville: University of Virginia Press, 2007.

Tuveson, Ernest Lee. *Redeemer Nation: The Idea of America's Millennial Role*. Chicago: University of Chicago Press, 1968.

Van der Veer, Peter. *Imperial Encounters: Religion and Modernity in India and Britain*. Princeton, NJ: Princeton University Press, 2001.

Vaughn, Stephen L. *Holding Fast the Inner Lines: Democracy, Nationalism, and the Committee on Public Information*. Chapel Hill: University of North Carolina Press, 1980.

Walters, Ronald G. *American Reformers, 1815–1860*. New York: Hill and Wang, 1978.

Ward, Robert D. "The Origin and Activities of the National Security League, 1914–1919." *The Mississippi Valley Historical Review* 47, no. 1 (June 1960), 51–65.

Watson, Alexander. *Ring of Steel: Germany and Austria-Hungary in World War I; The People's War*. New York: Basic Books, 2014.

Weber, Timothy P. *Living in the Shadow of the Second Coming: American Premillennialism, 1875–1925*. New York: Oxford University Press, 1979.

Weigley, Russell F. *The American Way of War: A History of United States Military Strategy and Policy*. Bloomington: Indiana University Press, 1973.

Weinberg, Carl R. *Loyalty, Labor, & Rebellion: Southwestern Illinois Coal Miners and World War I*. Carbondale: Southern Illinois University Press, 2005.

Weiss, Richard. "Racism in the Era of Industrialization." In *The Great Fear: Race in the Mind of America*, edited by Gary B. Nash and Richard Weiss, 121–143. New York: Holt, Rinehart, and Winston, 1970.

White, Bruce. "War Preparations and Ethnic and Racial Relations in the United States." In *Anticipating Total War: The German and American Experiences, 1871–1914*, edited by Manfred F. Boemke, Roger Chickering, and Stig Förster, 97–124. Washington, DC: Cambridge University Press, 1999.

Wiebe, Robert H. *The Search for Order, 1877–1920*. New York: Hill and Wang, 1967.

Williams, Chad L. *Torchbearers of Democracy: African American Soldiers in the World War I Era*. Chapel Hill: University of North Carolina Press, 2010.

Williamson, Joel. *The Crucible of Race: Black-White Relations in the American South since Emancipation*. New York: Oxford University Press, 1984.

Wilson, Charles Reagan. *Baptized in Blood: The Religion of the Lost Cause, 1865–1920*. Athens: University of Georgia Press, 1980.

Winkler, Allan M. *Life under a Cloud: American Anxiety about the Atom*. New York: Oxford University Press, 1993.

———. *The Politics of Propaganda: The Office of War Information, 1942–1945*. New Haven, CT: Yale University Press, 1978.

Witcover, Jules. *Sabotage at Black Tom: Imperial Germany's Secret War in America, 1914–1917*. Chapel Hill, NC: Algonquin Books of Chapel Hill, 1989.

Zieger, Susan. "She Didn't Raise Her Boy to Be a Slacker: Motherhood, Conscription, and the Culture of the First World War." *Feminist Studies* 22 (Spring 1996), 7–39.

Ziegler-McPherson, Christina. *Americanization in the States: Immigrant Social Welfare Policy, Citizenship, and National Identity in the United States, 1908–1929*. Gainesville: University Press of Florida, 2009.

INDEX